Writing for a Lifetime
Contemporary Readings
from Popular Sources

Jane Maher
Nassau Community College

Prentice
Hall

Upper Saddle River, New Jersey 07458

Library of Congress Cataloging-in-Publication Data

MAHER, JANE (date)
    Writing for a lifetime : contemporary readings from popular sources / Jane Maher.
        p. cm.
    ISBN 0-13-674664-0
    1. College readers.   2. English language—Rhetoric—Problems, exercises, etc.   3. Report
writing—Problems, exercises, etc.   I. Title.

PE1417 .M39 2000
808'.0427—dc21

00-062349

Editor in Chief: Leah Jewell
Acquisitions Editor: Craig Campanella
Production Editor: Joan E. Foley
Prepress and Manufacturing Buyer: Mary Ann Gloriande
Marketing Manager: Rachel Falk
Cover Designer: Bruce Kenselaar

This book was set in 10/12 New Baskerville by DM Cradle Associates
and was printed and bound by Courier Companies, Inc.
Covers were printed by Phoenix Color Corp.

© 2001 by Prentice-Hall, Inc.
A Division of Pearson Education
Upper Saddle River, New Jersey 07458

Printed in the United States of America
10 9 8 7 6 5 4 3 2 1

ISBN 0-13-674664-0

Prentice-Hall International (UK) Limited, *London*
Prentice-Hall of Australia Pty. Limited, *Sydney*
Prentice-Hall Canada Inc., *Toronto*
Prentice-Hall Hispanoamericana, S.A., *Mexico*
Prentice-Hall of India Private Limited, *New Delhi*
Prentice-Hall of Japan, Inc., *Tokyo*
Pearson Education Asia Pte. Ltd., *Singapore*
Editora Prentice-Hall do Brasil, Ltda., *Rio de Janeiro*

Contents

Chapter 3
The Art (and Hard Work) of Parenting *44*

Chapter 4
School: The Best Place to Learn?   67

Chapter 5
Adolescence: Leaving Childhood Behind   91

Chapter 6
Parents and Guardians: What They Mean to Us   *128*

Chapter 7
Class and Race in Our Society: Are We Really Created Equal?   *166*

Chapter 8
Working: Pursuing Our Passions or Paying the Bills?   *208*

Preface

"I hope you realize that I'm the one who has to write about this stupid vacation next fall."

(© *The New Yorker* Collection 1999 Peter Steiner from cartoonbank.com. All Rights Reserved.)

The caption says it all: Many students spend their elementary and even their high school years writing about topics such as what they did on their summer vacation. You have probably had at least one experience—probably many more than one—in which you were required to write about something that meant little or nothing to you. And no matter how good a writer you are, or how much you like writing, such topics can really make you dread writing. Hopefully, you were one of the lucky students who got to write about things that were important to you, and who got to use writing to discover things about yourself and your world.

Be assured that whatever type of writing experiences you have had in the past, *Writing for a Lifetime* will provide you with the opportunity to see how meaningful and rewarding the acts of reading and writing can be in your education, in your career, and in your life.

Now that you are in college, the "what I did on my summer vacation" assignments are gone forever; instead, the topics you will be asked to write about will be more relevant, more intellectually stimulating, and more academically challenging than anything you have been asked to write about in the past. *Writing for a Lifetime: Contemporary Readings from Popular Sources* will help to prepare you for this type of writing. This textbook has been designed to help you develop your writing skills in three ways: (1) by providing you with published essays and articles that are well written, meaningful, and interesting; (2) by presenting pre-writing assignments and other activities that will help you to discover and practice those actions and skills that are essential to good writing; and (3) by offering you a selection of writing topics that are not only meaningful and interesting but will help you to prepare for the type of writing that will be assigned in your college courses.

This book is called *Writing for a Lifetime: Contemporary Readings from Popular Sources* because the readings in each chapter deal with a topic that we have encountered or will encounter in our own lives—from childhood to old age—and everything in between, including adolescence, education, parenting, class and race in our society, careers, and relationships. These topics will help you to think about where you have been and where you are going; what you have done in the past and what you hope to do in the future; the people who have helped you get where you are and the people whom you will help as you become more independent and self-sufficient. In short, these topics will bring you through a "lifetime" of reading and writing—enabling you to use your own life experiences and knowledge to develop and build your writing skills.

Each chapter of this book contains activities designed to guide you through a writing process that will help you to produce a finished product that will give you a feeling of satisfaction and accomplishment. Each activity is defined and described below.

Pre-reading Activity

Each chapter begins with a pre-reading activity. You will be able to draw on your knowledge and experience as you write on a topic that is related to the readings and the writing assignments in the chapter. For example, Chapter 1 is about writing, so you will be asked to consider your own writing experiences: why you like or dislike writing, whether you are a "successful" writer, with whom you share your writing.

This pre-reading activity will help you to make connections between your own experiences and the experiences of the professional writers whose essays and articles are presented in the chapter. Educational researchers have discovered that we can best learn new information and make the most sense of what we read when we are able to connect it with information that we already possess and with events that we have already experienced—and that is the process that will occur as you respond in writing to the questions posed in each chapter's pre-reading activity.

Readings

Each chapter contains several readings about the topic covered in the chapter. They have all been published in either magazines, newspapers, or books; however, that does not mean they were all written by professional, experienced writers. In fact, several of the readings were written by high school and college students, and they reflect ideas and experiences similar to those that you have probably had.

The readings are presented in each chapter in order of difficulty, from easiest to hardest. In each chapter, the last reading is the longest and most difficult, similar to the type of reading that will be assigned to you in a college-level, credit-bearing course in various disciplines: English, sociology, psychology, anthropology, history, or human sexuality. Your instructor may or may not assign this last, most difficult reading to you, but even if it is not assigned, if you are up to a challenge, go ahead and read it on your own. You will learn something new, and you will be preparing yourself for the kind of reading assignments you will encounter in your college classes.

Each chapter also contains at least one poem. These poems are meant to help you realize that poetry can be informative and inspiring, that poets choose their words very carefully so that you not only can *understand* their meaning, you can actually *feel* their meaning.

Too often, students are turned off by poetry because they are either asked to memorize a poem or they are asked to figure out what each word, each metaphor, each simile, each image means. You will not be asked to do that when reading the poems contained in *Writing for a Lifetime*; instead, reading these poems will show you how your understanding of a topic can actually be improved and increased just by letting the poets' words seep into your mind and heart without worrying about their exact meaning or precise interpretation.

The readings in *Writing for a Lifetime* reflect many different modes of writing; in addition to poetry, there are letters, articles, memoirs, essays. This diversity of writing styles and modes will help you to understand and appreciate the many uses of writing—for enjoyment, for exploration, for information, even for getting things off our chests.

You can use these readings to evaluate your comprehension and reading speed. As you read the more difficult and challenging reading assignments at the end of each chapter, time yourself to see how long it takes you to read the entire article; then divide that time by the number of pages. In that way, when you are given a reading assignment in your college classes, you will have some idea of how much time you should allow for that assignment. If you find that you are having difficulty understanding the material, you will know that you need to seek out help, either from your instructor, from a tutor, from another student, or from a friend or family member. *Never* be afraid to ask for help.

Vocabulary Lists and Knowing When to Use (or Avoid) a Dictionary

Although there is a list of vocabulary words before each reading, you will probably still encounter words that are new to you. As you come across these words, don't let them stop you from enjoying the meaning of the reading. Remember that new words are an opportunity to learn and grow, and remember that you do not always have to look up the meaning of a word in order to understand the sentence or the paragraph.

Before you go to a dictionary, try to understand the meaning of the entire sentence by looking at the words *around* the unfamiliar word. Chances are good that if you do this, you will still be able to get a general understanding of the sentence or paragraph without having the flow of your reading broken.

For example, in Chapter 1, the last (and most difficult) reading of the chapter begins with this sentence: "Seating stressed-out and revelry-minded people in a cramped cylindrical space for hours on end while serving them powerful depressant beverages at high altitude and encouraging them to think they deserve royal treatment is probably not the best way to elicit model human behavior." One look at that sentence could lead a student to think that all of the sentences that follow will be equally difficult—with words like "revelry" and "cylindrical" and "depressant" and "elicit."

However, the very next sentence explains the meaning of the first sentence: "Support for this theory comes from reports filed by airline personnel about unruly passengers." The phrase "support for this theory" refers to the entire first sentence, and the phrase "reports filed by airline personnel about unruly passengers" helps the reader understand that the action is taking place on an airplane. "The stressed-out and revelry-minded people" are the airline passengers; the "cramped cylindrical space" is the airplane, the "hours on end" indicates a very long flight; "serving them powerful depressant beverages" refers to the alcoholic drinks served on airplanes. In other words, if the students who read the first sentence stopped to look up the words *revelry, cylindrical, depressant,* and *elicit,* they would not have gotten to the second sentence for about five or ten minutes. And even if they had taken the time to look those words up, it is doubtful that the dictionary definition of *cylindrical* would have helped them to realize that the writer was referring to an airplane; it is doubtful that the definition of the word *revelry* would have helped them to realize that the writer was referring to passengers who were probably on their way to a vacation spot; it is doubtful that the definition of the word *depressant* would have helped them to realize that the passengers were drinking, and it is doubtful that the definition of the word *elicit* would have helped them to realize that serving the passengers drinks would not bring out the best in them.

In short, before you look up a word in a dictionary, read on for a few more sentences; if you are still having trouble, then go to the dictionary. But first be certain to check the vocabulary list that is provided before each reading. These vocabulary words were selected as a result of class testing.

Suggestions for Free Writing

Free writing is a phrase that you have probably heard before, perhaps in a writing class. It refers to the practice of writing freely, without stopping, for a certain length of time, and without worrying too much about spelling, punctuation, grammar, usage, or even meaning. Free writing provides an opportunity for you to get your thoughts onto paper, where you can see them, think about them, evaluate them. Often, the words, phrases, and sentences you put down on a piece of paper during a free-writing session become the ingredients that you will later use to write a more formal essay.

However, the free-writing suggestions are not so "free" that you can just write about anything that pops into your mind. Instead, the free-writing suggestions in this book are carefully designed to help you focus on the topic that you will be reading about and then writing about. For example, in Chapter 2, the free-writing suggestion that appears before a memoir about a young boy who misbehaved asks you to think about a time when you were a child and did something wrong. You are asked to describe the event, and then to answer several questions.

By answering these questions in a free write, you are not only able to "collect" your thoughts; you are able to let your thoughts run freely about a particular incident or event or topic—providing you with an opportunity to remember details, to picture images, to recall dialogue, and finally, to consider the importance of all of these thoughts and images. As a result, by the time you are ready to read the essay and then to write about the essay, you will have already gathered much of the information and ideas you will need to be a better reader and writer.

During the first few free-writing sessions, you may think that you have nothing to write about. Hang in there; don't give up. Just try to jot down words or phrases. After a few sessions, you will notice that the very act of writing ideas and details enables you to remember more ideas and details.

Questions for Reflection and Discussion

After each of the readings, there are two questions. The first question usually asks you to think more carefully about the reading, and the second question usually asks you to think about the similarity between your experiences and the experiences described in the reading. By considering these questions, either on your own, in a small group discussion, or in a class discussion, you will have an opportunity to better understand the reading. These questions give you an opportunity to talk about the readings and to listen to others talk about the readings; it is by talking and listening that we are better able to understand what we read.

Topics for Writing

After each reading you will be given a choice of two writing topics. These questions have been carefully designed to enable you to combine the information you gained by reading the article with information you already possess as a result of your own experiences and observations.

Often, you will be asked to return to the reading to find specific information to include in your essay. You will be asked either to put the information in quotation marks or to put the information in your own words. This is a skill that is essential not only in college writing assignments.

The second topic for writing will always refer back to the free-writing topic. Therefore, if you choose the second writing topic, you will already have ideas available to you to use as you organize and write your essay. However, even if you choose the first topic for writing, you will always be able to use the ideas you gathered in your free write and when you talked about the Questions for Reflection and Discussion. In deciding which question to respond to, always remember that you should choose the question you know the most about and have the most interest in.

Each chapter contains one poem, and one of the two writing topics following the poems in each chapter asks you to write your own poem. You are being asked to write poems so you can have the opportunity to experiment: to be playful with words and phrases, to express your ideas in new and unexpected ways, to say what you really feel, without worrying about the rules of essay writing. Don't be intimidated, and don't think that your words have to rhyme. Go ahead and have fun with these assignments.

Additional Topics on the Chapter Theme

At the very end of each chapter, there are always two additional writing topics that relate to the general theme of the chapter. The first question will often ask you to review and incorporate all of the information you gained from reading the entire chapter; this type of writing assignment will help you to develop those reviewing and analyzing skills that are so crucial in college-level classes.

The second question will always ask you to return to the first activity you completed at the beginning of the chapter—the pre-reading activity. In that way, you will be able to use the general information about the topic that you recorded in your first free write, combined with all of the information you gained by reading and writing about the topic as you completed the chapter.

In other words, by the time you complete each chapter, you will have become an expert on that topic as a result of combining what you already knew with what you learned. That is the way true learning takes place. True learning is not memorizing, it is not copying from a textbook. Rather, it is the ability to take new information, combine it with what you already knew, and then create new ideas, new theories, even new questions. However, that's only the half of it: You must also have the ability to *communicate* these new ideas, theories, and questions. Of course, you will have developed that ability to communicate—through writing—as a result of completing all of the activities provided in this book.

I hope you benefit from using this book as much as I have benefited from writing it. As I decided on the chapter topics, as I chose the readings, as I defined the vocabulary words, as I composed the free-writing and essay topics, as I wrote and rewrote, and rewrote again, I always kept my students in mind. Because I have been teaching basic writing for more than 20 years, I can no longer remember all of my students' names. But I do remember how hard they worked, both in my classroom and at home, to develop their writing skills, to produce clear and interesting essays, to improve their reading comprehension, to balance the demands of work and family with the demands of school, to prepare for the final placement examination that enabled them to pass out of basic writing and into the more difficult college classes that awaited them.

I wrote this book for those students—and for you. Use it well, enjoy it, and good luck as you embark on your college career. I believe the writing skills that you develop through this book will serve you well in college. But I also believe that the writing skills you develop by using *Writing for a Lifetime* will serve you well for the rest of your life.

As you begin using this book, you may agree with the young boy in the cartoon: that writing topics can be—and often are—boring and useless. But by the time you finish *Writing for a Lifetime*, I hope you will agree with Charlie Brown when he says that "life is a thousand word essay." And what an interesting essay that can be!

(PEANUTS reprinted by permission of United Feature Syndicate, Inc.)

Jane Maher

Chapter
1

Why Do We Write?
What Do We Write?
For Whom Do We Write?

As you begin your college career, you may find yourself doing more writing than you have ever done before. Or perhaps you have always done a lot of writing. In either case, this is a good time for you to answer the questions asked in the title of this chapter—that is, to understand, perhaps for the first time, exactly what writing means to you.

If your writing experiences have been limited to school assignments that were returned to you with grades and comments (often written in what one student described as "bloody red ink"), then perhaps you are not yet aware that writing can be an opportunity for you to learn about yourself, about other people, about the world. And even more important, this is a good time in your life to discover that writing can also be an opportunity to communicate with others—to give them information about yourself, about the people who are important to you, about your world. Writing can also help you to think more clearly, to understand information more completely, and to examine ideas and issues—not only in school but in all aspects of your life. As the novelist E. M. Forster said, "How do I know what I think till I see what I say?"

The reading selections contained in this chapter were chosen not only because they are well written; they were chosen to help you realize there is no one "correct" or "successful" type of writing. In fact, these selections were written by people who are very different from each other in age and background and interests; they were written for a variety of purposes, and they were written in very different styles. These selections will help you to understand the many reasons why people write: for pleasure, for understanding, to communicate ideas, to record important information, to remember important events, to express frustration or anger, to make an argument, even to work up the courage to do something.

These selections will also help you to see the way our writing voices can change, depending on the circumstances and reasons for our writing. For example, an entry made in a log has a very different tone and style (it is far more informal) than an essay written for publication in a magazine or journal. Most important, by reading the selections presented in this chapter, you will see that writing isn't just something that will be required of you as a student (although you will be required to write a lot in college); writing can be very useful—and highly pleasurable–in a wide variety of circumstances. It is something you will do long after you complete your education; hopefully, it is something you will do (and enjoy) for the rest of your life.

Pre-reading Activity

Before you read the selections in this chapter, take about 10 minutes to respond to the following free-writing topics. They will help you to think about your own writing experiences.

List all the reasons why you like (or dislike) writing, then describe the circumstances that led to these feelings. Next, try to answer as many of the following questions as possible: What is the most successful writing you have ever done? What is the least successful? Who is your favorite audience or reader? Your least favorite? With whom do you share your writing? If you had all the time in the world to write, what would you write? A novel? A children's book? Letters? Journal entries? Short stories? Poems? E-mail? Have you been a successful writer in school? Have you ever thought about having your writing reach a larger audience through publishing?

Reading 1–1

UNAFRAID OF THE DARK (EXCERPT)

Rosemary L. Bray

In the following *excerpt* (an excerpt is a part of a longer work), taken from a book entitled *Unafraid of the Dark* by Rosemary L. Bray, the author explains the pride she felt as a young girl over her first successful writing experience: a poem she wrote shortly after learning of the death of President John F. Kennedy.

Vocabulary

thesaurus (paragraph 2)   reference book that lists words with similar and different meanings
retrospect (6)   looking back at something at a later time

Suggestions for Free Writing

Before you read the excerpt, take about 5 minutes to free-write on the following topic:

> What public event that has occurred in your lifetime has had a significant impact on you? Recall as much as you can about the event, including how you learned about it and where you were when it happened. Then explain how you felt about the event. Why do you think you still remember this event?

We all watched as Kennedy's coffin was rolled through the streets   1
of Washington, and as he lay in state in the Capitol rotunda. So many people crying, just the way I was crying, I thought. Lots of black people coming to see him lie there, standing in line for hours. I wished I could go, wished I could see him and say good-bye; it seemed so important. The saddest part of all was watching the funeral, looking at Jackie Kennedy standing there with her children. Caroline was only a little bit younger than I was, and I felt bad for her. Her daddy seemed like a nice man; whenever I saw pictures of him with his children, they were always laughing. What an awful thing to have someone kill your father when he was nice, I thought. When her little brother gave a salute on the steps of

St. Matthew's Cathedral, following the funeral mass, it seemed like the saddest thing in the world.

In school later that year, we had to try to write a poem about any- 2 thing we wanted, and so I wrote a poem about President Kennedy dying. It was the first thing I ever wrote to show anybody else. I remember the first of the three verses.

> When President Kennedy passed away,
> The world was very sad that day.
> The United States was wrapped up in grief,
> At the death of their commander in chief.

There was more, about how young he was and how nice he seemed, and how he had to be in heaven. I sat at the kitchen table for hours working on it, looking up words that would say what I meant, then trying to find a way to make them rhyme. My habit of reading reference books for fun was paying off; I had a dictionary and an old paperback thesaurus to find the words I wanted.

When I turned in the poem, my teacher asked me who had helped 3 me with the words. I told her I had done it myself. "Where did you learn a word like *span*?" she asked me, quoting from another of the verses. "It was in the dictionary," I said. I'd picked it because it let me talk about the fact that the president didn't live a very long time, and because it rhymed with *man*. But I didn't tell her all that, in case she thought I was trying to get smart with her. She just looked at me a little strangely, and told me to sit down.

I asked Mama if I could send the poem to Mrs. Kennedy so she 4 would know how sorry I was about her husband. She said yes, and bought me a stamp. I printed the poem over again on a clean piece of notebook paper so it wouldn't have any mistakes in it, folded it up to fit one of the small envelopes Mama had from Woolworth's, and put the stamp on the envelope and mailed it to the White House, because I didn't know where else to send it.

A few weeks later, Mama met me after school. She was very excited. 5 "You got a letter back from the White House," she said. I couldn't believe it; I thought she was kidding until she handed me the large, flat package. When I opened it, there was a letter from Mrs. Kennedy, thanking me for my poem and telling me that it would be saved and placed one day in the John F. Kennedy Library that the family planned to build in Boston. There was also a black-and-white picture of the Kennedy family, taken before the president was killed.

Even Daddy was excited about my news. He told all his friends, and 6 Mama told all the neighbors and showed them the picture. I walked around with the letter all that day, reading it over and over again. It's long gone now, and I realize in retrospect that it probably wasn't from Mrs. Kennedy, but from a member of her staff. But none of that mattered then. What mattered was that I had written something to express the way I felt about something that was important to me. I had sent it to someone I'd never met. That person had read it and liked it and wanted to keep it, even though she had never met me. It was a good feeling, to think of her reading my words.

Questions for Reflection and Discussion

1. Rosemary Bray's teacher looked at her "a little strangely" because the teacher suspected that Rosemary didn't write the poem herself. Have you ever had a similar circumstance when you were suspected or accused of not writing something yourself? (People who are suspected of stealing the writing of another person or of having someone else write for them are accused of "plagiarism.")
2. If you were going to write about someone you admire, who would it be? Why? Would you write it in the form of a poem or in some other form?

Topics for Writing

1. Describe the most successful, or the most unsuccessful, writing experience you have ever had. Be sure to include background information and details about the writing itself so that the reader can fully understand when, where, why, and how the writing was created and why it was successful or unsuccessful.
2. Return to the free write that you completed before you read Rosemary Bray's excerpt, and use the information there to write a full and complete description of a public event that made a lasting impression on you, just as watching John F. Kennedy's funeral on television made a lasting impression on Bray. Remember to include details, descriptions, and explanations, so that your reader can "see" and "feel" what you felt when the event occurred.

Reading 1–2

A LETTER

The next selection is a letter that was published in *Elementary English,* a journal for elementary school English teachers. It was written by Mark Levensky, who is now a successful college professor at a very highly regarded university. The letter describes a period in Levensky's life when he was struggling and suffering as an elementary school student.

Vocabulary

humiliation (paragraph 1)   a feeling of shame and embarrassment

Suggestions for Free Writing

Before you read this letter, take about 5 minutes to free-write on the following topic:

List the names of as many elementary or high school teachers that you can remember. Next to their names, write two or three phrases or sentences that describe their teaching ability and/or their concern for their students.

Teachers
Perkins School
43 & College
Des Moines, Iowa 50311

Dear Teachers:

This morning, just as I woke up. I remembered something that I   1
have thought about off and on for years. I remembered taking spelling tests when I was in grade school at Perkins. As I remembered this, I experienced some of the feelings that I experienced when I prepared for these tests, took them, and got them back. I experienced fear, anxiety and humiliation.

I remember the spelling books that we used. The color, size and   2
shape of the books. How the words to be learned were grouped on the page. And I can remember how hard I tried to learn these words. Doing just what my teachers said. Printing the words over and over again. Spelling a word to myself with my eyes closed and then opening my eyes

to check if I was right. Spelling the words for my parents before bed. Going over them again and again right before the test. I can also remember what it was like to take the spelling tests. A piece of wide margined paper and a pencil. The teacher saying the words aloud. Fear and anxiety. I struggled to remember how to spell each word. Erase. No matter how I spelled a word, it looked wrong. Fear. I crossed out, printed over, went back, tried again. "One minute left." Anxiety. When my spelling papers came back they were covered with red marks, blue marks, check marks, correction marks, and poor grades. It was so humiliating. And it was always the same. No matter how much I prepared or how hard I tried, I couldn't spell most of the words. And no matter how many spelling tests I took and failed, there were always more spelling tests to take and fail. We got a new book of spelling words at the beginning of each term.

At the time my teachers tried to help me. They told me what I had to do in order to improve: "Print the words over and over again. Spell a word to yourself with your eyes closed and then open your eyes to check if you are right. Spell the words for your parents before bed. Go over them again and again right before the test." My teachers also said that unless I learned to spell I would never get into high school, or out of high school, or into college, or out of college. And the last thing that they always told me was that I couldn't spell. 3

What I want to say to you teachers now is this. I couldn't spell very well then, and I still can't. I got into high school, and out of high school, and into college, and out of college. While my teachers at Perkins didn't teach me to spell, they did manage to have an effect on me. For example, this morning, twenty five years later, I woke up and remembered their spelling tests, and experienced the fear, anxiety and humiliation that I felt when I prepared for these tests, took them, and got them back. If you are still giving children these spelling tests, please stop doing so at once. 4

Sincerely yours,

Mark Levensky
Associate Professor
Department of Humanities
Massachusetts Institute of Technology
Cambridge, Massachusetts

Questions for Reflection and Discussion

1. In his letter, Mark Levensky tries to convince his former teachers at the Perkins School to stop giving spelling tests "at once." If you were an elementary school teacher, would you be convinced by his letter? Why?
2. Do you think the ability to spell words correctly is related to one's ability to succeed in school? In a profession? In life?

Topics for Writing

1. Using Mark Levensky's letter as a model, write a letter to a former teacher, counselor, coach, principal, or other administrator, and explain to that person why he or she should stop engaging in a certain practice or enforcing certain rules that had a negative impact on you.
2. Return to the free write you completed before you read Levensky's letter, and write a letter to a former teacher explaining why you admire him or her and how you have benefited from him or her as a teacher. Be certain to provide background information, details, and examples so that the person knows precisely why you feel the way you do.

Reading 1–3

THEME FOR ENGLISH B

Langston Hughes

The next selection, "Theme for English B," is a poem written in 1959 by an African-American poet, Langston Hughes. Hughes is recognized as one of the finest American poets of the twentieth century.

Vocabulary

colored (stanza 2) term used to describe African Americans before the civil rights movement; today, of course, the use of this term to describe an African-American person would be considered insulting and degrading

Winston-Salem, Durham (2) cities in North Carolina

college on the hill above Harlem (2) Columbia University

Bessie (4) Bessie Smith (1898?–1937), famous blues singer

Bach (4) Johann Sebastian Bach (1685–1750), famous classical music composer

Suggestions for Free Writing

Before you read this poem, take about 5 minutes to free-write on the following topic:

If you were asked by your writing instructor to write a one-page essay describing yourself, what are some of the things you would want to write about? What are some of the things you would not want to write about?

The instructor said,   1

> *Go home and write*
> *a page tonight.*
> *And let that page come out of you—*
> *Then, it will be true.*

I wonder if it's that simple?   2
  I am twenty-two, colored, born in Winston-Salem.
  I went to school there, then Durham, then here

Source: From *Collected Poems* by Langston Hughes. Copyright 1994 by the Estate of Langston Hughes. Reprinted by permission of Alfred A. Knopf, a Division of Random House, Inc.

to this college on the hill above Harlem.
I am the only colored student in my class.
The steps from the hill lead down into Harlem,
through a park, then I cross St. Nicholas,
Eighth Avenue, Seventh, and I come to the Y,
the Harlem Branch Y, where I take the elevator
up to my room, sit down, and write this page:

It's not easy to know what is true for you or me   3
　　at twenty-two, my age. But I guess I'm what
I feel and see and hear, Harlem, I hear you:
hear you, hear me—we two—you, me, talk on this page.
(I hear New York, too.) Me—who?

Well, I like to eat, sleep, drink, and be in love.   4
　　I like to work, read, learn, and understand life.
I like a pipe for a Christmas present,
or records—Bessie, bop, or Bach.
I guess being colored doesn't make me *not* like
the same things other folks like who are other races.
So will my page be colored that I write?

Being me, it will not be white.   5
　　But it will be
a part of you, instructor.
You are white—
yet a part of me, as I am a part of you.
That's American.
Sometimes perhaps you don't want to be a part of me.
Nor do I often want to be a part of you.
But we are, that's true!
As I learn from you,
I guess you learn from me—
although you're older—and white—
and somewhat more free.

This is my page for English B.   6

Questions for Reflection and Discussion

1. When Langston Hughes wrote this poem in 1959, before the civil rights movement, there was much discrimination against African Americans in the United States, leading him to write: "Sometimes perhaps you don't

want to be a part of me, Nor do I often want to be a part of you." Do you think this feeling still exists, or have race relations improved since 1959?

2. Hughes says that he learns from his (white) professor, and his professor learns from him. What are some of the things your professors can learn from you?

Topics for Writing

1. Although you will probably not be asked to write poetry in college (unless you take a creative writing course), writing poetry is a wonderful way to express ideas and feelings without having to worry about the rules of essay writing. Using Langston Hughes's poem as a model, write a three-stanza poem for your instructor. Use the first stanza to explain your background, use the second stanza to explain your present circumstances, and use the third stanza to explain your goals and hopes for the future.

2. Return to the free write you completed before you read Hughes's poem, and use the information there to write an essay describing yourself to your writing instructor. Be sure to include details, descriptions, and examples so that your instructor can get to know you.

CAN YOU WRITE THE WRONGS
OF THE PAST?

Guy Nassiff

The next selection is an essay written by a man who is trying to gather up the courage to write a letter to his father, whom he has never met.

Vocabulary

indifferent (paragraph 10) not caring
inexplicably (10) something that is impossible to explain or understand
adversely (10) having a bad effect
condoning (12) approving of

Suggestions for Free Writing

Before you read this essay, take about 5 minutes to free-write on the following topic:

Think about someone important to you whom you haven't seen in a long time: a childhood friend, a relative, a teacher, a co-worker, a former neighbor. Make a list of all the things you would like to tell that person about yourself, including all that has happened to you and that you have done since you last saw the person.

For six years, I've been debating with myself about writing to my father. Where do I start? What do I say? I sit down with a pen, but the words don't come. After all, how do you write to a man you've never met?   1

Hello, Mr. Nassiff, I'm the 36-year-old son you never knew you had. I   2
don't think so. I don't want the guy to have a heart attack. Every Father's Day since my son, Michael, was born, I've agonized about writing this letter, because I can't imagine a day without seeing or talking to my own little boy. And I feel a sense of obligation now. I feel my father has the *right* to know.

Source: "Can You Write the Wrongs of the Past?" by Guy Nassiff, *Brooklyn Bridge*, Vol. 2, #11, July, 1997. Reprinted by permission of Brooklyn Bridge.

My mother, Virginia, was a housewife, and my father, Donald, a
World War II Navy vet. They lived in Florida, and my dad had a lot of
trouble finding steady work after the war. For years he bounced from job
to job, and at times they struggled to make ends meet.

In the early '50s my grandmother on my mother's side passed
away. A few months later my mother lost a baby. These two events led to
a nervous breakdown. I believe my father was unable to handle my
mother's depression, and, on top of their financial problems, it pushed
him over the edge. He became a different man. He grew solemn and
unresponsive. He withdrew from my mother and shouted at her whenever he wanted something. As time passed, he began to show signs of
aggression, and, although he never struck my mother, she grew to fear
him.

One day when she was cleaning the house in November 1958, she
found a gun hidden in a closet. It horrified her. My father had never
kept one around before, and she didn't know where he'd gotten it, or
how he was going to use it. She called her father—my grandad—
Gaetano DeGiose, and he told her to hop on the first plane to New York.
She came home to Brooklyn, not knowing she was pregnant. My mom
filed for divorce, and my father didn't fight it. She always said she never
had any regrets.

By then she knew she was pregnant with me, and having lost
one baby, decided to do everything possible not to lose another. This
meant not telling my father for fear he might try to take me away, in
one way or another. When she died in 1982, she'd still kept her
secret.

My grandfather was my dad until I was six, and after he passed on,
my uncles and older cousins, always generous with their time, took over
as father figures. I never felt I lacked in any way by not having a "real"
father—it was a tribal experience, I told myself. And a great deal of
credit has to go to my mother, who did a terrific job of raising me.

As a boy I never wanted for anything, but when I started grade
school the other kids would ask about my dad and, not wanting to look
stupid, I'd just say he'd died. But I got sick of lying and finally told the
truth. I pretended it didn't bother me, even when people would say I'd
lost out, or had been cheated. After all, my uncles were throwing the ball
around with me all the time, and I was going to baseball games and car
shows with my cousins—what was so bad? And when the day came, they
even showed me how to use my hands to defend myself. I had a wonderful time that I wouldn't trade with anybody, and I learned things I
plan on passing down to my own son.

My mother, of course, painted word portraits of my father that
were far from flattering. And since this *was* my mother, my guiding
force, I couldn't listen objectively. How could anyone *mistreat my mother?*
For a 9-year-old, the idea was unthinkable.

And so I went through life indifferent, if not hostile, to the notion   10
of my father. Then one day—because this is America—I kind of lost it at
the movies. I went to see Kevin Costner in *Field of Dreams*. I saw it alone
on a hot summer afternoon, and enjoyed it immensely. During the final
scene, where Costner asks his dad if he wants to play some catch, inexplicably, I felt tears well up in my eyes. I sat there in the darkness, long
after the movie had ended, thinking, longing. My wife, Carol, and I were
expecting a baby at that point, and when I went home, I lay awake all
night, wondering if not having had a father would adversely affect my
ability to raise my own child.

In the summer of 1990 Michael was born. Soon I was hearing his   11
first words, helping him with his first steps, taking him to the park and
doing all the things I hadn't done with my old man. I got to thinking: *I
wasn't the one who'd been cheated. My father was.* In a way I even felt
guilty that he'd missed out on raising me.

And now I keep thinking that he's a lonely old man (he's 71),   12
living in a trailer park somewhere down in Florida. I imagine him
sitting in the glow of a black-and-white TV tube, watching the world
go by on a 19-inch screen. It would be great for both of us, I think, if
I could pick up the phone and say hello, or ask him for some advice.
It's been 15 years since my mother passed away. I see things differently
now. I'm more understanding: a family and all of its reponsibilities
will do that to you. Maybe I even understand what my pop might have
gone through in 1958. Don't get me wrong, I'm not condoning his
hostility, or withdrawal, or suggesting that the pressures of family life
gave him a reason to flip out. . . . It's just that I'm old enough to know
now that life rarely goes as planned, and that a lot of people can't
handle it. Whatever the reason, I must confess that I no longer look
upon my father unfavorably. I want to believe that if I let him know
about me, he'll come up north and meet the son and grandson he
never knew he had.

Perhaps we'll share some happy moments, making up for all those   13
that were lost. Yet, I'm afraid. What if he takes the letters and photos I
plan on sending him and throws them in the garbage? I want to believe
that doesn't matter anymore, but it's gotten to the point where I want
to put an end to this chapter in my life, one way or the other—be it
happy or sad.

I think I'm going to be able to do it this year. I'm finally going to   14
sit down and write that letter. When I'm done this time I'll have a completed letter, not a wastebasket filled with crumpled pieces of paper.
This year will be different. I'm going to do it. Forget about a phone
call, I did that once and when he said who he was, I just froze up. No,
it's a letter I'll write. I'll do it right after I have a cup of coffee. Yeah,
right after that.

Questions for Reflection and Discussion

1. What are the factors that led Guy Nassiff to realize that he wanted to contact his father?
2. Reread the last paragraph in this essay very carefully. Will Nassiff write the letter to his father?

Topics for Writing

1. Think of something you have been putting off doing because it is very difficult or painful. Write an essay in which you explain the advantages and disadvantages of finally doing this thing.
2. Return to the free write you completed before you read Nassiff's essay, and use the information there to write a letter to someone whom you have not seen for a while. In the letter, explain what kind of person you have become. Be sure to list and then describe and explain as many qualities (both good and bad) about yourself as possible so that the recipient of your letter will really know what kind of person you are.

Reading 1–5

HIGH CRIMES AND MISDEMEANORS: THE FLIGHT LOGS OF UNCIVIL AVIATION

Tom Kuntz, Editor

The next selection is a collection of flight log entries written by airline attendants; they were reprinted in *The New York Times*. Many of us imagine that being a flight attendant is a wonderful and exciting job, one that includes meeting interesting people and traveling for free to exotic destinations. However, it is clear from these entries that the attendants' jobs are difficult, sometimes even dangerous.

You will notice that some of the words in the article are in brackets; that means that the person who edited the article for the newspaper inserted the words to make the meaning clearer for the reader. This article is similar to the type of reading that would be assigned to you in a college-level career development or industrial psychology course.

Vocabulary

misdemeanors (title)   a minor offense; less than a crime
revelry-minded people (paragraph 1)   people who want to party and have fun
elicit (1)   get; obtain
mayhem (2)   total confusion or lack of control
defecated (3)   had a bowel movement
foibles (4)   small faults or weaknesses in human nature
discreet (8)   keeping things quiet
implying (9)   suggesting something rather than saying it outright
retaliate (9)   get back at someone
nonplused (10)   to be confused or disturbed
aft galley (15)   the galley in the back of the plane

Suggestions for Free Writing

Before you read these log entries, take about 5 minutes to free-write on the following topic:

Recall a time when you observed someone having a difficult time dealing with a customer, a client, a student, or a patient. Or recall the reverse, when you

Source: "High Crimes and Misdemeanors: The Flight Logs of Uncivil Aviation" by Tom Kuntz, *The New York Times*, Week in Review, December 8, 1996. Copyright 1996 by the New York Times Co. Reprinted by permission.

observed someone having a difficult time dealing with a salesperson, a teacher, a doctor, a waiter, a flight attendant, or someone else (not a relative or friend).

Seating stressed-out and revelry-minded people in a cramped cylindrical space for hours on end while serving them powerful depressant beverages at high altitude and encouraging them to think they deserve the royal treatment is probably not the best way to elicit model human behavior. 1

Support for this theory comes from reports filed by airline personnel about unruly passengers and other problems. Incidents of airplane mayhem appear to be on the rise, as air traffic gets more congested and planes more crowded. 2

Among recent, well-publicized cases is that of a United Airlines passenger from Connecticut who, swacked out of his mind and cut off from the airline's hooch, defecated on a food cart. Then there's the rich widow who is suing American Airlines after the pilot tied her up with her dog's leash in a dispute over stowing the pet (a Maltese named Dom Pérignon). Not to mention the guy on a British Airways flight from India to London who began rubbing butter all over his body while chanting. 3

American Airlines says the number of incidents of verbal and physical abuse against its crew members nearly tripled from 1994 to 1995, to almost 900. While many incidents are amusing for the foibles they expose, airline employees say the threat of violence on the job is no joke. Prodded by American Airlines and flight attendants' unions, the Federal Aviation Administration last month signaled a sterner line, urging a range of airline procedures to curb (rather than tolerate) abusive passengers. 4

Here are flight attendants' accounts of incidents on a variety of airlines, some of which resulted in arrests. (In-flight interference is a Federal crime and can draw the heat of the F.B.I.) The accounts are excerpted from incident reports made available by the Association of Flight Attendants. The union withheld the names of airlines and people involved. 5

On a Newark-to-San Francisco flight in May 1994: 6
Passenger upset that flight attendant didn't have her special meal, used abusive language and then threw her wine in his face, and then hit him on the head with the empty wine bottle. . . .

On a Chicago-to-Orlando flight in October 1994: 7
Following completion of the safety demo, [passenger] in 16C struck flight attendant. . . in the head. Flight attendant explained that this behavior was unacceptable and tried to calm him down. Flight attendant smelled alcohol on his breath at this time. . . . Five minutes into flight, flight attendant witnessed [the passenger] spit on another pas-

senger seated in 16D. The second officer came back to talk with [the passenger] and the decision was made to go back [to the airport] . . .

On a San Francisco-to-Las Vegas flight in October 1994, off-duty airline 8
employees were trouble:
Flight was uneventful until passengers in seats 20 E&F ordered their drinks and then flashed [an employee] ID badge when it came time to pay for their drinks. . . . The party was sarcastic and loudly blurted out, "I take a gamble when flying [this airline]!" Flight attendant then responded, knowing they were employees, [that] they should be more discreet. Female passenger then yelled at flight attendant that [the attendant] . . . was servng her and "she is the customer because she is flying 'full fare.' " After landing, and during deplaning, the male passenger approached flight attendant, intoxicated, and demanded his badge. When flight attendant refused, passenger shoved flight attendant and as flight attendant tried to move away from them they both tried to block him while yelling obscenities. . . .

On a Jan. 20, 1996, flight from Taipei, Taiwan, to San Francisco, an 9
incident involved a passenger who was evidently an influential Taiwanese:
I never served a passenger like this. . . . I was in the galley [and] he came. . . to ask [for] wine and try to talk to me and ask me out. But I said "no" and I refused to give him wine because he was drunk. Then he walked down to first class yelling and disturbing the passengers. . . . I called cockpit to ask [them] to turn on the seatbelt sign so I could ask him to return back to his seat. After he returned to his seat, he pushed the call button and I went to answer. He asked for another drink. I said, "You should take a good rest; we don't have any wine left anymore." He said, "I got a better idea," then grabbed my arm and tried to kiss me. I pushed him away and said, "If you dare to touch me again, I'm going to sue you." . . . He came to the galley and said . . . "You want to be in big trouble?" [implying he could use his influence to retaliate against her if she told] . . . I really don't know how to handle this situation.

Before takeoff of a Feb. 13 flight from Los Angeles to Chicago, a flight 10
attendant learned that a passenger on the previous flight had left the plane a
mess. Superiors seemed nonplused:
Flight attendants on inbound aircraft relayed to me that a passenger lost control of all bodily functions in back galley and also the lav. . . . I immediately went back to see for myself and was appalled at what I saw. . . . Cabin service personnel were starting to clean it with a dust mop, squirt bottle, coffee grounds and [the airline's brand of] cologne. They saturated the spots, making the floor squishy . . . The smell of the feces/cleaner/cologne made me gag. Halfway through the cleaning process the caterers changed the galley without the cabin service personnel cleaning the floors underneath the carts. I immedi-

ately went to the duty supervisor and told him I was uncomfortable with the situation and did not want to take the trip.

He showed little or no concern and said they would clean it . . . 11
Finally [a] supervisor came to the aircraft along with captain . . . Both doors were open with a draft going through and the captain said he didn't smell anything . . . He disagreed with my judgment but should be commended for showing concern for my feelings. . . .

On an April 14 flight from Chicago to Paris: 12
While I was doing the service in [first class] the man in 15H asked me to turn off the light so he could make love to his wife. . . . She didn't seem to be pleased. It looks like [this] was the cause of the argument. A couple of hours later he asked me to move his wife to another seat. She didn't want to at first . . . but to avoid any problem she moved.

Then the wife returned. . . [He] asked me to tell her to move back to 13
economy. She said: "I'm his wife. I want to stay here." He started screaming at her, using very vulgar language, and pushed her away. I asked the lady to go back to economy as it was the safest place for her. . . .

On a Nov. 14 flight from San Francisco to Narita International Airport 14
in Japan:
Passenger . . . seated at 22G indicated [to] flight attendant during cocktail service that he had to go to sleep without meal, therefore requested double scotch. He had another double drink before the meal service . . . [and was] served another double scotch during meal service. At the same time [he] expressed frustration/anger for not being able to smoke on flight. Requested drink from other flight attendant after meal service. Amount of liquor consumed is unknown but we purposely delayed delivery of drinks, so he purchased duty-free scotch and started drinking from the bottle. (This was observed/reported by passengers seated around him.)

Passenger . . . in 21H came back to aft galley and informed me that 15
[the unruly passenger] was smoking in 22G and disturbing all other customers in the vicinity. I asked him politely not to smoke and gently removed cigarette and extinguished it. Japanese passenger in 22F during all this time was extremely polite and accommodating. After the cigarette was removed I communicated with the Japanese passenger. . . . That's when [the drunken passenger] grabbed and held my wrist and told me to "shut up and listen" to him, and ordered me to speak in English only. That's when flight attendant came on to the scene and assisted me in escaping from this man's very strong grip. . . .

The assisting flight attendant reported this: I grabbed his hands, [and] 16
was able to make him release his grip on her. . . . I tried to explain to him again that smoking was not permitted anywhere on the aircraft and that his action of grabbing and pulling [the flight attendant] is against F.A.R.

[Federal air regulations] and is a serious problem. I then bent down to speak with him quietly, eye-to-eye level. As I was explaining to him the seriousness of his action . . . he put his hand on my left shoulder as if to say "O.K." and slid his right hand up and around my throat. . . . This done, he began pressing hard on my Adam's apple. The pressure became dangerous and my instinctive reaction was [to] grab his thumb and render it unusable. I then strongly informed him that he crossed the line. . . .

The captain arrived moments later . . . Again [the passenger] became verbally abusive . . . and tried to grab his hands. The captain strongly requested that he was not to be touched at any time and that he should return to his seat. . . . [He] returned to his seat, at which point I asked him to turn over his duty-free scotch . . . He complied . . . [The] other flight attendant requested that he just go to sleep and he did. (He passed out.) 17

[But later he] got out of his seat and walked to door 3R to 3L, crossing past all the lavs. [A passenger] . . . was sleeping. . . . What woke her up was someone pushing on the seat back. When she opened her eyes she saw [him] leaning over her, which made her think he was having a heart attack or ill, only to discover that he was unzipping his pants and began urinating. . . . 18

Questions for Reflection and Discussion

1. The attendants who completed the flight log entries did not have to write "formally"—that is, they did not have to write complete essays or even paragraphs. They simply had to record as precisely as possible what happened. Have you ever had a job in which you were required to write? Did your writing have to be formal, or could it be informal? Who read what you wrote? Did you feel that you were able to express yourself clearly and convincingly?
2. Do the passengers described in the flight logs have any traits in common? If yes, what are they?

Topics for Writing

1. Write an essay in which you give advice to flight attendants about how to handle abusive passengers and other difficulties. Remember, flight attendants are trained to act on the belief that the passenger is always right, and if they do not do this, they will either be severely reprimanded (corrected) or fired.
2. Return to the free write you completed before you read the logs written by the flight attendants, and write your own "log" entry describing a particularly difficult incident that you witnessed or one that happened to you. In your conclusion, compare your experience with the experiences described by the flight attendants, describing both the similarities and the differences between the two.

Additional Topics on the Theme of Writing

In this chapter, you read five selections that show some of the many purposes and uses of writing, and they are as varied as the writers themselves. The writers came from all walks of life: an African-American girl whose teacher did not believe she was capable of writing the poem about President John F. Kennedy's death; a highly successful college professor who still wakes up in the middle of the night in terror of the spelling tests he was forced to take in elementary school; a poet describing what a young African-American man would say to his white college instructor about himself; a new father explaining why he wanted to write a letter letting his own father know that he exists; and hardworking flight attendants recording in their logs how they were forced to endure unpleasant, even dangerous, treatment by passengers. Taken together, these selections show the varied and important uses of writing.

1. How has your opinion about the importance and uses of writing changed as a result of reading the five selections in this chapter? Be sure to refer to the selections themselves whenever necessary in order to give the necessary evidence and information needed to convince your reader of the change(s) that occurred. Remember, it is perfectly acceptable for you to use the exact words of the authors, as long as you place the words in quotation marks.
2. Return to the free write you completed at the beginning of the chapter, before you read any of the selections, and use the information there to write an essay on the following topic:

   If you could go back in time, what would you do differently to improve your writing skills and be a better writer? Be sure to provide details, examples, and background information so that the reader can fully understand what you would do differently.

Chapter
2

Childhood:
The Best Time
of Our Lives?

Researchers are discovering more and more about the way young children develop: how their brains form and function, how they learn to speak, and how they grow physically, intellectually, and emotionally during their earliest years. Researchers are also discovering that parents can do much to ensure that their infants develop into well-adjusted, happy, and healthy children—from giving them the attention and love they need to helping them gain independence and a sense of confidence in the world around them. The last selection in this chapter provides important information on this topic.

However, although childhood is the period when humans complete most of their physical and mental growth and development, it is also a time of personal exploration and experimentation—and very often, when children explore and experiment, they get into trouble. Two of the selections in this chapter describe the type of trouble children can get into, and they will probably remind you of some of the mischievous things you did as a child.

These reading selections will not only remind you of your own childhood; hopefully, they will help to prepare you when you have (or if you already have) your own children. They will remind you not only of the challenges of childhood but also of the beauty and the satisfactions of that stage of life as well.

Pre-reading Activity

Before you read the selections in this chapter, take about 5 minutes to free-write on the following topics. They will help you think about your experiences with children and your own childhood.

Are there children in your life now—either your own children, younger siblings, nieces, nephews, neighbors, children of friends? Do you have a good relationship with them? Do you like children? Why? Would you like to work with young children, in a day-care center perhaps, or as a kindergarten or first-grade teacher? Why? Do the children you know remind you of yourself when you were a child?

Reading 2-1

VICTIMS OF THE 14TH-FLOOR WINDOW
Thomas Beller

The first selection in this chapter, "Victims of the 14th-Floor Window," was written by Thomas Beller in the form of a *memoir* (a memoir describes something that actually happened to the author: an event, an incident, a period of time, or his or her entire life). Beller describes what seems to be a rite of passage among many children: throwing water balloons and pots of water onto people from very high places.

Vocabulary

expansive (paragraph 1)   generous, wide
a multitude (1)   many
contemplating (2)   considering
teetering (2)   barely balanced; about to fall
entranced conviction (2)   a pleasant type of concentration
trajectory (3)   the path an object in motion takes
malice (4)   hatred
revelations (4)   discoveries
monitor (5)   watch
impassive (5)   not showing emotion
transfixed (6)   completely absorbed
ambled (7)   walked slowly and casually
gait (7)   a type of step or walk
translucent (7)   solid but able to see through
corrupting (9)   causing a loss of innocence
random (9)   without a plan, to happen by chance

Suggestions for Free Writing

Before you read this memoir, take about 5 minutes to free-write on the following topic:

Try to remember a time when you were a child and you did something wrong. Describe the event. Did you know it was wrong? What were the results of your actions? Did you get caught? Do you really think what you did was wrong, or did you simply not know any better?

Source: "Victims of the 14th-Floor Window" by Thomas Beller, *The New York Times Magazine*, October 8, 1995. Copyright 1995 by Thomas Beller. Reprinted by arrangement with Mary Evans, Inc.

I grew up in an apartment on the 14th floor with what, if one were   1
feeling expansive, could be called a view—the sky, the tops of buildings,
a multitude of wooden water towers. The view that most fascinated me,
however, was the one to be had by looking directly down.

Once when I was 6, I suddenly rose from my bath, opened the   2
narrow bathroom window above it and leaned out. I balanced on my
wet stomach, arms and legs outstretched, contemplating what it
would be like to take the plunge and whether my life so far had contained enough satisfaction so that it could now reasonably come to a
close. I stayed teetering there for a while, looking at the distant pavement below. Then, with the same entranced conviction with which I
had got up on the ledge, I got down, closed the window and resumed
my bath.

Having decided that I would not throw my body out the window, I   3
began throwing smaller, less valuable objects. I do not recall with what,
exactly, I began, but soon I was depositing all kinds of things out the
window, including water balloons, whose wobbly downward trajectory I
always monitored until they hit the ground.

Things were different at my friend Will's apartment, which was also   4
on the 14th floor. We were 10 and new best friends, and Will was constantly surprising me with novel ways with which to express malice. One
of the biggest revelations came in the arena of throwing things out the
window—Will introduced the idea of a target, or, more specifically, a
human target. The windows of his apartment all looked out over the
Hudson River, and directly below was a broad, lonely patch of Riverside
Drive.

A sense of heightened drama existed at Will's house, mirrored   5
by the bit of Riverside Drive he lived above. Interesting and unusual
things kept happening there, which we would monitor from his
kitchen window. Since the street was so empty, everyone walking past
had the quality of a person stepping onto a stage and walking across
it. We once observed an attractive young woman with a bouquet of
flowers in her hands walking briskly toward a man who was standing
still with several suitcases around him. He stared at her, his body
impassive as she approached. It looked like a love scene. When she
arrived in front of him she bashed the bouquet across his face, scat-
tering the petals, and turned and walked away. The man didn't move
at all.

We were so transfixed by this scene that we forgot to pour our pot   6
of water on him.

Others were less fortunate. We would stand guard at the kitchen   7
window until someone ambled down Riverside Drive. We'd have a long
time to size them up—their gait, their posture, their clothes. At a certain
ideal moment we would pour, and the water would fall forward in one
solid, translucent mass, and then split in half, and then in half again and

again, so that what started as a single glob on the 14th floor ended as a thousand pellets of water on the ground. The pale pavement would darken and the victim would become completely still. This momentary freeze was, for some reason, the most delicious part of the whole thing.

I remember one set of victims with great clarity: a mother and her small child walking down the street. The child—a girl I think, though from that height it was hard to tell—walked with unsteady steps. The water hit the ground in a great hissing mass and they froze just like everyone else.   8

But in the several seconds between the pour and the splatter, as I watched the water fragment and descend, a tremendous pang of regret leaped up in my stomach to go along with the more familiar thrill. I wondered what this regret might feel like had it been me and not the water falling. And also, as I watched the jerky, awkward expressiveness of the little girl walking beneath the water's widening net, I understood that there was a small corrupting moment about to take place—one kid introducing another to the random world of fate and bad luck.   9

Questions for Reflection and Discussion

1. In the very last sentence of the memoir, Thomas Beller says he understands that by dropping the water balloon on the little girl and her mother, he is "introducing" the little girl to "the random world of fate and bad luck." One can imagine the little girl looking to her mother for some sort of explanation or help. If you were that little girl's mother, what emotions would you be feeling as you tried to explain what happened? What would you say to the little girl?
2. Have you ever been hit by a water balloon or been the victim of some other childish prank? Or did you do such things when you were younger? How did being either the doer or the receiver of such a prank make you feel? Do you feel differently now that you are an adult?

Topics for Writing

1. When children are little, they get into little troubles. Then, as they get older, they sometimes get into far more serious trouble. Based on your own experiences, your readings, and your observations, describe the trouble that children typically get into, from the time they are very young until high school graduation. Be sure to give examples so that your essay is interesting and convincing. In your conclusion, explain whether you think there are any advantages to getting into trouble.
2. Return to the free write that you completed before you read the memoir, and use the information there to write a full and complete description of

a time in your childhood when you did something wrong or mischievous. Be sure to include background information about the event so that the reader can fully understand when, where, why, and how the incident occurred. Then, in your conclusion, explain how committing the act made you feel then and how you feel about it now.

Reading 2-2

HER FIRST WEEK

Sharon Olds

The next selection is a poem entitled "Her First Week," written by Sharon Olds, a highly regarded American poet. In this poem, Olds reminds us how delicate a baby is, how miraculous it is that something so small and helpless can even survive.

Although it is sometimes hard to understand exactly what every word and every line of a poem mean, often it is easy to get a general understanding and a good deal of pleasure from a poem. So even if you don't understand everything the poet is saying, just try to get the *feeling* she is trying to impart (get across) to her readers.

Vocabulary

the puckered, moire sacs (line 13) the baby's tiny lungs
the first chordate (18–19) refers to the fact that all humans have gills when they are still in the womb
vertebrate (20) species of living things that have a backbone
miniscule (27) very tiny

Suggestions for Free Writing

Before you read this poem, take about 5 minutes to free-write on the following topic:

If you were going to write a poem about your own childhood, what topics would you choose to write about? Make a list of these topics. Then, next to each one, write a few phrases or sentences to describe your feelings as you recall these topics.

She was so small I would scan the crib a half-second   1
  to find her, face-down in a corner, limp
  as something gently flung down, or fallen
  from some sky an inch above the mattress. I would

Source: "Her First Week" from *The Wellspring* by Sharon Olds. Copyright 1996 by Sharon Olds. Reprinted by permission of Alfred A. Knopf, a Division of Random House, Inc.

tuck her arm along her side   5
and slowly turn her over. She would tumble
over part by part, like a load
of damp laundry, in the dryer, I'd slip
a hand in, under her neck,
slide the other under her back,   10
and evenly lift her up. Her little bottom
sat in my palm, her chest contained
the puckered, moire sacs, and her neck—
I was afraid of her neck, once I almost
thought I heard it quietly snap,   15
I looked at her and she swivelled her slate
eyes and looked at me. It was in
my care, the creature of her spine, like the first
chordate, as if the history
of the vertebrate had been placed in my hands.   20
Every time I checked, she was still
with us—someday there would be a human
race. I could not see it, in her eyes,
but when I fed her, gathered her
like a loose bouquet to my side and offered   25
the breast, greyish-white, and struck with
miniscule scars like creeks in sunlight, I
felt she was serious, I believed she was willing to stay.

Questions for Reflection and Discussion

1. The poet feared that something would happen to the infant because she was so tiny and delicate. She writes: "I was afraid of her neck, once I almost thought I heard it quietly snap." Think back to the last time you held a very young infant. Did you have the same feelings?
2. If you were going to write a poem about a newborn infant, what are some of the adjectives (words that describe) you would use? Make a list of them.

Topics for Writing

1. Imagine that you are going to become a parent (or think back to when you became a parent for the first time). Describe some of the things you will do (or did do) to ensure that the infant is safe, healthy, happy, and knows that he or she is loved and wanted.

2. Return to the free write you completed before you read the poem, and use the information there to complete this assignment. Although you will not be required to write poetry very often in college (unless you decide to major in creative writing), take this opportunity to write a poem about one period of time in your childhood or an event that occurred in your childhood. Don't worry about whether the poem contains rhymes (notice that "Her First Week" does not rhyme). Just try to choose the most effective words and phrases that capture some of the feelings and emotions you felt at the time.

BARBIE-Q

Sandra Cisneros

The next selection is a short story written by Sandra Cisneros entitled "Barbie-Q." It was published in 1991 as part of a collection of stories entitled *Woman from Hollering Creek*, stories that focus on the author's Mexican-American childhood. Notice that the writer adopts a child's way of thinking and speaking as she tells the story of two little girls' fascination with Barbie Dolls.

Vocabulary

stiletto (paragraph 1)   a very high-heeled shoe

Jackie Kennedy pillbox hat (1)   The wife of President John F. Kennedy was famous for her wonderful sense of style in dressing, and she often wore a "pillbox" hat, so called because it looked a little like a pill box, either square or round, and about three inches high. These hats sometimes had short see-through veils attached to them.

ensemble (3)   an entire outfit

Suggestions for Free Writing

Before you read this short story, take about 5 minutes to free-write on the following topic:

Think back to a time in your childhood when you couldn't have something you wanted very much. What was it? Why was it so important to you? What did you do to try to get it? Why couldn't you have it? How did not being able to have it make you feel?

Yours is the one with mean eyes and a ponytail. Striped swimsuit, 1
stilettos, sunglasses, and gold hoop earrings. Mine is the one with bubble
hair. Red swimsuit, stilettos, pearl earrings, and a wire stand. But that's
all we can afford, besides one extra outfit apiece. Yours, "Red Flair,"
sophisticated A-line coatdress with a Jackie Kennedy pillbox hat, white
gloves, handbag, and heels included. Mine, "Solo in the Spotlight,"
evening elegance in black glitter strapless gown with a puffy skirt at the
bottom like a mermaid tail, formal-length gloves, pink chiffon scarf, and

mike included. From so much dressing and undressing, the black glitter wears off where her titties stick out. This and a dress invented from an old sock when we cut holes here and here and here, the cuff rolled over for the glamorous, fancy-free, off-the-shoulder look.

Every time the same story. Your Barbie is roommates with my Barbie, and my Barbie's boyfriend comes over and your Barbie steals him, okay? Kiss kiss kiss. Then the two Barbies fight. You dumbbell! He's mine. Oh no he's not, you stinky! Only Ken's invisible, right? Because we don't have money for a stupid-looking boy doll when we'd both rather ask for a new Barbie outfit next Christmas. We have to make do with your mean-eyed Barbie and my bubblehead Barbie and our one outfit apiece not including the sock dress.

Until next Sunday when we are walking through the flea market on Maxwell Street and *there!* Lying on the street next to some tool bits, and platform shoes with the heels all squashed, and a fluorescent green wicker wastebasket, and aluminum foil, and hub-caps, and a pink shag rug, and windshield wiper blades, and dusty mason jars, and a coffee can full of rusty nails. *There!* Where? Two Mattel boxes. One with the "Career Gal" ensemble, snappy black-and-white business suit, three-quarter-length sleeve jacket with kick-pleat skirt, red sleeveless shell, gloves, pumps, and matching hat included. The other, "Sweet Dreams," dreamy pink-and-white plaid nightgown and matching robe, lace-trimmed slippers, hair-brush and hand mirror included. How much? Please, please, please, please, please, please, please, until they say okay.

On the outside you and me skipping and humming but inside we are doing loopity-loops and pirouetting. Until at the next vendor's stand, next to boxed pies, and bright orange toilet brushes, and rubber gloves, and wrench sets, and bouquets of feather flowers, and glass towel racks, and steel wool, and Alvin and the Chipmunks records, *there!* And *there!* And *there!* and *there!* and *there!* and *there!* Bendable Legs Barbie with her new page-boy hairdo. Midge, Barbie's best friend. Ken, Barbie's boyfriend. Skipper, Barbie's little sister. Tutti and Todd, Barbie and Skipper's tiny twin sister and brother. Skipper's friends, Scooter and Ricky. Alan, Ken's buddy. And Francie, Barbie's MOD'ern cousin.

Everybody today selling toys, all of them damaged with water and smelling of smoke. Because a big toy warehouse on Halsted Street burned down yesterday—see there?—the smoke still rising and drifting across the Dan Ryan expressway. And now there is a big fire sale at Maxwell Street, today only.

So what if we didn't get our new Bendable Legs Barbie and Midge and Ken and Skipper and Tutti and Todd and Scooter and Ricky and Alan and Francie in nice clean boxes and had to buy them on Maxwell Street, all water-soaked and sooty. So what if our Barbies smell like smoke when you hold them up to your nose even after you wash and wash and wash them. And if the prettiest doll, Barbie's MOD'ern cousin

Francie with real eyelashes, eyelash brush included, has a left foot that's melted a little—so? If you dress her in her new "Prom Pinks" outfit, satin splendor with matching coat, gold belt, clutch, and hair bow included, so long as you don't lift her dress, right?—who's to know.

Questions for Reflection and Discussion

1. There always seem to be fads in children's toys and games. Today, it seems that all young children want to collect Pokemon stuff. What were the "must-have" toys or fads when you were a child?
2. Notice the writer's attention to detail when she describes the clothing and accessories that come with Barbie Dolls. How do these precise and accurate details contribute to the effectiveness of the story? Do you get the "joke" of the letter Q in the title?

Topics for Writing

1. Write an essay in which you explain whether you think our society is far too concerned with owning (and showing off) expensive items, from toys to clothing to cars to the latest technological developments in entertainment. Be sure to give examples from your observations, your readings, and your experiences to support your position.
2. Return to the free write you completed before you read the short story, and use the information there to write an essay describing a time in your childhood when you couldn't have something you wanted very much. Be sure to include background information and details about what you wanted, why you wanted it, and why you couldn't have it, so that the reader fully understands how you felt at the time. In your conclusion, reflect on the impact that not being able to have something you wanted very badly had on you.

Reading 2–4

ANGRY FATHERS

Mell Lazarus

The next selection, "Angry Fathers," written by Mell Lazarus, is a memoir that describes a time in his childhood when he and two of his friends destroyed someone's property, and the consequences they had to endure as a result of their actions.

Vocabulary

listless (paragraph 2)   without energy
anonymous (4)   without knowing the name of the person who did something
consequences (4)   results
surveyed (6)   looked over
a tweak of remorse (7)   a tiny bit of regret
craving (7)   desiring
indignant (9)   feeling put out or angry
inconspicuous (10)   without being noticed
blighted (11)   badly damaged
approbation (11)   approval
abstractions (14)   concepts, ideas
emerged (18)   came out
reproach (23)   blame
corporal punishment (24)   physical punishment as opposed to verbal punishment
conspiracy (25)   to plan and act together, often secretly and for a bad purpose
spectacle (25)   to put on a show
outrageous (26)   completely unacceptable

Suggestions for Free Writing

Before you read this essay, take about 5 minutes to free-write on the following topic:

Consider the way your parents or guardians disciplined you when you did something wrong, and compare their disciplinary methods with the methods you use or will use with your own children.

Source: "Angry Fathers" copyright 1995 by Mell Lazarus. This article originally appeared in *The New York Times Magazine,* May 28, 1995. Reprinted by permission of the author.

"Daddy's going to be very angry about this," my mother said.   1

It was August 1938, at a Catskill Mountains boarding house. One   2
hot Friday afternoon three of us—9-year-old city boys—got to feeling listless. We'd done all the summer-country stuff, caught all the frogs, picked
the blueberries and shivered in enough icy river water. What we needed,
on this unbearably boring afternoon, was some action.

To consider the options, Artie, Eli and I holed up in the cool of the   3
"casino," the little building in which the guests enjoyed their nightly
bingo games and the occasional traveling magic act.

Gradually, inspiration came: the casino was too new, the wood   4
frame and white Sheetrock walls too perfect. We would do it some quiet
damage. Leave our anonymous mark on the place, for all time. With, of
course, no thought as to consequences.

We began by picking up a long, wooden bench, running with it like   5
a battering ram, and bashing it into a wall. It left a wonderful hole. But
small. So we did it again. And again. . . .

Afterward the three of us, breathing hard, sweating the sweat of   6
heroes, surveyed our first really big-time damage. The process had been
so satisfying we'd gotten carried away; there was hardly a good square
foot of Sheetrock left.

Suddenly, before even a tweak of remorse set in, the owner, Mr.   7
Biolos, appeared in the doorway of the building. Furious. And craving
justice: When they arrived from the city that night, he-would-tell-our-
fathers!

Meantime, he told our mothers. My mother felt that what I had   8
done was so monstrous she would leave my punishment to my father.
"And," she said, "Daddy's going to be very angry about this."

By 6 o'clock Mr. Biolos was stationed out at the driveway, grimly   9
waiting for the fathers to start showing up. Behind him, the front porch
was jammed, like a sold-out bleacher section, with indignant guests.
They'd seen the damage to their bingo palace, knew they'd have to
endure it in that condition for the rest of the summer. They, too, craved
justice.

As to Artie, Eli and me, we each found an inconspicuous spot on   10
the porch, a careful distance from the other two but not too far from our
respective mothers. And waited.

Artie's father arrived first. When Mr. Biolos told him the news and   11
showed him the blighted casino, he carefully took off his belt and—with
practiced style—viciously whipped his screaming son. With the approbation, by the way, of an ugly crowd of once-gentle people.

Eli's father showed up next. He was told and shown and went   12
raving mad, knocking his son off his feet with a slam to the head. As Eli
lay crying on the grass, he kicked him on the legs, buttocks and back.
When Eli tried to get up he kicked him again.

The crowd muttered: Listen, they should have thought of this   13
before they did the damage. They'll live, don't worry, and I bet they
never do that again.

I wondered: What will my father do? He'd never laid a hand on me   14
in my life. I knew about other kids, had seen bruises on certain school-
mates and even heard screams in the evenings from certain houses on
my street, but they were those kids, their families, and the why and how
of their bruises were, to me, dark abstractions. Until now.

I looked over at my mother. She was upset. Earlier she'd made it   15
clear to me that I had done some special kind of crime. Did it mean that
beatings were now, suddenly, the new order of the day?

My own father suddenly pulled up in our Chevy, just in time to see   16
Eli's father dragging Eli up the porch steps and into the building. He got
out of the car believing, I was sure, that whatever it was all about, Eli
must have deserved it. I went dizzy with fear.

Mr. Biolos, on a roll, started talking. My father listened, his shirt   17
soaked with perspiration, a damp handkerchief draped around his neck;
he never did well in humid weather. I watched him follow Mr. Biolos into
the casino. My dad—strong and principled, hot and bothered—what
was he thinking about all this?

When they emerged, my father looked over at my mother. He   18
mouthed a small "Hello." Then his eyes found me and stared for a long
moment, without expression. I tried to read his eyes, but they left me
and went to the crowd, from face to expectant face.

Then, amazingly, he got into his car and drove away! Nobody, not   19
even my mother, could imagine where he was going.

An hour later he came back. Tied onto the top of his car was a   20
stack of huge Sheetrock boards. He got out holding a paper sack with a
hammer sticking out of it. Without a word he untied the Sheetrock and
one by one carried the boards into the casino.

And didn't come out again that night.   21

All through my mother's and my silent dinner and for the rest of   22
that Friday evening and long after we had gone to bed, I could hear—
everyone could hear—the steady bang bang bang bang of my dad's
hammer. I pictured him sweating, missing his dinner, missing my
mother, getting madder and madder at me. Would tomorrow be the last
day of my life? It was 3 A.M. before I finally fell asleep.

The next morning, my father didn't say a single word about the   23
night before. Nor did he show any trace of anger or reproach of any
kind. We had a regular day, he, my mother and I, and, in fact, our usual
sweet family weekend.

Was he mad at me? You bet he was. But in a time when many of his   24
generation saw corporal punishment of their children as a God-given
right, he knew "spanking" as beating, and beating as criminal. And that

when kids were beaten, they always remembered the pain but often forgot the reason.

And I also realized years later that, to him, humiliating me was just 25 as unthinkable. Unlike the fathers of my buddies, he couldn't play into a conspiracy of revenge and spectacle.

But my father had made his point. I never forgot that my van- 26 dalism on that August afternoon was outrageous.

And I'll never forget that it was also the day I first understood how 27 deeply I could trust him.

Questions for Reflection and Discussion

1. How would you react if your child vandalized someone's property? Would you react as Artie's and Eli's fathers reacted, or as Mell's father reacted? Why?
2. Find as many examples as you can of the writer's use of very precise details that enable you to actually picture the events that occurred that day and evening.

Topics for Writing

1. Punishment of children has changed very much over time. Thirty years ago, it was acceptable to hit, even beat, a child if he or she did something wrong. In fact, it was expected, and parents who did not physically punish their children for wrongdoing were sometimes accused of spoiling their children. Today, however, society frowns upon physical punishment such as the beatings described in Mell Lazarus's essay.

    Interview a parent, relative, teacher, or friend who is old enough to remember what types of punishments were acceptable for children 20 to 30 years ago, and describe the differences between what was acceptable then and what is acceptable now. Be sure to include background information and details so that your reader can fully understand the differences you are describing.
2. Return to the free write you completed before you read this passage, and use the information there to write a full and descriptive essay explaining how you will (or how you do) discipline your children so they can learn from their mistakes.

Reading 2-5

POTS, BLOCKS & SOCKS

Debra Rosenberg and Larry Reibstein

The final selection in this chapter is entitled "Pots, Blocks & Socks." The article, which appeared in a special "Your Child" edition of *Newsweek* magazine, explains that most experts believe a baby probably does not need special toys or other equipment to "guarantee a life . . . of success." This article is similar to the type of reading that would be assigned to you in a college-level child psychology class.

Directly following this article is a chart, "A Century of Bringing Up Baby," that briefly explains the way that experts' ideas of good parenting have changed from generation to generation.

Vocabulary

From "Pots, Blocks & Socks":

immune (paragraph 1)   protected from

conscientious (1)   very determined

ivy-covered diplomas (1)   diplomas from one of the Ivy League colleges (Brown, Columbia, Cornell, Harvard, Princeton, Stanford, and Yale)

accouterments of success (1)   symbols of success

Einstein (2)   Albert Einstein, one of the greatest thinkers of the twentieth century

obsessive (2)   paying far too much attention to

stimulated (2)   excited

isolation (3)   alone, solitary

sibling (3)   a sister or brother

developmental psychologist (3)   one who studies children's intellectual, physical, and emotional development

neural pathways (3)   pathways in the brain

cognitive science (4)   the study of learning (cognition)

futile (4)   hopeless, useless

cadence fluctuates (5)   tone of voice changes

the next Leonardo (6)   refers to the Italian artist, Leonardo da Vinci (1452–1519), one of the greatest artists of all time

embodied (6)   contained in

concedes (6)   admits

anecdotes (6)   true stories used to prove a point

attuned (8)   used to

mesmerized (8)   giving something complete attention to the exclusion of everything else

Claude Monet (8)   French Impressionist painter (1840–1926), known for the way he reflected light in his paintings

From "A Century of Bringing Up Baby":

denounced (paragraph 1)   disagreed with and criticized as worthless

behaviorist (3)   one who believes that behavior can be changed gradually through training or stimulation

stoicism (3)   not showing emotion, being strong

nuclear families (5)   consisting only of the mother, father, and children, as compared with earlier times when grandparents and other relatives lived together in the same households

anti-establishment generation (6)   generation that questioned rules and authority

Suggestions for Free Writing

Before you read this article, take about 5 minutes to free-write on the following topic:

What are some of the techniques and practices you will use to make sure your children learn and grow happily and safely?

The baby is due soon, so you're out buying the normal stuff— diapers, receiving blankets, towels, powder, creams. Think you're done? Only if you're immune from guilt. Nowadays you'd be hard pressed to call yourself a conscientious parent unless you've also laid on black-and-white toys, flashcards, "scientifically designed" playthings and at least a dozen Mozart CDs—thereby supposedly guaranteeing a life full of ivy-covered diplomas and other accouterments of success.   1

Does any of this really make a difference? Can you stimulate your child into becoming another Einstein? Not likely. All of this obsessive parenting is based on the notion that a baby properly stimulated will develop faster, learn languages or music better and all in all be a smarter kid. The key phrase here is "properly stimulated," which is not the same as expensively stimulated or the worse fate, overstimulated.   2

Most experts advise parents to calm down. Sure, a baby requires certain stimulation to learn basic tasks, whether to speak or to use motor skills to build Lego bridges. But short of being raised in isolation, a baby will encounter enough stimulation in most households to do the trick—   3 anything from banging pots and pans together to speaking to a sibling. There's no evidence that specific kinds of toys or environments will somehow speed up skills or groom a child for the Olympics. "You could stimulate until the cow comes home and it's not going to make any difference," says David Henry Feldman, a developmental psychologist at Tufts University. "Evolution has made sure that the baby's brain is going to develop certain neural pathways."

Researchers also caution parents against expecting that they can make their kids smarter. "The fact is, it's very, very hard to raise anybody's IQ," says Edward Zigler, a Yale psychologist and a founder of Head Start. And even if a child learns to read early, there's no evidence that that accomplishment translates into higher grades, intelligence or later success, according to John Bruer, president of the James S. McDonnell Foundation, which studies cognitive science. Besides, he says, trying to determine a child's right age, or "critical period," to learn a skill is futile— no one agrees on when or even whether such windows occur in the brain.

If any stimulation is effective, it's plain old talking. Language development results from a child's talking to a mother or other caretaker— not from flashcards, says Zigler. Mothers worldwide naturally pick up a way of speaking that Zigler calls "motherese." They pause between words so that babies can concentrate on language sounds. Their voices rise in pitch and their cadence fluctuates almost melodically. There's nothing fancy about this.

To be fair, there are some experts who say kids can be specially stimulated into success. One of the more controversial is Glenn Doman, head of the Institutes for the Achievement of Human Potential, also known as the Better Baby Institute, near Philadelphia. His theory—strongly disputed by most experts—is that babies can learn anything and it's easiest to start at birth. "Every child has the potential to be the next Leonardo," he says. His technique, embodied in the book "How to Teach Your Baby to Read," first published in 1963, exposes babies to flashcards of words and phrases. Doman concedes he's gained little scientific recognition but says he has 20,000 supporting anecdotes. One of them is from Jo Ann Loeliger, a 43-year-old Philadelphian who began teaching her three children to read at the ages of 3 years, 9 months and at birth. She says her older kids were reading difficult books early, and her youngest could read single-word flashcards at 9 months. The older kids also started learning violin at the ages of 4 and 3. "It comes so easily to them," says Loeliger.

Some researchers also think that particular toys are more effective than others in stimulating children. Dr. Richard Chase, founder of Child Development Corp., says his company's age-appropriate toys, like the Rattle Cat, which contains high-contrast colors with a simple face for babies, can heighten kids' development. "We can make most children smarter and more interesting than we make them now," says Chase, an adjunct professor of psychiatry at Johns Hopkins University.

But most experts say that more important than a particular toy is 8
that parents be attuned to the kind of stimulation that interests their
child. Sue Cima, who lives in Orlando, Fla., found that when her
daughter Niki was 3 months, she was fascinated by black-and-white cardboard flashcards. "She just loved them. She was mesmerized," Cima
recalls. Pots and pans? Niki hardly looked. Beth Crim, a librarian in
Manassas, Va., noticed that as a newborn her son David seemed
intrigued by patterns of light. She would place him on his back where he
could watch the sunlight making shadows through the trees. "That's
about as low-tech as you can get," says Crim. So one kid will grow up to
be a great blackjack dealer in Las Vegas and the other the next Claude
Monet. But which one?

A Century of Bringing Up Baby

Parenting, even with the best advice, has never been easy. The 1
child-raising experts of one generation are often denounced by the children of the next. Here's a look at how much has changed since the
beginning of the century.

1920s: Education pioneer Maria Montessori lets a child's own 2
interests set the pace at her new schools; Swiss psychologist Jean Piaget
rethinks how children learn.

1930s: The Depression forces kids to grow up fast. Behaviorist John 3
Watson says stoicism builds character; never hug or kiss the child.

1940s: The war ends and a baby boom begins. Dr. Benjamin 4
Spock's best-selling book on child raising advises a new generation of
parents to replace schedules and scoldings with humor and hugs.

1950s: Nuclear families colonize the suburbs. Parents seek cues 5
from science and monitor Johnny's progress against the development
charts of Arnold Gesell, founder of Yale's Child Development Clinic.

1960s: The anti-establishment generation attempts to revolutionize 6
nearly everything, including family relations.

1970s: Divorce divides a record number of families and the 7
women's movement questions traditional parenting roles for both men
and women.

1980s: More moms enter the work force than ever before, pushing 8
some companies to provide day care. Feminists like Carol Gilligan ask
why researchers largely ignore girls' development.

1990s: Researchers examining cognitive development tap new 9
technologies to see the exciting world inside a child's brain.

Questions for Reflection and Discussion

1. What information contained in the article "Pots, Blocks & Socks" do you think is most useful for parents?
2. As you look at the "Century of Bringing Up Baby" chart, under which decade's theories do you think you were brought up? Which decade's theories make the most sense to you? The least sense?

Topics for Writing

1. Recall a time in your life when you had difficulty learning something, either in or outside of school. Describe how you overcame, or were unable to overcome, this difficulty. Be sure to give background information and details so that the reader can understand the circumstances and conditions that existed. In your conclusion, explain what you will do to ensure that your children do not experience the same difficulty.
2. Return to the free write you completed before you read this article, and use the information there, along with the information contained in the article, to write an essay describing some of the activities, techniques, and practices you will use (or do use) to ensure that your children have the best possible chance to learn and to develop their intellects to their fullest potential. It is perfectly okay for you to quote information from the article, as long as you place the words in quotation marks. (Remember, if you use the words of another writer and do not place them in quotation marks, you will be guilty of plagiarism.)

Additional Writing Topics about Childhood

This chapter contains five selections about childhood: the first four are highly personal accounts, whereas the last one is technical and scientific. However, taken together, they illustrate the many joys and challenges that children face: the poem in which the author understands how miraculous a tiny new life is; the two memoirs that recount the kind of trouble children get into without fully understanding the seriousness of their actions; the short story that relates how obsessed children can become with the latest "fashionable" toys; and finally, the article and chart explaining the latest theories being offered by researchers about the way children develop and thrive.

1. How has your opinion and attitude about childhood changed as a result of reading the selections in this chapter? Be sure to refer to the selections in order to give your reader the necessary evidence and information needed to convince him or her of the change(s) that occurred in your thinking. It is perfectly acceptable for you to use the exact words used in the selections, as long as you place the words in quotation marks.
2. Imagine that as a result of reading the selections in this chapter, you have decided to pursue a career in the field of child care. Return to the free write you completed at the beginning of the chapter, and use the information there to complete the following assignment:

> Write a letter to the director of a day-care center for children ages one to four, and explain how, if you were given a position at the center, you would interact with the children, which child development theories you will put into practice, and the way you would help children to learn. Be certain to begin or end your letter with an explanation of *why* you want to work with children.

Chapter
3

The Art (and Hard Work)
of Parenting

Chapter 2 dealt with some of the issues of childhood. In this chapter, we will consider what it is like to be a parent. It is a role that all of us are familiar with; all of us have had parents or parent replacements, and many of us will be (or already are) parents. Therefore, we know, based on our own experiences, how complex the role of parenting can be: the struggle to do the right thing no matter what other people think; the struggle to find the time and the patience to give children the love and attention they need; the personal and financial sacrifices that are often a part of parenting. In short, parenting may be one of the most difficult jobs in the world.

But parenting is also the most pleasurable, as some of the readings in this chapter will show. Through these selections, you will discover that parenting is a very individualized skill—no two parents are exactly alike. However, all of the parents who either wrote or who are described in the following readings have one thing in common: They love their children more than they love anything else, and they will do whatever they must to ensure their children's safety, comfort, and happiness—no matter what it takes.

Pre-reading Activity

Before you read the selections in this chapter, take about 10 minutes to free-write on the following topics. They will help you to think about your own experiences and knowledge of parenting.

Reflect on the relationship you have or had with your parents, and on the relationship you have (or will have) with your children. Are they similar or different? In what ways? What do you think are the most important qualities parents must possess? The least important? If you could change one thing about your parents, what would it be? What is the one thing you would never change? Do you think children who are raised in one-parent homes are at a disadvantage? Why? Is your relationship with your parents and/or your children as strong as you would like it to be? Will you raise your children differently than your parents raised you because the times have changed? For another reason? Explain.

Reading 3–1

LIVING WITH "THE LOOK"

Robert Hughes

In the essay entitled "Living with 'The Look,'" the author, Robert Hughes, describes the reaction of others when they see his 11-year-old autistic son, Walker. Autism is a mental condition with symptoms ranging from unusual behavior to an inability to communicate and do many of the things "normal" children can do. Only recently have scientists begun to discover the causes and possible treatments for this disorder. (As of now, there is no cure.) Hughes explains why some people's reactions (reflected in "the look" on their faces) bother him, and he then explains the way he is trying to develop his own "look" in response.

Vocabulary

autistic (autism) (paragraph 1)   a disorder that affects a child's ability to communicate and function socially

baffling (2)   confusing

the bourgeoisie (2)   typical people

threshold (3)   level

field anthropologist (5)   one who studies types and or groups of people

Rain Man (5)   a movie about an autistic adult

phenomenon (5)   unusual happening

gravitate (6)   move toward, head in the direction of

magnanimous (6)   extremely generous

conjecture (7)   try to figure out

deploys (8)   uses

a Ward and Beaver experience (9)   reference to a popular TV show in the 1950s,
"Leave It to Beaver," about a "perfect," "normal" family with no problems

unvarying (9)   never changing

Suggestions for Free Writing

Before you read this essay, take about 10 minutes to free-write on the following topic:

Source: "Living with 'The Look'" from *Newsweek*, September 1, 1997. Copyright 1997 Newsweek, Inc. All rights reserved. Reprinted by permission.

When you see someone who has a handicap, what is your first reaction? Or, if you have a handicap, how do people react to you when they first notice it? Is it possible to ignore a person's handicap completely? Is it a good idea to ignore it completely? Why?

I am walking down a busy Chicago street with Walker, my autistic 11-year-old son, and people are staring at him. He's a boy blessed with terrific good looks—tall and straight, with big dark eyes, glossy hair and a movie star's smile—but this isn't what's turning heads.   1

Walker isn't actually walking down the street; he's running and somehow skipping at the same time. And he isn't talking to me; he's loudly singing "Jingle Bell Rock," though this is the middle of July. And he isn't, like me, trying unsuccessfully to look everywhere but into people's eyes; he's looking and smiling directly at everyone he passes with his fingers in his ears, his elbows flared out on either side. And, further baffling the bourgeoisie, he occasionally stops, shouts, spits twice and pulls up his shirt.   2

Although I'm secretly proud of every bit of this sidewalk routine of his, I'm all too aware of the faces of the people we pass. Some smile, even laugh appreciatively, at his obvious joy. Some nod to me sadly and knowingly: "Ah, I know how hard your life must be," they seem to say. Some flinch in exaggerated horror as though from some ghastly space alien from Warner Brothers. Others are cool, spot him far off and pretend not to see him when they pass. Still others are so used to such surpassing weirdness in the city that our little show comes nowhere near their threshold of surprise.   3

One reaction, however, is more puzzling to me than all the others. I have come to think of it as "The Look." The passerby's face becomes still and thoughtful. The eyes become narrow, like those of the cunning psychiatrist in an old movie when he asks a patient what the inkblots look like. A hand goes up to the lips and, shifting into field anthropologist mode, the eyewitness stops and stares and nods silently as though making a mental note to write this one down in the journal. It's a locked-on-target look. A piano falling onto the pavement nearby wouldn't jar the stunning logical processes at work.   4

Having been upset by The Look about a thousand times, and being something of an amateur field anthropologist myself, I have often asked this question: "Why do these people act this way?" The best answers that I have been able to come up with are these: 5

(a) They are heartless and rude and should be tortured in some hideous way for upsetting a really nice father.

(b) They are ignorant and think that humans come in solidly "normal" and "abnormal" forms and have no doubt about what kind they themselves are.

(c) They saw the movie "Rain Man" and are now experts on autism.

(d) They are fearful and are trying to achieve distance from a scary sight by trying to regard it as a rare scientific phenomenon.

(e) They are curious, as the father would be, too, in their situation, at seeing a normal-looking boy acting strangely.

(f) They aren't even aware that they have an expression on their faces and actually feel sympathetic toward the boy.

(g) They really are psychiatrists, and their work is a big help to humanity.

Which answer I choose is largely dependent on my mood. If I'm feeling defensive and hypersensitive (most of the time), I gravitate toward letters a, b and c. If I'm feeling wise and magnanimous (not very often), I go for letters d, e and f. And if I'm feeling lighthearted (once or twice a year), I amuse myself with some variation of g. 6

But I know that I can conjecture forever and never really be sure what The Look means. 7

One thing I am sure of is the look on Walker's face. Unable to talk normally, he deploys a heavy arsenal of expression and movement to communicate. The beaming smile, the direct gaze, the skip-running and shout-singing, even the vigorous spitting—all of it—tells me Walker is working his audience hard. "Here I am! Look at me! I'm having fun! Aren't you impressed?" The message goes out, and some people, remarkably, seem to pick it up. Most, understandably, do not. 8

But what about my face, my look? Inside the house I do a fair job of attempting to see the world as Walker sees it and understanding him as far as possible on his own terms. Thus a game of catch is, for us, not a Ward and the Beaver experience in the backyard. Performed Walker style, catch is an "extreme sport," with rules that are reinvented by him daily. Currently the game must be played in the house while Walker jumps wildly on his exercise trampoline, and there must be loud music playing, and he must catch the ball and throw it back while airborne. At unpredictable moments, Walker must leap off the trampoline and dash in and out of the room. The one unvarying rule is this: Dad must never stop paying attention. The result is that I long ceased aching for the "normal" game of catch and learned to love the in-house version we share. 9

At home, I stretch my notions of the "appropriate" to accommo-date Walker's ideas on: a bedroom (the dining room, lights on); break-fast, lunch and dinner (cooked spaghetti, no sauce), and entertainment (every morning, the video of "The Wind in the Willows"). 10

When I step outside the house, however, a different, less noble point of view grips me, and I start to speculate needlessly on how out-siders see my son. Lost in a fog of anger or avoidance or criticism, I must present an uninviting picture for him and the world to look at. Why shouldn't passersby stare at the friendly son when the father's face is cloudy with conflict and questioning? 11

So I'm working on my look. I'm shooting for, at minimum, a near-frequent smile. I want to face the sidewalk parade as Walker does, with joy and hope and, most important of all, with a saving sense of fun.   12

Questions for Reflection and Discussion

1. Robert Hughes described the various ways people reacted when they saw his autistic son running and skipping and singing "Jingle Bell Rock," with his fingers in his ears, his elbows flared out on either side, and all the while shouting, spitting, and pulling up his shirt. How do you react when you see someone behaving differently? Reread paragraphs 3 and 4 and decide if your reaction fits into any of the categories described there.
2. Think about someone you have known or had contact with who has a physical or mental disability. How is that person's life being affected, both negatively and positively, by his or her handicap?

Topics for Writing

1. Think of an action or an inappropriate or cruel reaction you have seen someone (a teacher, a parent, an employer, a salesclerk) have to a child. Write an essay in which you describe the action or reaction, being sure to give complete details and answering the important who, what, where, when, why, and how questions. In your conclusion, explain why you think the person behaved in this way, just as Hughes tries to figure out why people behave the way they do when they see his son.
2. Return to the free write you completed before you read Hughes's essay, and use the information there to write an essay describing and explaining the way you react to people with handicaps, or the way people react to your handicap. In your conclusion, explain whether Hughes's essay had any effect on the way you will react in the future to people with a handicap.

Reading 3–2

THE COLOR OF WATER (EXCERPT)
James McBride

The next selection is an *excerpt* (an excerpt is part of a longer work) from a wonderful and inspiring book about family life entitled *The Color of Water* by James McBride. In his book, he describes the extraordinary energy and devotion of his mother, Ruth McBride, who raised 12 biracial children on her own after her second husband died. The McBride's family life was anything but typical; however, as the author says at the end of the book, his mother's methods may have been unusual, but she managed to put all 12 of her children through college.

Vocabulary

chaos (paragraph 1)   total confusion
microscopic (1)   very tiny
indignities (1)   humiliations or embarrassments
denizens (1)   citizens or representatives
scavenging (2)   searching, as in the jungle or other wild place
foraged (2)   searched for
Red Hook (2)   neighborhood in Brooklyn, N.Y.
benevolent (2)   good; kind
pillage (2)   steal
commiserate (3)   sympathize with one another
a Third World country (4)   a developing country
dissipate (4)   lessen, then disappear
artifact (4)   evidence
fossilize (4)   harden

Suggestions for Free Writing

Before you read this excerpt, take about 10 minutes to free-write on the following topic:

Source: From *The Color of Water* by James McBride. Copyright 1996 by James McBride. Used by permission of Riverhead Books, a division of Penquin Putnam, Inc.

Think about the busiest, most hectic, craziest time in your household. Jot down everything you can remember that goes on; in other words, "write" a picture of what is happening so your reader can "see" it.

Mommy's house was orchestrated chaos and as the eighth of twelve children, I was lost in the sauce, so to speak. I was neither the prettiest, nor the youngest, nor the brightest. In a house where there was little money and little food, your power was derived from who you could order around. I was what Mommy called a "Little Kid," one of five young'uns, microscopic dots on the power grid of the household, thus fit to be tied, tortured, tickled, tormented, ignored, and commanded to suffer all sorts of indignities at the hands of the "Big Kids," who didn't have to go to bed early, didn't believe in the tooth fairy, and were appointed denizens of power by Mommy, who of course wielded ultimate power.

My brothers and sisters were my best friends, but when it came to food, they were my enemies. There were so many of us we were constantly hungry, scavenging for food in the empty refrigerator and cabinets. We would hide food from one another, squirreling away a precious grilled cheese or fried bologna sandwich, but the hiding places were known to all and foraged by all and the precious commodity was usually discovered and devoured before it got cold. Entire plots were hatched around swiping food, complete with double-crossing, backstabbing, intrigue, outright robbery, and gobbled evidence. Back in the projects in Red Hook, before we moved to Queens, Mommy would disappear in the morning and return later with huge cans of peanut butter which some benevolent agency had distributed from some basement area in the housing projects. We'd gather around the cans, open them, and spoon up the peanut butter like soup, giggling as our mouths stuck closed with the gooey stuff. When Mommy left for work, we dipped white bread in syrup for lunch, or ate brown sugar raw out of the box, which was a good hunger killer. We had a toaster that shocked you every time you touched it; we called our toast *shock*toast and we got shocked so much our hair stood on end like Buckwheat's. Ma often lamented the fact that she could not afford to buy us fruit, sometimes for weeks at a time, but we didn't mind. We spent every penny we had on junk food. "If you eat that stuff your teeth will drop out," Mommy warned. We ignored her. "If you chew gum and swallow it, your behind will close up," she said. We listened and never swallowed gum. We learned to eat standing up, sitting down, lying down, and half asleep, because there were never enough places at the table for everyone to sit, and there was always a mad scramble for Ma's purse when she showed up at two A.M. from work. The cafeteria at the Chase Manhattan Bank where she worked served dinner to the employees for free, so she would load up with bologna sandwiches, cheese, cakes, whatever she could pillage, and bring it home for the hordes to devour. If you were the first to grab the purse when she got home, you ate. If you missed it, well, sleep tight.

The food she brought from work was delicious, particularly when 3 compared to the food she cooked. Mommy could not cook to save her life. Her grits tasted like sand and butter, with big lumps inside that caught in your teeth and stuck in your gums. Her pancakes had white goo and egg shells in them. Her stew would send my little brother Henry upstairs in disgust. "Prison stew," he'd sniff, coming back a few minutes later to help himself before the masses devoured it. She had little time to cook anyway. When she got home from work she was exhausted. We'd come downstairs in the morning to find her still dressed and fast asleep at the kitchen table, her head resting on the pages of someone's homework, a cold cup of coffee next to her sleeping head. Her housework rivaled her cooking. "I'm the worst housekeeper I've ever seen," she declared, and that was no lie. Our house looked like a hurricane hit it. Books, papers, shoes, football helmets, baseball bats, dolls, trucks, bicycles, musical instruments, lay everywhere and were used by everyone. All the boys slept in one room, girls slept in another, but the labels "boys' room" and "girls' room" meant nothing. We snuck into each other's rooms by night to trade secrets, argue, commiserate, spy, and continue chess games and monopoly games that had begun days earlier. Four of us played the same clarinet, handing it off to one another in the hallway at school like halfbacks on a football field. Same with coats, hats, sneakers, clean socks, and gym uniforms. One washcloth was used by all. A solitary toothbrush would cover five sets of teeth and gums. We all swore it belonged to us personally. Our furniture consisted of two beautiful rocking chairs that Ma bought from Macy's because on television she saw her hero President John F. Kennedy use one to rock his kids, a living room couch, and an assortment of chairs, tables, dressers, and beds. The old black-and-white TV set worked—sometimes. It wasn't high on Mommy's list of things to fix. She called it "the boob tube" and rarely allowed us to watch it. We didn't need to.

Our house was a combination three-ring circus and zoo, complete 4 with ongoing action, daring feats, music, and animals. Over the years we assembled a stable of pets that resembled a veritable petting zoo: gerbils, mice, dogs, cats, rabbits, fish, birds, turtles, and frogs that would alternatively lick and bite us and spread mysterious diseases that zipped through our house as if it were a Third World country, prompting health clinic visits chaperoned by Ma where bored doctors slammed needles into our butts like we were on a GMC assembly line. Ma once brought home a chick for Easter, and it grew and grew until she came home from work one night, opened the door, and saw eight kids chasing a rooster around the living room. "Get him out!" she screamed. He was removed and eventually replaced by a fierce German shepherd named Abe who bit us all and would occasionally leave a mound of dog poop in a corner somewhere, then growl and dare us to beat him for it. The mound would sit, untouched. After a day the odor would dissipate and we'd avoid it further until it dried up and hardened like a rock, whereupon some brave soul would kick the offending artifact under the radiator, where it would fester and further fossilize into dust or extinction or discovery.

We never consulted Mommy about these problems. Her time merited only full-blown problems like, "Is the kitchen floor still under two feet of water since y'all flooded it?" and school, which was a top priority. Excuses for not doing homework were not accepted and would draw a beating. Cursing was not allowed. We weren't even allowed to say the word "lie," we had to use "story."

5

Questions for Reflection and Discussion

1. Ruth McBride cared about the education of her children more than she cared about anything else. She believed it was the one thing they would need to be successful. What, in your opinion, is the most important thing parents can do to ensure that their children will have happy and successful lives?
2. Ruth McBride was a single parent as a result of her second husband's death. What are some of the disadvantages single parents face? What are some of the advantages?

Topics for Writing

1. Write an essay describing the characteristics (habits, traits, qualities) of a family member whom you know very well. Begin each paragraph of your essay with a description of the characteristic. Then, in the rest of the paragraph, provide details, descriptions, and examples so that the reader can "see" the person whose characteristics you are describing.
2. Return to the free write you completed before you read the excerpt, and use the information there to write an essay describing your household, using a style similar to the one McBride uses. He begins each paragraph with a topic sentence and then offers many details and examples to support his topic sentence. For example, in paragraph 3, he notes in his topic sentence that the food his mother brought home from work was delicious when compared with the food his mother cooked because she "could not cook to save her life." He then describes her terrible cooking by giving examples—from her lumpy grits to her gooey pancakes to her "prison stew." And when he describes his mother's housework, he gives lists of the items and objects that were scattered all over the house.

Devote each paragraph of your essay to a description and explanation of one particular aspect of your household. You could describe such aspects as the appearance of your home (messy or neat), cooking, cleaning, discipline, mealtime, bedtime, homework time, a time when everyone is trying to get ready for work or school. Be certain to give as many details and examples as possible so that the reader can "see" what is going on.

THE CALL

Kathy Boudin

The next selection is a poem, written by Kathy Boudin, an inmate (and poet) who, because she is serving a long sentence in a New York state prison, has been unable to live with her son, who was raised by other family members and close friends. This poem shows the suffering the poet endures as a result of being separated from her child (he is now a college student). However, although Boudin cannot see her son very often, they are still able to have a strong and valuable parent-child relationship, as reflected in the phone call she describes in her poem—a call placed to her son from the crowded, noisy prison where she has little privacy.

Vocabulary

submerged (stanza 3)   buried under
careening (3)   bouncing off
QE II ticket stub (9)   souvenir of a cruise on the *Queen Elizabeth II*

Suggestions for Free Writing

Before you read the poem, take about 10 minutes to free-write on the following topic:

Recall a time when, as a child, you were separated from one or both of your parents or guardian. Write down all the words and phrases that come to mind to express the feelings you had. Then recall when you all were reunited, and write down all the words and phrases that come to mind to express the feelings you had.

You might not be at the other end   1
of eight cells,
one garlic-coated cooking area
vibrating with the clatter of popcorn
on aluminum pot covers
two guards peering through blurry plexiglas,
the TV room echoing with
Jeopardy sing-song music and competing yells for

Source: "The Call," a poem by Kathy Boudin. Reprinted by permission of the author.

answers—
all lying between
my solitude and the telephone.

Or   2
you might answer
with a flat "hello,"
and I will hear your fingers
poking at plastic computer buttons,
your concentration focused on
the green and blue invaders and defenders.
My words only background
to your triumphs and defeats.

But I long for your voice.   3
Even the sound of your clicking fingers.
I journey past
eight cells submerged
in rap, salsa, heavy metal and soul
careening along the green metal corridor,
the guards perched on their raised platform,
dominoes clacking on plastic tabletops.
Past the line of roaches weaving
to the scent of overflowing garbage pails
voices shouting down the corridors,
legs halted by the line
that cannot be crossed.

Finally I sit on the floor   4
of the chairless smoky butt-filled room
to call you
who answers with an ever-deepening voice,
who barely sounds like my son.

"Hi, what are you doing?"   5
"I'm lying down, burning incense, listening to music.
        Do you want to hear it?"
With such relief
I barely utter "Yes," pushing my ear into the telephone,
my nose into the air.
Your flutes and organs become a soft carpet I walk along
in the musty sweetness and fruit smells
of orange peels and raspberries.
You begin to describe your new room
One wall the dream catcher, a set of hatchets
        and white feathers wrapped with beads
        of turquoise sky and sunset.

Your bed opposite a full length mirror
Perfect, you say, to view yourself,
a new body, six and a half inches in one year.

Then you invite me 6
into your special boxes,
gifts from your father
made behind bars.
"I keep all my treasures."

I nod breathlessly 7
My son has taken my voice.
His words fill me in
A naming ceremony.

Slowly his hand lifts 8
    a coffee brown belt
name carved across,
a menu of favorite food
    shared on the overnight visit.
Father-love.

The QEII ticket stub from 9
    the final ocean trip with Grandma.
"Eat breakfast, pack your clothes, then you can watch
    TV,"
his grandfather's voice echoes
    from a note left by his bed.
He moves to the Christmas calendar
    of shared favorite books
Tales of Peter Rabbit to *Huck Finn*
    the story of fourteen years.
A birthday card
    A photo
My son and I stand back to back.
His head inches past mine.

Then you dangle one sandstone earring 10
    the other in a box in my cell,
"We'll put them together when you get out."
    Your words hang like a glider.
Mother-love.

Then guitar notes rise and fall, 11
and I say, as always, "I love you,"
and you say, as always, "I love you,"
and the phone clicks off.

Questions for Reflection and Discussion

1. Kathy Boudin describes the prison surroundings at the beginning of her poem in great detail, and she describes her son's room later in the poem, in equally great detail. Why do you think she does this?
2. If you knew you were going to be separated from your teen-aged child for one year, what advice would you give to him or her to follow in your absence?

Topics for Writing

1. There is much discussion today about whether certain people should be permitted to adopt and raise children: single men or women, gay couples, people of a different race than the child they want to adopt. Write an essay in which you describe and explain whether you think a child should only be raised in a "conventional" household with a father and a mother, or whether you think it is okay for people with alternative lifestyles or circumstances to adopt children.
2. Although you will probably not be asked to write poetry in your college classes (unless you major in creative writing), writing poetry offers us the opportunity to say what is really on our minds and in our hearts by freeing us from having to worry about sentence structure, organization, topic sentences, and so on.

   Return to the free write you completed before you read Boudin's poem, and use the information there to write a poem that deals in some way with your relationship with the person or persons who raised you: parents, grandparents, siblings, aunts or uncles, or guardians. Include details so that the reader can "see" what you mean, just as Boudin uses very specific details (fingers on the computer buttons, the sounds in the prison corridor, the "chairless smoky butt-filled room," the fruit smells, the bed and mirror, the contents of the boxes) to enable her reader to "see" the relationship she has with her son.

Reading 3–4

THE MYTH OF QUALITY TIME
Laura Shapiro

In "The Myth of Quality Time," published in *Newsweek*, Laura Shapiro explains the difficulty that working couples have in raising their children; the demands of their careers often do not leave them with enough time—or energy—to be the kind of parents they want to be. This article is similar to the type of reading that will be assigned to you in a college-level sociology class. (Sociology is the study of groups of people.)

Vocabulary

myth (title)   an accepted belief that is often wrong
deluding ourselves (paragraph 2)   fooling ourselves
hovering (2)   hanging over
complicity (2)   going along with
cognitive (3)   having to do with the brain, with learning
nuances (3)   small differences
domestic (3)   in the home
rituals (3)   acts performed regularly
jettisoned (3)   thrown out
apathy (5)   lack of interest
spawns (5)   creates
deviant (5)   behavior that is not normal
a class phenomenon (7)   occurring only in certain classes of society
jibes (7)   agrees with
a marginal role (8)   less involved, on the sidelines
sacrosanct (11)   sacred, special
underutilized (12)   under used
trolling (13)   looking for
utopia (16)   a perfect world

Suggestions for Free Writing

Before you read the article, take about 10 minutes to reflect on the following topics:

> Children who come from school to a house where no one is home (because their parents or guardians are at work) are often called "latchkey" kids. Do you think these children suffer as a result of having to spend several hours alone each afternoon? In what way? Do you think there are benefits to being "latchkey" kids? What are they? Many parents say they do not have very much time to spend with their children, but the time they do spend with their children is "quality" time—time that is carefully planned to be enjoyable and beneficial to the parent/child relationship. Do you think it is possible to have limited "quality" time with children, or do you think parenting is a 24-hour, 7-days-a-week job?

For the New York lawyer, it all hit home in the grocery store. She had stopped in with her 6-year-old to pick up a few things, but since the babysitter normally did the shopping, she was unprepared for what was about to happen. Suddenly there was her son, whooping and tearing around the store, skidding the length of the aisles on his knees. "This *can't* be my child," she thought in horror. Then the cashier gave a final twist to the knife. "Oh," she remarked. "So *you're* the mother." That was the moment when the lawyer was forced to admit that spending "quality time" with the kids didn't seem to be working. She and her husband, a journalist, had subscribed in good faith to the careerists' most treasured rule of parenting: it isn't how much time you spend with your kids, it's how you spend the time. But despite those carefully scheduled hours of parental attention between dinner and bed, their two kids were in danger of turning into little brats. "I don't want to come home and find my kids watching cartoons and demanding every new product Disney put out this week," she says. "It's not that sitters do a bad job, but sitters don't raise kids. Parents do." Next month the family is moving to a suburb, and she'll go to work part-time.

Not every family can, or wants to, make a life change on that scale. But many are starting to question whether time devoted to their children really can be efficiently penciled into the day's calendar, like a business appointment with a couple of short, excitable clients. No wonder a growing number of psychologists and educators who work with children would like to get rid of the whole idea of quality time. "I think quality time is just a way of deluding ourselves into shortchanging our children," says Ronald Levant, a psychologist at Harvard Medical School. "Children need vast amounts of parental time and attention. It's an illusion to think they're going to be on your timetable, and that you can say 'OK, we've got a half hour, let's get on with it'." For parents who love their kids and also love their work, there's no more insistent wake-up call than Arlie Hochschild's new book, "The Time Bind," just published and already hovering in the nightmares of anyone who has ever sung a lullaby over the phone. Hochschild's most chilling insight is our complicity in depriving our children. "Many working families," she writes, "are both prisoners and architects of the time bind in which they find themselves."

Quality time arrived on the scene in the early '70s, featured in a wave of research including a now famous study by Alison Clarke-Stewart of the University of California, Irvine. She found (and recent brain research backs her up) that the more actively mothers were involved with their babies, talking and cooing and so forth, the better it was for the babies' cognitive and social development. Babies who spent time with their mothers but didn't get as much of the goo-gooing and eye contact did less well. "But to be able to have that high-quality time, you have to invest a certain amount of pure time," says Clarke-Stewart. "It's not just 10 minutes a week." Such nuances quickly dropped away as baby-boomer couples found quality time an immense help in juggling two careers and a potty chair. Today it's not even clear what most people mean when they use the term—is playing patty-cake supposed to be a higher-quality activity than driving to ballet lessons? Does family dinner count if the TV is on? Very softly? All we reliably know is that whenever time with kids is in short supply, calling it "quality time" makes parents feel better.

Experts say that many of the most important elements in children's lives—regular routines and domestic rituals, consistency, the sense that their parents know and care about them—are exactly what's jettisoned when quality time substitutes for quantity time. "Mom is working until 4:30 and has to get the groceries and do the laundry and the chores and pick somebody up from soccer and drop somebody off at ice skating," says Chicago psychologist Vicki Curran. "The structure of the day disappears. But the structure, and the availability to one another, provide the safe arena we know as home." Nor do kids shed their need for parental time when they get to be teenagers. "One of the functions of parents is monitoring—you monitor their homework, their friends, what they're really doing in their spare time," says Jeanne Brooks-Gunn, a developmental psychologist at Columbia University. "I don't think we've said enough to parents about how the demands on them change when early adolescence hits, and kids may start to engage in drugs or sex. Monitoring is critical."

Parents who race in the door at 7:30 p.m. and head straight for the fax machine are making it perfectly clear where their loyalties lie, and the kids are showing the scars. "I see apathy, depression—a lack of the spunkiness I associate with being a kid," says Levant. "These kids don't have the self-esteem that comes from knowing your parents are really interested in you, really behind you." Kevin Dwyer, assistant executive director of the National Association of School Psychologists, says teachers are reporting increases in discipline problems and classroom disruptions. "One of our concerns is that parents are not spending enough time with their kids," he says. "Most of the parents we see are really drained at the end of the day." The result is inconsistent discipline and all the problems it spawns. "There's a tremendous amount of research showing that inconsistency leads to kids' being more aggressive, more deviant and more oppositional," says Dwyer.

In "The Time Bind," Hochschild analyzes in depth a large corporation she calls "Amerco." She spent months interviewing employees, from the CEO to the factory shift workers, and found many who complained about long workdays and hectic home lives. But few of the employees were taking any steps to carve out more time with their families—they weren't taking unpaid family leave even if they could afford it, and they weren't applying for flextime or job sharing. Hochschild's startling conclusion was that for many workers, home and office have changed places. Home is a frantic exercise in beat-the-clock, while work, by comparison, seems a haven of grown-up sociability, competence and relative freedom. Quality time has been a crucial component of this transformation. "Instead of nine hours a day with a child, we declare ourselves capable of getting the 'same result' with one, more intensely focused, total quality hour," she writes. Hochschild describes some of the Amerco kids as essentially on strike against their assembly-line lives. "They sulk. They ask for gifts. They tell their parents by action or word, 'I don't like this'."

Not all researchers agree with Hochschild's analysis or her view of its consequences for kids. "What she's describing is a class phenomenon," says Rosalind Barnett, a psychologist and senior scholar at Radcliffe College. "I don't think most ordinary Joes confuse work with family. Work is work." Barnett and journalist Caryl Rivers are the authors of "She Works/He Works," which describes the results of a four-year, $1 million study of 300 two-earner couples in the Boston area. The authors and their team of interviewers found that both men and women in this random sample reported high levels of satisfaction with their lives, despite the stress, and warm, close relationships with their children. "Most see their families as the center of their emotional lives," they write. Barnett says their study jibes with many others—for instance, a 1995 survey of more than 6,000 employees at DuPont, showing that nearly half the women, and almost as many men, had traded career advancement to remain in jobs that gave them more family time. Fran Rodgers, CEO of Work/Family Directions in Boston, agrees that national surveys give results different from Hochschild's focus on one company. "What people really want is both to be good parents and good at work," she says.

Underlying at least some of the criticism of Hochschild's work is the fear that to acknowledge problems with our kids is to invite a backlash against women's working. That's mighty unlikely to change. Not only do women work for the same reason men do—they need the money—but surveys have also consistently shown that employed women are happier, healthier and feel more valued, even at home, than women who are full-time homemakers. "Even if women *did* go home, it wouldn't be the best solution," says Stephanie Coontz, author of "The Way We Never Were," an examination of the real, as opposed to the mythic, world of the '50s. Her new book, "The Way We Really Are," takes a similarly unblinkered look at the present. "Suppose the wife quits work for a year when the kids are little," she says. "She becomes the specialist in child nurturing, and the man never catches up. He doesn't have the initial skills, and she's got a year's head start. Research shows that men do more and better child care when their wives aren't home." Studies also clearly indicate that children whose fathers are thoroughly involved in their care do better socially and cognitively than kids whose fathers play a more marginal role. What's more, the involved fathers are happier than the marginal ones—you know, the daddies talking intently into cell phones during the entire Little League game.

In light of this data, one way to start solving the problems posed by quality time seems obvious: guys, go home. It's 5 p.m. Women may feel guiltier than men about working, women may choose to cut back their careers, but if our kids are hurting for lack of family time, it's not a women's issue, it's a family issue. And studies overwhelmingly show that men's contribution to housework and child care ranges from a third to a half of what women do even though the numbers have been inching closer in recent years. Then there was the 1993 survey by the Families and Work Institute that asked dual-earner couples how they divided responsibility for child care. "We share it 50-50" was the response of 43 percent of the men—and 19 percent of the women.   9

James Levine, director of the Fatherhood Project at the Families and Work Institute, says change is happening slowly, but it's happening. Time with their children is increasingly important to men, he says, but some are unwilling to confront a corporate culture that values long hours and face time above all. "I find guys doing all kinds of strange things to avoid publicly acknowledging that they have parental responsibilities," says Levine. "They'll sneak out to pick up their kids at day care, or wait just a few minutes after their boss leaves to go themselves. People need to break this pattern and start taking responsibility."   10

Some men do break the pattern, though it's easier at the high end of the pay scale. New York attorney Franz Paasche tried hard to keep weekends with his family sacrosanct. But he found that work was lasting later and later on Fridays, and starting up earlier on Sundays. So he changed to a new job with more flexible hours. Now, he says, he never misses walking his daughter to the school bus and buckling her seat belt; and even if he has to work at night, he has dinner with the family and reads bedtime stories first. "These days are not replaceable," he says. "My   11 children are different every day. That may be the myth of quality time—that time is interchangeable."

The family-friendly policies introduced by some companies with much fanfare—job sharing, flexible hours and the like—often don't hold up in practice. "The easiest thing for the corporate world to do is fall back on family-friendly benefits," says Lotte Bailyn, a professor at MIT's Sloan School of Management. "They're wonderful, but they're underutilized. Men hardly ask for them, and if they do they're seen as wimps. If women take them, they're put on the mommy track." Bailyn heads a research team that develops new organizational structures designed to help companies become more productive while eating up less of their employees' time. "We're reversing the idea of quality time," she says. "Quality time belongs at work. Quantity time belongs with the family."   12

Unfortunately, there's little in the current business climate that encourages most employees to do anything about their long hours except cling desperately to their jobs as colleagues disappear around them. Now more than ever, people have powerful financial incentives to resist making more time for families. And men, who still tend to make more money than their wives—and work about eight more hours per week—are caught in a special time bind: if they do cut back for the family's sake, the family suffers financially. But Elizabeth Perle McKenna, whose book "When Work Doesn't Work Anymore" will be published in September, says corporate downsizing might well prompt some men to look harder at their values. "When motherhood hit the baby-boomer women, we were forced to stop and really look at work for the first time, and ask, 'Is this worth it to me?' " she says. "I think all the downsizing in business, and its effect on men's lives, could make them do the same thing." She also believes that younger workers, men and women starting their careers now, will have a major impact on how corporations treat families. "I interviewed young women who have no intention of sacrificing their lives for their jobs," she says. "If you're company X and you're trolling for the best people, you won't be able to ignore those issues anymore."   13

Corporate utopia may be a long way off, but men and women can change their own lives right now. Cutting back on work hours—and income—might seem an impossible dream; but Seattle psychologist Laura Kastner often reminds her clients that they do have choices. Maybe they can move to a cheaper neighborhood; maybe they can move closer to work and cut their commuting time. Marlene and Keith Winsten, who live outside Providence, R.I., with their two kids, are up and running by 5:30 a.m.; most of their family time is on the weekend. So they're cutting back on the hikes and museums that used to jam Saturday and Sunday; sometimes they all just hang out. "We've been trying hard to calm things down," says Marlene. "Quality time is going at their pace."   14

Want to hear about some people who don't have to "juggle" work   15
and family because it's so easy for them to carry both? They work in the
state attorney general's office in Bismarck, N.D. "Most of the workers go
home at noon—they get in their cars and drive home and have lunch
with their kids," says Jean Mullen, who moved to Bismarck after working
in Washington, D.C., for two decades. "If you look at the computer bulletin board, where the attorneys sign out when they're going someplace,
you'll see people have written down things like 'car pool.' They leave at
3 p.m. to pick up their kids from school and take them home. The
building generally empties out at 5.

"The men are eligible for the same family leave as the women, and   16
they take it. They take flextime as much as the women. There's total
acceptance of the fact that you'll take off time to go to your child's
school conference. It's not free time—they expect you to make it up—
but you can openly say that's where you're going." Mullen talks on and
on—about taking her kids to the dentist, about receiving phone calls
from them during a staff meeting, about being taken seriously as a professional woman, family and all. Maybe utopia does exist. Or maybe the
attorney general's office in Bismarck, N.D., is just the way real life runs,
when people acknowledge what's important to them—and live that way.

Questions for Reflection and Discussion

1. If you are a male, do you intend to be (or are you) fully active and involved
   in raising your children (feeding, bathing, dressing, helping with homework, playing, advising, teaching)? If you are a female, how much partici-
   pation will you expect (or do you expect) your children's father to provide
   in the care and raising of the children?
2. Would you be willing to sacrifice a promotion or a raise at work if it were
   necessary in order for you to be a better parent?

Topics for Writing

1. Based on the information in "The Myth of Quality Time," and on your own
   experiences and observations, which parent do you think is more involved
   in the day-to-day responsibilities of raising children, the father or the
   mother? Be certain to take information from the article to prove your point.
   Remember, it is acceptable, even desirable, for you to use exact words from
   the article; just be sure to place them in quotation marks so your reader will
   know that you are not trying to "steal" them from the author.
2. Return to the free write you completed before you read "The Myth of
   Quality Time," and use the information there to write an essay in which

you argue that it is better for children if both parents work, or that it is better for children if one parent remains at home to care for them on a full-time basis.

Additional Writing Topics about Parenting

1. The essays and poem in this chapter show that parents face many difficult decisions and circumstances: Robert Hughes's child suffers from autism; Ruth McBride is a single mother responsible for the care and feeding of 12 children; Kathy Boudin is separated from her son; and couples who work outside the home suffer from guilt and exhaustion as they juggle parenting with careers.

   However, all of the parents share one very important thing in common: They express a strong desire to be the best parents they can be. Review all of the readings, and write an essay in which you describe and give examples of the things they are doing and the actions they are taking to make sure they are good parents. You may use the same words that are used in the article as long as you place the words in quotation marks. In your conclusion, describe how your opinion of parenting has changed as a result of reading these selections. If it has not changed, explain how your opinion was reinforced (made stronger) as a result of reading these articles.

2. Return to the free write you completed before you read the selections in this chapter, and use the information there to write an essay on the following topic:

   You will face or you are facing many challenges as a parent that your own parents or guardians did not have to face when they were raising you. Write an essay in which you describe some of the challenges facing you and your generation as you raise your children that your parents or guardians did not have to deal with.

Chapter
4

School:
The Best Place to Learn?

School has played a major role in your life: You have probably spent at least 12 years in a classroom attending elementary, junior high, and high school, and now you have decided to continue your education in college. It is possible that you have spent as much time in school as you have in any other place, except for home. But just because you spent a lot of time in school does not necessarily mean that you learned all that you could have while you were there or that you had a satisfying educational experience.

Many factors influenced what you learned, how you learned, and even whether you learned in school. For example, consider the quality and concern of your teachers and counselors: Did they have confidence in your ability and encourage you to do the best you could? Were they well qualified and willing to work hard? What about the values and interests of your peers: Was doing well in school important to them, and thus to you? Were the students interested in learning, or did they actually keep other students from learning? The amount of time and energy you were able to devote to your studies is another factor: Were you more interested in sports or socializing? Did you have to work after school to earn money for necessities? The circumstances that existed in your home were also important: Were there problems or issues occurring at home that distracted you or prevented you from studying?

The selections in this chapter deal with incidents that occur in school, and they reflect the various factors that can affect whether students learn: illness, the cruelty or bullying of students, poverty, cultural conflicts between teachers and students. By reading these selections, you will end up with a far better understanding of the way outside pressures and influences may have affected your performance in school, and you may end up, as well, with a clearer understanding of the way you can control those forces in the future as you begin your college career.

Pre-reading Activity

Before you begin to read the selections in this chapter, take about 10 minutes to free-write on the following topics. They will help you to think about your educational experiences.

Think all the way back to elementary school right up through high school, and describe the most successful year you spent in school: Why was it successful? Also, think about the most unsuccessful year you spent in school: Why was it unsuccessful? Answer the following questions for both your most successful and least successful school years: Who or what had the most influence on your performance and behavior in school? Teachers, parents, friends, peers, family? After-school activities such as sports or clubs, work? Hobbies? Circumstances such as a move from one school to another, or another serious change in your life such as the illness or death of someone important to you? Did you ever witness or participate in cruelty toward another student in school, or were you ever a victim of it? Finally, why are you attending college? What are your goals for the future? Do you need a college education to achieve these goals?

Reading 4–1

BULLY BASICS: WHAT EVERY TEACHER
SHOULD KNOW ABOUT BULLIES

Gerry Sheanh
Jamie Kyle McGillian, Editor

In the course of our educational careers, we have all had a bully (or two or three) in our classrooms. And we all remember how destructive the actions and behavior of a bully can be not only to individual students but to the entire class. In the article and sidebars (a sidebar is a shorter article that gives additional information about the topic) presented below, the problem of bullying in the classroom is discussed; suggestions for controlling or stopping children from being bullies are given; teachers suggest ways to stop bullying in the classroom; and there is even a quiz to help students determine if they are bullies.

Vocabulary

modified (paragraph 1)   changed
provocative language (1)   language meant to cause trouble
opt (1)   choose
calculated (2)   carefully planned out
spontaneous (2)   without advance planning
reprisal (3)   punishment
diminishing (4)   reducing
distorted view (4)   inaccurate view that is not based on reality
carte blanche (6)   total freedom
unnerving (8)   upsetting
proximity (8)   closeness to
provocation (8)   actions or words that cause anger
precipitators (8)   causes
makes amends (9)   makes up for in order to gain forgiveness
malice (9)   evil
a penchant (10)   a tendency
a persecution complex (10)   a belief held by people that everyone is against them
inept (10)   unskilled
empathy (10)   the ability to understand the way other people are feeling

Source: "Bully Basics" and "Trade Secrets" edited by Jamie Kyle McGillian, *Creative Classroom,* November/December 1996. Reprinted by permission of The Creative Classroom LLC.

Suggestions for Free Writing

Before you read the article, take about 10 minutes to free-write on the following topics:

> Think about your educational experiences—from elementary school on—and think about the bullies in your classroom. Who were they? Were the bullies boys or girls? What did they do? How did they make other students feel? Were you ever a bully? Were you ever the victim of a bully? What, if anything, did the teacher do to stop the bully's behavior? Do you know what became of the bullies? Did they change, or did their behavior finally lead them to bigger trouble? Is there one bully who stands out in your mind as the absolute worst? Write a short paragraph describing this person's actions and behavior.

Nobody is born a bully. Bullying is a behavioral pattern that 1 appears to have its roots in whatever has caused these kids to become powerless in their personal lives. There is both good news and bad news in this: the good news is that the behavior can be modified; the bad news is that such change requires massive effort, patience, and the willingness to concede that the attempt may fail. Bullying is about using whatever tools are available to gain power and control, to elevate the bully's feelings of self-esteem, and to achieve status within the peer group. Bullies use provocative language and physical violence to create and enhance their sense of control over others. Lacking positive experiences, they opt to earn success in negative ways that elicit attention from teachers and parents (other adults, too) and that instill fear in most of their peers. Bullying, in essence, is a deliberate attempt to manipulate others for the bully's own personal satisfaction.

Put-downs are one tool the bully uses, but the act of putting others 2 down is committed by many others, often without the bully's goal of control. These put downs are a less calculated and more spontaneous response to others, at least in a defensive sense. Put-downs used as an offensive tactic are closer to bullying and achieve similar results: a measure of power and control. Again, put downs are more difficult to stop because they become a pattern of behavior for a far greater number than does bullying.

Bullying: The first thorn   3

We will probably encounter bullies throughout our lives, from the kid who scribbled all over our kindergarten masterpieces, to the kid on the soccer field who tripped us if we tried to get by him, to power-drunk adults who simply want to wield their power, to the boss who makes life difficult for us just because he can do so without fear of reprisal. Our natural instincts are twofold: to protect ourselves and to get back at the bully. We use a number of strategies to accomplish both, but the most important concept in dealing with bullies, and one that is sort of a rallying cry, is this: If you give a bully what he wants, the bully wins.

So, what is bullying, and what are its underlying bases? The ideas that follow are helpful in thinking about these questions.

4

- Bullying is another way of gaining and wielding power. Power is the absolute number one issue with bullies.
- Bullies can't bear to lose, and losing face or sense of dignity will always invite an attempt to regain power. Bullies find they like the feeling of power and tend to want more, thus beginning a cycle of bullying with no foreseeable end.
- Bullying is a means of gaining self-esteem by diminishing the self-esteem of others.

  In effect, the bully can't bear the success of others, seeing such success not as success for the other person, but as failure for himself.
- Bullying is an attempt to gain peer status. In some ways, every bully thinks that if he can't have status as a good student, a good athlete, or a well-liked person, then he'll seek a reputation as the toughest, strongest, meanest kid in the school.
- Bullying sometimes emerges from a distorted view of what is truly funny. "Funny" to these kids normally involves pain, suffering, or humiliation. Bullies are the ones who think it is uproariously funny if someone falls and is injured. They find continual amusement in the classroom mistakes of others and are quick to point out the weaknesses they perceive in others. Sadly, some of our popular television shows tend to reinforce this type of humor. Watch *America's Funniest Home Videos* or *America's Funniest People* and make note of how many of the clips shown involve someone getting hurt or humiliated. Bullies love these shows.

What does bullying look like?

5

Bullies do a variety of things in their attempt to gain attention, to strike fear into the hearts of others, or simply to "flex their bullying muscles" for all to see. Most of these actions fall into these categories:

- Acts intended to cause pain: spitting, punching, kicking, slapping, pinching, biting, scratching, striking, tripping, choking, and more seriously, cutting, stabbing, strangling, shooting
- Acts of petty vandalism: breaking, hiding, discarding, stealing, destroying, confiscating, or vandalizing the personal belongings of others
- Acts that "level the playing field" in sports: playing dirty, cheating to win, and beating up any challengers

What does bullying sound like?

6

Bullies believe that they have carte blanche to say whatever they want and, if the target rises to the challenge, the bully will unleash the weapons in his considerable arsenal. These statements are only samples:

"Wanna make something out of it?"
"I could beat you up with one hand tied behind my back."
"Go ahead, take the first punch."
"Take that back or I'll pound you."
"You're dead after school."
"You had it coming."
"I'm going to teach you a lesson."

Assertiveness: The most effective strategy for dealing with bullies 7

Assertiveness is an often misunderstood concept, with many believing that it means to stand our ground, trade provocative comment for provocative comment, and win the conflict through superior verbal abilities. This more accurately describes aggressiveness and results in the escalation of conflict, not in de-escalation. Being assertive actually involves stating your position firmly but clearly without throwing fuel on the fire of conflict. Not an easy task, but with training and practice, a manageable one. Assertiveness says: "This is my position," while aggressiveness says: "This is my position, you stupid idiot."

Six major aspects of assertiveness 8

1. **Eye contact.** It is a natural reaction to want to avoid eye contact with someone who is verbally attacking us. The bully knows this, so when we face up to him and maintain steady eye contact, he can find it unnerving. It is important, though, not to glare, but to look at him as though you were watching a parade go by—engaged but neutral.
2. **Facial expression.** When we are under attack, a worried or even angry facial expression, which mirrors our inner anxiety, is quite normal. An expression of fear, or one of defiance, can subtly escalate the conflict in the mind of the bully, who is a master at taking cues from any evidence of resistance or anger. This is why it is useful to adopt a neutral facial expression.
3. **Body language.** Instinctively, we tend to turn away, quite literally, from unpleasantness, and this is certainly true when we are being provoked by a bully. It is important to face the bully squarely.
4. **Proximity.** While it is difficult to know if and when to back down, it is equally important not to place yourself too close to the bully.
5. **Tone of voice.** Critically important, tone of voice is very difficult to control, since the anger that results from provocation is difficult to manage. A clear, steady tone is the goal. Whining, sarcasm, yelling, or any attempt to one-up the bully will be interpreted as a willingness to escalate the conflict, which is exactly what the bully wants.
6. **Choice of words.** Name-calling, trading insults, and other forms of verbal provocation are by far the most common precipitators of fights and arguments. It is tempting to fight back with words, but doing so is just as provocative as throwing a punch.

Acceptable vs. unacceptable teasing

9

Teasing falls into two categories: acceptable and unacceptable. Acceptable teasing has the following characteristics:

- It is done by a trusted, close friend, or family member. If someone we are close to makes a teasing comment, we can usually accept it because we know it's not meant to provoke or anger us.
- It is not repeated continually to exhaust our patience and make us angry. When bullies and put-down artists try our patience, they call it teasing; however, the victim calls it bullying.
- It isn't meant to hurt. If by chance, it does hurt, the teaser usually observes this and makes amends.
- It is not directed at something over which we have no control. Unusual or atypical physical characteristics normally provide enough anxiety in themselves; being teased about them only makes things worse.
- It is said to the person, not about the person. Being teased in front of a group is never comfortable.
- The tone is friendly and devoid of sarcasm or cynicism. We can sometimes accept teasing if we see there is no malice intended.

Unacceptable teasing displays directly the opposite characteristics of those listed above. In short, unacceptable teasing originates from someone other than a friend or relative and it is intended to hurt.

Bullies

10

- lack impulse control
- lack anger-management skills
- often can't see the connection between actions and consequences
- display a penchant for blaming the victim
- often display a persecution complex
- appear mad at the world
- are intensely competitive, even in areas where they can't possibly win
- are socially inept
- have poor decision-making skills
- have abnormally high tolerance for conflict
- lack empathy

Are you a bully?

11

For each question, have students circle the response that best describes the way they feel.

1. Do you always have to win the game?
   yes   no   sometimes
2. When you do lose, are you very worried about what other people think of you?
   yes   no   sometimes
3. Do you enjoy teasing others?
   yes   no   sometimes

4. If you do like to tease, do you stop if you are upsetting someone?

      yes   no   sometimes

5. Do you laugh at other people's mistakes or misgivings?

      yes   no   sometimes

6. Do you often pick on people who are smaller than you?

      yes   no   sometimes

7. When you become angry, is it difficult for you to let go of the angry feeling?

      yes   no   sometimes

8. Do you always feel the need to blame someone else for what happens to you?

      yes   no   sometimes

9. If a person makes you look bad do you seek revenge to make that person pay for it?

      yes   no   sometimes

10. Do you want to be thought of as the toughest, strongest, meanest person at your school?

      yes   no   sometimes

Scoring

- Give yourself two points for each question that you answered yes.
- If your score was less than 6. you are not a bully, and definitely not in danger of becoming one. In fact, you're probably an easygoing person.
- If your score was 10 or more, try to become more aware of your behavior. Go out of your way to make sure you are treating people the way you'd want them to treat you.
- If your score was 12 or more, you may need to start making serious changes in the way you interact with people.

Trade secrets: How do you handle bullies?

Here's what master teachers do to bully-proof their classrooms.

I have some rules for my third graders. Each student signs an agreement saying that he or she will never cheat, lie, steal, or act like a bully. These written agreements carry a lot of weight. They are hung on a wall in my classroom and whenever a student breaks a rule, he or she is given the statement to read aloud before the class. A banner saying NO BULLIES ALLOWED hangs from our ceiling. Bullies are simply not welcome in my room. (*Jay Pickel, Laguna, CA*)

12

Often bullies become bullies because they themselves have been picked on. They don't like being treated unfairly, so they decide to treat someone with the same cruelty that they have known. I prevent this from happening by talking to my students whenever something or someone is bothering them. During private meetings with me, students release tension and bad feelings. Doing this lets them feel better about themselves. They are less likely to act like bullies and are more confident when it comes to defending themselves in the presence of a bully. (*Marshall Kramer, Lake Grove, NY*)

13

Positive reinforcement is the name of the game. After several warn- 14
ings, a difficult child still may not let up. You've made threats, taken away
privileges. Still, the behavior persists. Positive reinforcement to the
rescue.

The student goes on trial and is asked to evaluate his own behavior
every day for a week using a rating scale from one to ten. It's interesting
to see how quickly a bully will reform out of a desire to receive a good
score. I give an award to acknowledge a consistently high score. After a
week of high scores, the student gets a chance to be class leader for a
day. Children quickly discern the difference between a leader and a
bully. (*Randy Sutton, Baltimore, MD*)

15

It's inevitable! Every year there's sure to be a bully in my third-
grade class. But it's never too late to reform him or her. My resident
trouble-maker will spend a lot of time in the Bully Corner. He or she is
given time to let off steam, collect thoughts, and explain to me the
reason he or she is there. Then we role play. The child becomes the
teacher and I the student. The "teacher" has to find a fair solution to the
"student's" problem. (Example: Return a stolen nickel to Ted and apologize to Ted for bossing him around.) Together we find a fair solution.
After being sent to the Bully Corner several times, the student understands about unacceptable behavior. In most cases, the bully is
reformed. (*Judy King, Troy, NY*)

Questions for Reflection and Discussion

1. The information in the article about bullies does not mention the role that
   parents play. What do you think parents can do to stop bullying? Or do you
   think parents are the cause of the problem?
2. Reread the quiz to determine if you are a bully (paragraph 11). Take the
   quiz yourself and find your score. Are you surprised at the result?

Topics for Writing

1. It is clear from the information in the article that bullying is a problem that
   can disrupt classrooms, creating an uncomfortable, even dangerous
   climate, and that can prevent the teacher from teaching and keep the students from learning. But bullying is only one of the factors that negatively
   affects learning.

   Think back over your elementary, junior high, and high school years,
   and write an essay in which you identify and describe the various factors
   that prevented you and/or other students from learning. Devote each
   paragraph of your essay to one factor, identifying the factor in the topic

sentence and then using the rest of the paragraph to explain, define, describe, and give examples so the reader can fully understand how that factor negatively affected the learning environment. In your conclusion, explain the result that these factors had on your ability to receive a good education.

2. Return to the free write you completed before you read the article about bullying, and use the information there to write an essay in which you describe the worst bully you encountered in all of your educational experiences. Be sure to provide your reader with as much background information (who, what, when, why, where, and how) as possible so the reader can actually see and feel and hear and imagine the bully and his or her behavior. In addition, be sure to describe the effect the bully had on others, especially on his or her victims. In your conclusion, explain what became of the bully, if you know, and if you don't know, predict what you think happened to him or her.

Reading 4–2

AUTOBIOGRAPHY OF A FACE (EXCERPT)
Lucy Grealy

In the next reading, an *excerpt* (part of a longer work) taken from a book of nonfiction (nonfiction is a true story) entitled *Autobiography of a Face,* Lucy Grealy describes the way the boys in her junior high school tormented her because of her appearance. Grealy had surgery on her jaw to remove a cancerous growth, and as a result her face was badly disfigured and scarred. Her appearance affected her so much that she says (in another part of the book) she felt so ugly that she did everything she could to avoid looking into a mirror.

Vocabulary

contagious (paragraph 1)   something you can catch, usually an illness or disease
apprehension (2)   nervousness; fear
sidling (2)   to move sideways
suitability (3)   acceptability
tactic (4)   plan; method
spur them on (4)   encourage them
camouflage (4)   cover; disguise
inquisitor (4)   one who asks questions
saunter (4)   walk slowly
reprimand (5)   correct
simplistic (6)   childlike
definitively (6)   accurately, precisely
chemotherapy (6)   injections to treat cancer that often result in serious side effects such as nausea and vomiting

Suggestions for Free Writing

Before you read this excerpt, take about 10 minutes to free-write on the following topics:

Why do you think students, especially teenagers, are sometimes cruel to students who are weaker or different? Were there students in your high school who were treated differently, even cruelly, because they were different in some way? Describe the circumstances. Were you ever treated unfairly or cruelly by other students? Describe the circumstances. Did you ever treat anyone cruelly? Describe the circumstances. Do you regret your actions? What, if anything, did the teachers or guidance counselors do to prevent such behavior when it occurred?

The summer passed, and junior high school loomed. Jan, Teresa, and Sarah were all very excited at the prospect of being "grownups," of attending different classes, of having their own locker. Their excitement was contagious, and the night before the first day of school, I proudly marked my assorted notebooks for my different subjects and secretly scuffed my new shoes to make them look old. 1

Everyone must have been nervous, but I was sure I was the only one who felt true apprehension. I found myself sidling through the halls I'd been looking forward to, trying to pretend that I didn't notice the other kids, almost all of them strangers from adjoining towns, staring at me. Having seen plenty of teen movies with their promise of intrigue and drama, I had been looking forward to going to the lunchroom. As it happened, I sat down next to a table full of boys. 2

They pointed openly and laughed, calling out loudly enough for me to hear, "*What* on earth is *that?*" "*That* is the ugliest girl I have *ever* seen." I knew in my heart that their comments had nothing to do with me, that it was all about them appearing tough and cool to their friends. But these boys were older than the ones in grade school, and for the very first time I realized they were passing judgment on my suitability, or lack of it, as a girlfriend. "I bet David wants to go kiss her, don't you, David?" "Yeah, right, then I'll go kiss your mother's asshole." "How'll you know which is which?" 3

My initial tactic was to pretend I didn't hear them, but this only seemed to spur them on. In the hallways, where I suffered similar attacks of teasing from random attackers, I simply looked down at the floor and walked more quickly, but in the lunchroom I was a sitting duck. The same group took to seeking me out and purposely sitting near me day after day, even when I tried to camouflage myself by sitting in the middle of a group. They grew bolder, and I could hear them plotting to send someone to sit across the table from me. I'd look up from my food and there would be a boy slouching awkwardly in a red plastic chair, innocently asking me my name. Then he'd ask me how I got to be so ugly. At this the group would burst into laughter, and my inquisitor would saunter back, victorious. 4

After two weeks I broke down and went to my guidance counselor to complain. I thought he would offer to reprimand them, but instead he asked if I'd like to come and eat in the privacy of his office. Surprised, I said yes, and that's what I did for the rest of the year whenever I was attending school. Every day I'd wait for him, the other guidance coun- 5 selors, and the secretaries to go on their own lunch break. Then I'd walk through the empty outer office and sit down in his private office, closing the door behind me.

As I ate the food in my brown paper bag, which crinkled loudly in   6 the silence, I'd look at the drawings his own young children had made. They were taped to the wall near his desk, simplistic drawings in which the sky was a blue line near the top and the grass a green line near the bottom and people were as big as houses. I felt safe and secure in that office, but I also felt lonely, and for the very first time I definitively identified the source of my unhappiness as being ugly. A few weeks later I left school to reenter chemotherapy, and for the very first time I was almost glad to go back to it.

Questions for Reflection and Discussion

1. Do you think the boys who tormented Lucy Grealy can be defined as bullies based on the information in "Bully Basics"? What, if anything, would you do if you saw someone being tormented the way the boys tormented Lucy Grealy? Do you think the counselor could have done something more to help her rather than just giving Lucy a private place (his office) to eat her lunch?

2. In the last paragraph of this excerpt, Lucy Grealy explains that she would sit in the counselor's office and look at the drawings made by his children that were hanging on the wall. Reread this passage carefully, and discuss why you think Grealy included this detail in her account of the boys' cruelty to her.

Topics for Writing

1. Write an essay in which you describe the most embarrassing incident that ever happened to you in school. Be sure to include descriptions, details, and examples so that the reader can really "see" the incident or event. In your conclusion, explain whether this incident or event had a temporary or permanent effect on you.

2. Return to the free write you completed before you read the excerpt, and use the information there to write an essay describing either an example of cruelty that you witnessed in school or an example of kindness. Your essay can describe behavior between or among students, but it can also describe an example of cruelty or kindness shown by a teacher, counselor, principal, or coach to a student.

Reading 4–3

WHEN MONEY IS EVERYTHING, EXCEPT HERS

Dirk Johnson

The next selection is a newspaper article describing the way that Wendy Williams, a 13-year-old-girl who lives and attends school in Dixon, Ill., is tormented by her peers because she is poor. As you read this article, notice the similarities between the way the students treated Wendy Williams and the way the students treated Lucy Grealy. Also notice the differences in the behavior of the guidance counselors.

Vocabulary

scarcity (paragraph 4)   having too little of something
mocking (5)   to make fun of
affluence (14)   wealth
a poor boy nicknamed Dutch (15)   the nickname for Ronald Reagan, former U.S. president
relentless (20)   never giving up
ostentatious (23)   showing off
fret (33)   worry
taunts (43)   cruel teasing

Suggestions for Free Writing

Before you read the article, take about 10 minutes to free-write on the following topic:

Think back to a period of your education—elementary school, junior high school, high school—and explain whether there were popular and/or unpopular groups of students there. Then write a brief description of those factors (for example, appearance, clothes, type of car, athletic ability, intellectual ability) that made students popular and accepted, and a brief description of those factors that made students unpopular or unaccepted. Finally, decide if you think those factors are fair ones to use in judging someone's worth. If you do not think they are fair, what factors do you think should be considered in judging someone's worth?

Source: "When Money Is Everything, Except Hers" by Dirk Johnson, *The New York Times,* October 14, 1996. Copyright 1996 by the New York Times Co. Reprinted by permission.

Dixon, Ill.—Watching classmates strut past in designer clothes, 1
Wendy Williams sat silently on the yellow school bus, wearing a cheap
belt and rummage-sale slacks.

One boy stopped and yanked his thumb, demanding her seat. 2

"Move it, trailer girl," he sneered. 3

It has never been easy to live on the wrong side of the tracks. But 4
in the economically robust 1990's, with sprawling new houses and three-
car garages sprouting like cornstalks on the Midwestern prairie, the
sting that comes with scarcity gets rubbed with an extra bit of salt.

Seen through the eyes of a 13-year-old girl growing up at Chateau 5
Estates, a fancy name for a tin-plain trailer park, the rosy talk about the
nation's prosperity carries a certain mocking echo.

The everyday discussion in the halls of Reagan Middle School in 6
this city about 100 miles west of Chicago touches on computer toys that
can cost $1,000, family vacations to Six Flags or Disney World and stylish
clothes that bear a Nike emblem or Tommy Hilfiger's coveted label.

Unlike young people a generation ago, those today must typi- 7
cally pay fees to play for the school sports teams or band. It costs $45
to play in the youth summer soccer league. It takes money to go
skating on weekends at the White Pines roller rink, to play laser tag
or rock-climb at the Plum Hollow Recreation Center, to mount a
steed at the Horseback Riding Club, to gaze at Leonardo DiCaprio
and Kate Winslet at the Plaza Cinemas, to go shopping for clothes at
Cherryvale Mall.

To be without money, in so many ways, is to be left out. 8

"I told this girl: 'That's a really awesome shirt. Where did you get 9
it?' " said Wendy, explaining that she knew it was out of her price range,
but that she wanted to join the small talk. "And she looked at me and
laughed and said, 'Why would you want to know?' "

A lanky, soft-spoken girl with large brown eyes, Wendy pursed her 10
lips to hide a slight overbite that got her the nickname Rabbit, a humiliation she once begged her mother and father to avoid by sending her
to an orthodontist.

For struggling parents, keenly aware that adolescents agonize over 11
the social pecking order, the styles of the moment and the face in the
mirror, there is a no small sense of failure in telling a child that she
cannot have what her classmates take for granted.

"Do you know what it's like?" asked Wendy's mother, Veronica 12
Williams, "to have your daughter come home and say, 'Mom, the kids say
my clothes are tacky,' and then walk off with her head hanging low."

This is not the desperate poverty of Chicago housing projects, 13
where the plight of empty pockets is worsened by the threat of gangs
and gunfire. Wendy lives in relative safety in a home with both
parents. Her father, Wendell Provow, earns $9 an hour as a welder.

Her mother works part-time as a cook for Head Start, the Federal education program.

Unlike students in some urban pockets, isolated from affluence, Wendy receives the same education as a girl from a $300,000 house in the Idle Oaks subdivision. The flip side of that coin is the public spectacle of economic struggle. This is a place small enough where people know the personal stories, or, at least, repeat them as if they did.   14

Even in this down-to-earth town, where a poor boy nicknamed Dutch grew up to become President, young people seem increasingly enchanted with buying, having, spending and status.   15

R. Woodrow (Woody) Wasson, the principal at Reagan Middle School, makes it a point to sit down with every child and ask them about their hopes and dreams.   16

"They want to be doctors, lawyers, veterinarians and, of course, professional athletes," said Mr. Wasson, whose family roots here go back to the 19th century. "I don't remember the last time I heard somebody say they wanted to be a police officer or a firefighter. They want to do something that will make a lot of money and have a lot of prestige."   17

He said a teacher in a nearby town has been trying to recruit high school students for vocational studies to become tool-and-die artisans, a trade that can pay $70,000 a year.   18

"The teacher can't fill the slots," Mr. Wasson said. "Nobody's interested in that kind of work."   19

It is not surprising that children grow up believing that money is so important, given the relentless way they are targeted by marketers.   20

"In the past, you just put an ad in the magazine," said Michael Wood, the director of research for Teen-Age Research Unlimited, a marketing consultant in suburban Chicago. "Now savvy marketers know you must hit them at all angles—Web sites, cable TV shows, school functions, sporting events."   21

He noted the growth of cross-promotions, like the deal in which actors on the television show "Dawson's Creek," which is popular among adolescents, wear clothes by J. Crew and appear in its catalogue.   22

But young people get cues in their everyday lives. Some spending habits that would once have been seen as ostentatious—extravagant parties for small children, new cars for teenagers—have become familiar trappings of middle-class comfort.   23

The stock market, although it is sputtering now, has made millionaires of many people in Main Street towns. Building developers here recently won approval to build a gated community, which will be called Timber Edge.   24

"Wendy goes to school around these rich kids," her mother said, "and wonders why she can't have things like they do."   25

A bright girl with a flair for art, writing and numbers, Wendy stays up late most nights, reading books. "The Miracle Worker" was a recent favorite. 26

But when a teacher asked her to join an elevated class for algebra, she politely declined. "I get picked on for my clothes and living in the trailer park," said Wendy, who never brings anyone home from school. "I don't want to get picked on for being a nerd, too." 27

Her mother, who watched three other daughters drop out of school and have babies as teen-agers, has told Wendy time and again: "Don't lose your self-esteem." 28

One time a boy at school was teasing Wendy about her clothes— "They don't even match," he laughed—and her humble house in the trailer park. 29

She listened for a while. He kept insulting her. So she lifted a leg— clothed as it was in discount jeans from the Farm & Fleet store—and kicked him in the shins. 30

He told the authorities. She got the detention. 31

It became clear to Wendy that the insults were not going to stop. It also became clear that shin-kicking, however deserved, was not going to be the solution. 32

She went to a guidance counselor, Cynthia Kowa Basler, a dynamic woman who keeps close tabs on the children, especially girls who fret about their weight and suddenly stop eating lunch. 33

"I am large," she tells the girls, "and I have self-esteem." 34

Wendy, who knew that Mrs. Basler held sessions with students to increase their self-confidence, went to the counselor. "I feel a little down," Wendy told her. The counselor gathered eight students, including other girls like Wendy, who felt embarrassed about their economic station. 35

In this school named for Ronald Reagan, the students were told to study the words of Eleanor Roosevelt. 36

One of her famous quotations was posted above the counselor's desk: "No one can make you feel inferior without your consent." 37

As a group, the students looked up the definition of inferior and consent. 38

And then they read the words out loud. 39

"Again," the counselor instructed. 40

"Louder," the counselor insisted. 41

Again and again, they read the inspirational words. 42

In role-playing exercises, the children practiced responses to taunts, which sometimes called for nothing more than a shrug. 43

"Mrs. Basler told us to live up to our goals—show those kids," Wendy said. "She told us that things can be a lot different when you're grown up. Maybe things will be the other way around then." 44

Wendy smiled at the notion. 45

Life still has plenty of bumps. When Wendy gets off the school bus—the trailer park is the first stop, so everyone can see where she lives—she still looks at her shoes. 46

She still pulls her shirt out to hide a belt that does not quite make the grade. And she still purses her lips to hide an overbite. But her mother has noticed her smiling more these days. And Wendy has even said she might consider taking an advanced course in math, her favorite subject. 47

"I want to go to college," Wendy said the other day. "I want to become a teacher." 48

One recent day, she popped in to the counselor's office, just to say hello, then walked back down the halls, her arms folded around her schoolbooks. 49

Mrs. Basler stood at the doorway and watched her skip away, a student with so much promise, and so many obstacles. 50

For the girl from Chateau Estates, it is a long way from the seventh grade to college. 51

"She's going to make it," the counselor said, with a clenched fist and a voice full of hope. 52

Questions for Reflection and Discussion

1. What similarities do you see between Wendy Williams and Lucy Grealy? What are the important differences between them in terms of the way their problems were handled and how they are handling their problems? Do you think the kids who tormented Wendy can be defined as bullies based on the information in the article "Bully Basics"?
2. Why do you think clothing and appearance are so important to high school students? Now that you are attending college, do you notice a difference in what matters to college students compared with what matters to high school students?

Topics for Writing

1. Sometimes it's very helpful to use writing as a way of getting things off our chests. Imagine that you are Wendy Williams and you have an opportunity to write an editorial (an essay that gives an opinion about something) for the school newspaper. Explain what you (Wendy) are going through day after day as a result of the behavior and attitudes of the students in your school. In the conclusion to your editorial, suggest a solution or solutions to the problem.

2. Return to the free write you completed before you read the article, and use the information there to write an essay describing the various "groups" or "types" that existed in your elementary, junior high, or high school. Devote one paragraph of your essay to each group, and begin each paragraph with a topic sentence naming and describing the group, then using the rest of the paragraph to give descriptions, details, and examples. In your conclusion, explain whether you think the existence of these groups or types was a good thing or a bad thing for the students in your school.

Reading 4–4

"INTRUSION," "THE CLASS CLOWN," AND "A POEM FOR ZAC" (THREE POEMS)

Dan Holt

The next selection is a set of three poems written by Dan Holt, a high school English teacher in Michigan. Although it is not easy to write poetry, one of the most important reasons why people do so is because it is often the best way to express their feelings and emotions about something that is very important to them. In these poems, it is clear that Dan Holt's students are important to him.

Vocabulary

From "Intrusion":

intrusion (title)   interrupting or disturbing someone's privacy
hordes (stanza 2)   large groups
agitated (3)   upset, disturbed

From "The Class Clown":

tolerance (stanza 2)   to put up with something or someone without complaining
invoked (2)   put a rule into effect
banishment (2)   to order someone to leave
barrage (10)   a large amount, one right after the other

From "A Poem for Zac":

stealth (stanza 2)   doing something in secret, unseen
bobbers and weavers (2)   a boxing term meaning not staying still for even a moment
anal (2)   uptight, taking something too seriously
linear (5)   straight, in order

Suggestions for Free Writing

Before you read the three poems, take about 10 minutes to free-write on the following topic:

Source: "Intrusion," "The Class Clown," and "A Poem for Zac" by Dan Holt. Reprinted by permission of the author.

Think about a teacher you have had, or a student who was in one of your classes, who was clearly different, highly unusual, a comedian, maybe even "one of a kind." Picture this person in your mind so you can "see" him or her acting in a different or unusual way. Then write down as much as you can in the form of details, descriptions, and examples, to prove that this person was different than any other teacher or student you had ever encountered.

Intrusion

It was a cold and snowy winter, even by Michigan standards and Tracy, a small, quiet girl, was waiting as usual for me to unlock my door. 1

Tracy was pleasant enough, and so I usually didn't mind her presence—no, that's not true. I resented her being there so early in the morning, because I liked getting to school before the hordes of students and colleagues arrived so that I could think about the day, organize my thoughts, prepare myself for the job. I needed time to ease into teaching. But there she was, everyday, leaning against the door, waiting to be let in so she could stand by the heater and stare out of the window until first hour. 2

"Tracy, don't you ever sleep in?" I asked her one day when I felt more agitated than usual. 3

"I like getting up early." She was holding her hands above the blower. "And besides, it's so warm here." 4

I laughed out loud, and she appeared hurt; her look had some shame in it. "Well, don't you have heat at home?" 5

"No" was all she said, and then she turned away. 6

The Class Clown

Marty Bolinger was my first really funny student. In fact, I kicked him out of the class the first day of Creative Writing. Marty said something that I considered disrespectful, so I told him to wait in the 1 hall for the hour to be over. I talked to him about what he had said—I don't remember what it was now—and he agreed to watch his mouth.

That turned out to be impossible for Marty, so rather than send him away every day, I learned tolerance and only invoked banishment in the most extreme situations. 2

And Marty was funny. One time, he raised his hand in the middle of class and refused to be ignored. 3

"Marty, do you have something to add?" 4

"Yes, but first I'd like all the guys in class to stand up." I looked at the class and saw their amused looks. 5

"OK," I said. "Will all the guys please stand up?" 6

"You too, Mr. Holt." I had been sitting on a small stool in front of the class. 7

"OK Marty, we're all standing." 8

"Good, now all the guys, including Mr. Holt, walk to the nearest wall." There were a few snickers in the class, and the guys were rolling their eyes but we all did exactly as Marty asked. 9

"Good, now everybody, including Mr. Holt, turn and face the wall." I had a brief vision of getting hit in the back with a barrage of water balloons or turning around to find that the entire class had vanished, but I reluctantly agreed to turn my back on the class. 10

"Excellent," said Marty, clearing his voice. "OK, now one of us has his fly unzipped." 11

A Poem for Zac

This is a poem for   1
those in the back row
for those who are grateful
for the geeks
in the front row.

This is a poem for   2
stealth students
flying beneath radar
and for bobbers and weavers
hiding from a teacher
who is frankly a little too
anal about poetry.
                                                              3
This is a poem for those
who have out of body experiences
in the middle of English,
their minds floating like smoke rings
vanishing beneath the hum of
fluorescent lights.
                                                              4
This is a poem for those
who think "not working up
to ability" is a compliment
and "capable of better grades"
is beside the point.
                                                              5
This is a poem for all
those who sit in straight rows
even though their spirits
are anything but linear.

Questions for Reflection and Discussion

1. Based on the information in Dan Holt's poems, what kind of teacher do you think he is?

2. Based on the information contained in the three poems, describe some of the challenges faced by Holt and other high school teachers.

Topics for Writing

1. Although you will probably not be asked to write poetry in college (unless you take a creative writing course), writing poetry is a wonderful way for us to express our ideas and feelings without having to worry about the rules of essay writing. Using Dan Holt's poems as a model, write a poem in which you describe an incident or event that occurred in school and that made a lasting impression on you.

2. Return to the free write you completed before you read Holt's three poems, and use the information there to write an essay describing the "one of a kind" teacher or student whom you described in your free write. In your opening paragraph, be sure to explain why this person is exceptional. Then use each of your body paragraphs to describe, explain, and give examples of each of the traits or behavior that made this person so exceptional. In your conclusion, reflect on the effect this person had on you and others.

Additional Writing Topics about School

1. Schools are places where students should be able to learn and grow intellectually and emotionally while feeling safe, comfortable, and secure. However, much of the information contained in the readings portray a very different picture: bullies who disrupt the classroom and make life miserable for their victims; cruel behavior by students that make life miserable, even unbearable, for other students; poverty, as reflected in Holt's poem about the young girl who has no heat in her home and by Wendy Williams's experiences.

   Consider these problems, and consider your own educational experiences, and write an essay in which you describe those factors that cause so many of our schools to be ineffective in their mission to provide their students with a good education. Be sure to begin each paragraph of your essay with a description of the factor, followed by explanations, details, descriptions, and examples so that your reader can fully understand your meaning.

2. Return to the free write you completed at the beginning of this chapter, and use the information there to write an essay in which you describe either the most successful or the most unsuccessful year of your educational career. Include details, descriptions, and examples, and be sure to answer the who, what, where, why, when, and how questions. In your conclusion, consider the impact that that school year had on you both as a student and as a person.

Chapter
5

Adolescence: Leaving Childhood Behind

The period known as *adolescence* (between puberty and maturity—the teenage years) is a complex, interesting, and important time in our lives. It is when we begin to leave the innocence and ignorance of childhood behind: We find out who we are, what we like, what we need, what we believe, what we want to do. And it is the time when we begin to realize just how complex life is: We begin to see our parents and guardians as real people, with real problems; we begin to realize that the decisions we make will have a permanent effect on our futures; we begin to realize that we have needs and wants and problems that cannot be satisfied or solved immediately. And because we are no longer children, we gain new freedoms, new insights about ourselves and others, and new opportunities to explore the world around us.

The selections in this chapter reflect the various challenges and pleasures faced by adolescents today, beginning with advice from a 17-year-old on how to deal with turning 13 to advice from a columnist for *The Chicago Tribune* on how to live the rest of your life—and everything in between, from the pain of having a disabled father to discovering that there are people in the world who have had advantages and privileges you never even knew existed. These selections reflect the fact that although adolescents certainly do face serious problems and challenges, they do their best to deal with them thoughtfully, carefully, and maturely.

Perhaps you will see yourself and your experiences reflected in these selections. Hopefully, they will help you to understand the many forces and

issues that you dealt with during this period of your life. And most importantly, they will prove that adolescents are doing a fine job of controlling
themselves and preparing for adulthood.

Notice that the readings in the chapters are beginning to get longer.
There is a reason for this: When writers are explaining something, they know
the importance of including background information, details, examples, dialogue, and explanations. As you read these longer selections, notice that they
contain all the information you need to understand fully and exactly what the
writer is saying. When you write essays, try to pay the same attention to these
important writing elements.

Pre-reading Activity

Before you begin to read the selections in this chapter, take about 10
minutes to respond to these free-writing topics. They will help you think about
your own adolescent experiences.

> Was the "passage" from childhood to adolescence (this "passage" occurs any-
> where between the ages of 10 and 14) a difficult one for you? Why? What were
> some of the issues you faced in school, at home, and with friends? Did your rela-
> tionship with family members (particularly your parents or guardians), with your
> classmates, and with your friends change? In what way? What were the advan-
> tages of entering adolescence?

TEEN ANGST? NAH!

Ned Vizzini

In the following essay, Ned Vizzini, a 17-year-old "survivor" of adolescence, promises that turning 13 doesn't have to be painful. In fact, he says, adolescence is actually a good time in life to "sit back, make some friends, and maybe discover what you're good at." Vizzini has discovered that he is good at writing; although he was still a high school student when he wrote this essay, he got it published in *The New York Times*, something that even professional, mature writers are often unable to do.

Vocabulary

angst (title)   worry or suffering
assail (paragraph 1)   to attack with arguments
niggling (3)   little; nagging
sordid (4)   dirty; vile
lurid (4)   harsh or shocking
affiliation (6)   connection with; membership in
repellent (6)   to drive away
indulge (10)   be nice to yourself; treat yourself well
anecdote (12)   a true story told to prove a point
discreetly (13)   quietly; without being noticed
sleight of hand (13)   trick
inebriation (13) drunkenness
domineering (15)   controlling

Suggestions for Free Writing

Before you read this essay, take about 10 minutes to free-write on the following topics:

What were some of the greatest challenges you faced as you entered adolescence and throughout your teenage years? What were some of the greatest satisfactions and pleasures? Of all the changes you went through as you passed from childhood to young adulthood, which was the most significant? Which was the most difficult? Which was the most pleasurable? Based on your responses to these questions, what advice would you give to children who are just entering adolescence?

Source: "Teen Angst? Nah!" by Ned Vizzini, as it appeared in *The New York Times Magazine*, May 17, 1998. Reprinted by permission of the author.

So, you've turned 13, and suddenly you feel as if you're in Death 1
Valley. You come home from school and Oprah is on, talking about
"America's Youth in Crisis"; your parents assail you after dinner with
antidrug literature, asking what you've been "experimenting" with
lately; and from every corner—school, home, church—you're being
told: "Be careful! These are four of the most important years of your
life!"

Well, relax. I've been there, and let me tell you: your teen years 2
aren't that important at all. The important years come when you want
them to. Ray Kroc was a two-bit, middle-aged, milk-shake-machine
salesman when he founded a little company called McDonald's. His
most important years started right there.

As for me, I'm a junior at Stuyvesant High School in Manhattan. 3
Although I'm still in the thick of my teen-age years, I think I've learned
a thing or two by now. And as far as I can tell, being a teen-ager is just
like being a kid, except that you've got five extra niggling concerns: sex,
money, smoking, drinking and getting into college.

First things first: sex. You already know all about sex (at least the 4
mechanics of it), so I'll spare the birds-and-bees stuff. The most important thing to remember about teen-age sex is that television is not a
study guide. Watching "Dawson's Creek," you get the idea that every
American over the age of 11 has a steady boyfriend or girlfriend, and
that sordid, love-triangle sex kicks in by age 15. The reality is far less
lurid, I promise.

Your friends are an equally unreliable study guide. Starting at 12, 5
their bragging begins: "I did blah-blah-blah with so-and-so." As a general
rule, take everything your friends tell you about sexual experience and
cut it in half. Then you'll have a reasonably accurate picture of what's
going on.

As for dating, here are some tips. Boys: join a rock band. Or a 6
sports team. Or anything. What girls are really attracted to is affiliation.
Buff up your brooding skills and don't talk much. Never underestimate
the repellent power of dandruff. When you find out a girl has a crush on
you, act fast—it'll last two weeks at most.

Girls: you'll never be rejected if you ask a guy out. He'll be so 7
dumbfounded or thrilled that he'll just shut up and nod. Another thing:
those quizzes in YM magazine are totally useless. And glitter makes you
look messy, not cute.

Despite what I've just said, however, don't sweat the small stuff. 8
Romance will eventually come your way. No matter how dorky you are,
you'll most likely get your first kiss in the next four years, if you haven't
already. Other people's mouths taste strange at first, but you'll get used
to them. You'll go for a nice walk in the park; you'll fall deeply in *luuuv*;
you'll do all the cute stuff. It will be fun.

Next up: money. Let's see, you're probably living rent-free, with   9
free food and free clothes. In addition, you can earn extra cash by, say,
working part time in a store. The next four years could be pretty profitable. Question is, how will you use your earnings?

Most likely, you'll wake up Saturday mornings thinking you've been   10
robbed, but soon realize that you've spent the week's money on the silly
scraps of teen-age life: school supplies, movies, haircuts, T-shirts. Why waste
it? As weak as it sounds, I say save your money. Wait until you can afford
something really cool, then indulge. The $50 mini-backpacks can wait.

Now we hit the naughty stuff. In the next four years, you'll   11
inevitably meet up with cigarettes and marijuana. You already know what
smoking's like. Haven't you ever been stuck with a puffing relative at a
family funeral? Smoking a cigarette yourself is similar—it tastes nasty
and burns your throat. As for pot, it shares smoking's characteristics with
one extra benefit: it makes you act really dumb.

But you've been told that before. All teen-agers have. Yet   12
somehow they all end up at a party where somebody offers them a
joint, and they have nothing to say but, "Uh, sure." Well, here's what
you say: "Nah, I tried that stuff once; it really messed me up." Proceed
to tell a ridiculous anecdote about the time you "tried that stuff." If the
story's funny enough to get everybody laughing, you'll slip out of the
situation. Alternatively, simply shake your head, act uninterested and
get into a conversation with somebody else. The quick, silent rebuttal
is devastating.

Drinking is also a tricky issue. From an early age, you've seen ads   13
that promise that the moment you crack open a beer, football players
will magically pop up on your front porch with bikini-clad girlfriends in
tow. Real teen drinking scenes are far less glamorous, I'm sad to say—
we're talking glassy-eyed party-goers slouched on couches. But there's an
easy way to handle parties without getting stinking drunk. Take a
drink—anything, whatever they give you—and walk around pretending
to sip it. (You'll need a plastic cup for this trick to work. A glass will give
you away.) After an hour, discreetly put the drink down on a table.
Nobody will notice this sleight of hand. And it'll be entertaining to
watch the inebriation (real or feigned) of others.

Finally, you've got to contend with college. Now, you already know   14
what school is like: you come in; you keep quiet; you don't break anything; you leave. High school is the same, except on the horizon,
looming over you, are these monstrosities: the SAT's, the Achievement
Tests, college interviews. A word of advice: don't worry so much about
college. To be sure, you can learn a lot at a university. At the same time,
plenty of successful people—Thomas Edison, Bill Gates, even my grandfather—never went, or dropped out as soon as possible. At a high-pres-
sure school like mine, teachers push the idea that your college will

absolutely determine your future, but nothing is set in stone. If you want to go, go; but don't freak out about it.

The media present adolescence as hell on earth, chock full of evil   15 cliques (the cliques in grade school are worse), domineering parents and wrenching decisions that will determine the rest of your life. Nah. Adolescence is a time to sit back, make some friends—and maybe discover what you're good at. Don't believe the hype.

Questions for Reflection and Discussion

1. Vizzini lists the five biggest concerns of entering adolescence as sex, money, smoking, drinking, and getting into college. Do you agree, or did you have different concerns? What were those concerns?
2. With what advice and information given by Vizzini do you most agree? Why? Least agree? Why? Do you think that Vizzini speaks for all adolescents in his essay? Why? Based on the conditions and experiences you had as an adolescent, does he speak for you?

Topics for Writing

1. Vizzini states that plenty of successful people did not attend or did not complete college. As he says, "If you want to go, go; but don't freak out about it." Write an essay in which you explain your reasons for attending college, devoting each of the paragraphs of your essay to one reason. In your conclusion, based on what you say in your essay, state whether you agree or disagree with Vizzini's position about attending college.
2. Return to the free write that you completed before you read Vizzini's essay, and use the information there to write an essay in which you agree or disagree with Vizzini's belief that adolescence is actually a pretty good time in one's life. Based on the position you take, use one of the following titles for your essay: "Teen Angst? Nah" or "Teen Angst? Most Definitely Yes!" (The word *angst* means "worry" or "unhappiness.") Be sure to clearly state in your opening paragraph whether you agree or disagree with Vizzini (this statement becomes the thesis or main idea of your essay), and then begin each of your paragraphs with a topic sentence giving the reason why you agree or disagree. Then, in the rest of the paragraph, give reasons, background information, details, and examples to support your topic sentence.

NOT MITZVAH

Celeste Fremon

The next selection is a mother's account of the way she provided her adolescent son with a "rite of passage" to celebrate his thirteenth birthday—a way of welcoming him "into the male world" and a way of helping him cope with his father's illness.

Vocabulary

bar mitzvah (paragraph 1) a sacred Jewish ceremony that signifies a boy's entry into manhood. Girls are bas mitzvahed.

crème fraîche (1) a culinary delicacy, more sour than whipped cream; a creamy color

calligraphy (1) beautiful handwriting

preadolescent hormones (8) hormones that control a human's sex drive

surly (9) grumpy

encodes and decodes speech (10) the ability to speak and understand speech

neuropsychologist (11) one who studies the workings of the brain and nervous system

calamitous (14) disastrous

sidewinder (20) rattlesnake

eccentricity (20) unusual behavior

stoic (20) without showing emotion

acquiescence (20) acceptance

talisman (22) a good luck charm; something to ward off evil

humongous (22) huge

mortified (23) embarrassed

boisterous (24) loud

jabberwocky (24) a language that no one understands (from *Alice in Wonderland*)

loopy (27) crazy, silly

Suggestions for Free Writing

Before you read this essay, take about 10 minutes to free-write on the following topic:

Source: "Not Mitzvah," by Celeste Fremon, as it appeared in *Utne Reader*, September/October 1999. Reprinted by permission of the author.

Think about when you had some sort of ceremony or celebration marking an important time or event: a bar mitzvah, a bas mitzvah, or other religious ceremony; a birthday celebration; a graduation. Recall as many details as possible about this event—why it was held, where it was held, when it was held, who was there, what you did, how it made you feel, how it changed you, how others reacted to you.

Three weeks before my son, Will, turned 13, he received his first bar mitzvah invitation. It was elegantly engraved on paper the color and texture of crème fraîche and came in an envelope professionally addressed in $5-a-pop calligraphy. He opened it with an expression of awe. [1]

Most of Will's socializing prior to this point had consisted of birthday parties that featured those giant, inflatable bouncy things you can rent for the backyard by the hour, or a trip to Magic Mountain plus a sleepover. The bar mitzvah invitation indicated a whole new universe of social intercourse. "I'm supposed to mark whether I want steak or salmon for dinner," he noted as he held the reply card delicately by its corners. [2]

"I think I'd like a bar mitzvah," he announced the next day, when I picked him up from school. As far as I knew, he'd barely heard the term, and even now had only the wooziest idea of what such an event entailed. [3]

"Honey," I said, "if you wanted a bar mitzvah, you should have planned a lot further ahead." He shot me a suspicious look. "You should have worked it out to get yourself born into a Jewish family." [4]

"You have to be Jewish?" he asked, narrowing his eyes as if he thought I might be manufacturing this restriction just to torment him. [5]

"Well, yeah," I told him. "It's kind of a religious thing." [6]

"That sucks," he said. [7]

Just about a year before, Will had gone through a rough period when preadolescent hormones invaded his body like spring floodwaters. He'd also graduated from our nice, low-key community Topanga Elementary and was attending a middle school for gifted kids where the homework load produced nightly cases of irrational dread. And on top of everything else, there was the father issue. [8]

At that time, a friend suggested that I hold some kind of welcome-to-manhood celebration for him. "Boys need a rite of passage," said the friend, who is not at all your sensitive New Age guy but an ex-Marine with a slightly surly demeanor. "It'd be good for your son, especially since he doesn't have a dad to, you know, show him the ropes." [9]

Actually, Will does have a dad: George, my ex-husband, who suffered a cerebral aneurysm several years back. A tiny vascular balloon exploded in the left temporal lobe of his brain, damaging the mechanism that encodes and decodes speech. Now his words are a jumble of English and a language of his own devising. George does his best to reach Will from inside his psychic terrarium; sometimes they play cards [10] together, or chess. But never again will George be able to show his son any kind of ropes.

A week or two after the aneurysm occurred, I took Will to meet with a neuropsychologist, who explained in simple terms the recovery one could expect. Will sat next to me listening quietly, his body listing against mine like a tree blown against the side of a barn. Whatever his dad's progress, the psychologist said, it would most likely top out at three years. 11

The truth seemed to help Will gain emotional footing. He would tell anybody who asked, "My dad is recovering from a stroke." But last spring, the three-year alarm rang inside Will. "My dad's mentally disabled," is now the way he answers all father-related inquiries. 12

To me he was even more specific. One night, when I asked him why he was in a bad mood, his cheek twitched, and he turned away from me bitterly. "I'm in a bad mood because I need a dad and my dad's half dead." 13

I read *Iron John*, Robert Bly's book about the importance of male initiation, when it came out in 1990 because I was curious about the best-seller fuss. But I didn't take it seriously until I began researching a book of my own on gang life in East Los Angeles. Night after night, I watched fatherless boys attempt to initiate each other into masculine mysteries, with calamitous results; I'd find them on street corners, and they'd talk to me about their absent, drunken, strung-out, dead, incarcerated dads, their voices full of rage and longing. 14

At first I failed to connect their anguish with my own son's distress. After all, Will had me as a mother, did he not? And surely with my superior education and resources I could mend most of the damage inflicted by the loss of his dad's influence. But then the hormones hit, the father alarm rang, and I discovered my arrogance. Will began kicking furiously away from me, as a swimmer kicks off from the side of the pool to speed through the water. But his kicks had a desperate, angry, isolating quality that I recognized from my years with those boys across town. 15

Hoping for a magic formula, I bought books about the art of parenting boys. "Coaches can be excellent mentors," I read. "A grandfather holds a valuable position in the boy's life as the elder of his personal tribe." But Will had zero interest in team sports. George's dad was dead. And my father, with whom Will had been close, died the year before George got sick. 16

Finally I did what many mothers cannot afford to do: I marched Will to a therapist. A male therapist. If I couldn't provide my son with fatherly advice the old-fashioned way, I would buy it by the hour. 17

The shrink was kind, smart, and able to rattle off skateboarding jargon with impressive fluency. A few sessions in, he asked to speak to me alone. "Will says his 13th birthday is coming up," he said. "Have you thought of doing some kind of . . . uh . . . ceremony for him?" 18

I knew my son wasn't going to put up with vision quests or inspirational hikes to mountaintops, so I decided on something simple. A "not mitzvah," I called it. I set the party for 2 p.m. on the third Sunday in November; the guests arrived, looking jumpy. Will emerged wearing his favorite skateboard T-shirt over baggy shorts and looking elaborately unconcerned. 19

I instructed him to sit down and picked up my Navajo peyote rattle, which makes a noise like sidewinders on amphetamines. "Not the rattle!" said Will, but it was a halfhearted protest. I shook the thing in an arc around his head and shoulders, while he endured my eccentricities with stoic acquiescence. 20

"Yesterday you crossed over the borderline from kidhood to the road that will take you to adulthood," I said. I'd rehearsed a speech earlier in the shower, but I'd forgotten it. "Traditionally, when a boy or a girl makes that crossing, he or she is welcomed on the other side by the community—which includes your family and those who care about you. That's why we're here." 21

I'd asked the guests to bring Will a talisman, plus a wish or piece of wisdom applicable to his future. The father of a classmate handed Will a worn Swiss Army Knife. "It's been with me for 20 years," he said, "and it's served me well. I hope it serves you." Our ex-neighbor, who'd often yelled at the kids for running through his garden, presented Will with a seven-foot plum tree ready for planting, "so you'd know the joy of watching things grow." My brother clasped Will in a bear hug, said he loved him, then handed him a humongous new power drill. "Welcome," he said with a manly man's grin. "Now you have everything you need to take apart the house." 22

In all, about 20 people spoke, including women and a few kids. One friend, who'd told me he thought the whole thing was stupid, got emotional when his turn came. "I found this out on Anacapa Island," he said, dropping a small white shell into Will's palm. "It's to remind you to be in the wilderness as much as possible, and to try to protect it whenever you can." Will seemed somewhat mortified by the attention, but he never protested. He just took it in. 23

His father went last. All afternoon I'd heard George gamely chatting up the guests with his strange, boisterous jabberwocky. This couldn't have been easy for him. A year after the aneurysm, we'd tried to go to a local restaurant to celebrate Will's 10th birthday; George spent half the night curled fetuslike on my bed, panicked at the thought of running into people who had known him when his brain was intact. Now he moved toward Will with ungainly dignity. He'd managed to type something on the computer and he indicated I should read it aloud. "I know how you feel about me," George wrote. "Our challenge is to transform the dragons that try to live with us. Blaming is a waste of time. We are responsible for our freedom. We are not our dragons." 24

When I finished reading, George lurched forward to hug his son. Will 25
ducked his head and hugged him back, whispering, "Thanks, Dad." I shook
the rattle once more and muttered something about the door of manhood.
"You have to walk through that door on your own," I said, "but we want you
to know that we're all behind you—me, your dad, all of us here." Finally, I
asked if there was anything Will would like to tell us in return.

"I think somebody let the cat outside," he said. And it was finished. 26

It has been six months now since Will's birthday celebration, and 27
things at our house are so improved that I find myself saying cautious
little prayers of thanks. On the surface of it, that loopy afternoon of rat-
tling and wishing wasn't any big deal. And yet it was a very big deal that
so many men in Will's life showed up to tell him that he mattered, that
they took him seriously, that they were there for him if he needed them.

"Never being welcomed into the male world by older men is a 28
wound in the chest," writes Robert Bly. Last year, my son was wounded
and I was terrified. This year, he came to understand that he was welcomed after all.

Questions for Reflection and Discussion

1. Consider the adolescent experiences and challenges of Will Fremon (the
author's son), and then think back to the first essay in this chapter, "Teen
Angst? Nah!" in which Ned Vizzini discusses his adolescent experiences.
Decide whose experiences most closely resemble your own, and explain why.
2. If someone were going to plan a ceremony to help you know you are loved
and appreciated, what would you want the ceremony to be like? Be as specific as possible.

Topics for Writing

1. Based on your own adolescent experiences, and based on your observations of friends, acquaintances, and classmates, write an essay in which you
describe some of the most difficult challenges faced by adolescents today.
Begin each paragraph with a topic sentence defining and describing the
challenge. Be sure to provide details, descriptions, and examples so that
your reader has a clear understanding of your meaning.
2. Return to the free write that you completed before you read Fremon's
essay. Use the information there to write an essay describing, with as much
detail as possible, the most important ceremony, celebration, event, or rite
of passage that has occurred in your life. Remember to answer the six
important questions that enable a reader to "see" and understand your
essay: who, what, where, when, why, and how. In your conclusion, explain
why this particular event was important and meaningful to you.

Reading 5–3

HANGING FIRE

Audre Lorde

DRIVING LESSONS

Neal Bowers

The following two poems, "Hanging Fire" by Audre Lorde, and "Driving Lessons" by Neal Bowers, reflect some of the more common concerns of adolescence: learning to drive, having acne, learning to dance, being in love, wearing braces, agonizing over what to wear, competing for good grades. But these poems also reflect a far deeper and more important adolescent theme: our relationship with our parents and our fear of losing them just when it seems we need them the most.

Remember, you do not have to understand every word or even every line of a poem; just read it through two or three times and let the meaning come to you. Sometimes poetry allows us to "feel" rather than "understand" what the poet is saying. For example, you may never be able to understand for sure what Audrey Lorde means when she ends each of her three stanzas with the words "and momma's in the bedroom with the door closed." But you can certainly *feel* that the 14-year-old speaker in the poem believes that her mother is not there when she needs her most. And although Neal Bowers describes actual "driving lessons" in his poem, as we read it, we can certainly *feel* that he is really talking about the lessons we need, not to get a driver's license but to get through life.

Vocabulary

From "Hanging Fire":

hanging fire (title)   waiting for something to happen

From "Driving Lessons":

maneuver (paragraph 1)   to move, manage or plan skillfully

clutch and gas (1)   in older model cars, a clutch pedal must be used when shifting gears

Suggestions for Free Writing

Before you read the two poems, take about 10 minutes to free-write on the following topics:

Think about your relationship with the person or persons most responsible for raising you: your parents, grandparents, or guardians. Then choose one person, and consider what kind of relationship you have by recording as many activities or events you can think of that represent (show) how you interact and get along with that person. Examples may be doing homework together, performing sports together, learning to drive, shopping, working together, cooking together, helping each other. Next to each activity or event, write several *adjectives* (words that describe) to show if the activity is pleasurable and productive, or uncomfortable and unproductive.

Hanging Fire

I am fourteen   1
and my skin has betrayed me
the boy I cannot live without
still sucks his thumb
in secret
how come my knees are
always so ashy
what if I die
before morning
and momma's in the bedroom
with the door closed.

I have to learn how to dance   2
in time for the next party
my room is too small for me
suppose I die before graduation
they will sing sad melodies
but finally
tell the truth about me
There is nothing I want to do
and too much
that has to be done
and momma's in the bedroom
with the door closed.

Nobody even stops to think   3
about my side of it
I should have been on Math Team
my marks were better than his
why do I have to be

the one
wearing braces
I have nothing to wear tomorrow
will I live long enough
to grow up
and momma's in the bedroom
with the door closed.

Driving Lessons

I learned to drive in a parking lot   1
on Sundays, when the stores were closed—
slow maneuvers out beyond the light-poles,
no destination, just the ritual of clutch and gas,
my father clenching with the grinding gears,
finally giving up and leaving my mother
to buck and plunge with me and say,
repeatedly, "Once more. Try just once more."

She walked out on him once   2
when I was six or seven, my father
driving beside her, slow as a beginner,
pleading, my baby brother and I
crying out the windows, "Mama, don't go!"
It was a scene to break your heart
or make you laugh—those wailing kids,
a woman walking briskly with a suitcase,
the slow car following like a faithful dog.

I don't know why she finally got in   3
and let us take her back
to whatever she had made up her mind to leave;
but the old world swallowed her up
as soon as she opened that door,
and the other life she might have lived
lay down forever in its dark infancy.

Sometimes, when I'm home, driving   4
through the old neighborhoods, stopping
in front of each little house we rented,
my stillborn other life gets in,
the boy I would have been if
my mother had kept on walking.

He wants to be just like her,   5
far away and gone forever, wants
me to press down on the gas;

but however fast I squeal away,
the shaggy past keeps loping behind,
sniffing every turn.

When I stop in the weedy parking lot,   6
the failed stores of the old mall
make a dark wall straight ahead;
and I'm alone again, until my parents get in,
unchanged after all these years,
my father, impatient, my mother
trying hard to smile, waiting for me
to steer my way across this emptiness.

Questions for Reflection and Discussion

1. Make a list of the adolescent problems that Audre Lorde mentions in her poem. Do you think she has captured the most important concerns that adolescent girls face? Why? If she has missed any important concerns, what are they?
2. In stanza 4 of "Driving Lessons," Neal Bowers mentions "the boy I would have been if my mother had kept on walking." Do you think his life would have been better or worse if his mother had, in fact, left him, his baby brother, and his father?

Topics for Writing

1. Write an essay in which you describe your relationship with the parent or guardian who has had the greatest impact on your life, either positive or negative. Remember to answer the important who, what, where, why, when, and how questions as you describe and explain this relationship so that your reader can fully understand the impact this person has had on you. In your conclusion, explain whether you want to have (or do have) the same kind of relationship with your own children. Explain why.
2. Although you will probably not be asked to create a poem in college (unless you take a creative writing class), writing poetry provides us with the opportunity to express our deepest ideas, feelings, and emotions without having to worry about the structure of an essay or the rules of formal writing. Return to the free write you completed before you read the two poems. Use the information there to write a poem (at least four stanzas long) in which you describe your relationship with a parent or guardian by describing one or several of the activities that you do together.

Reading 5-4

UNAFRAID OF THE DARK (EXCERPT)

Rosemary L. Bray

The next selection is an *excerpt* (an excerpt is a part of a longer work) taken from the book *Unafraid of the Dark* by Rosemary L. Bray. Recall the earlier excerpt from Bray's book in Chapter 1, in which she describes the pride she felt as a young child in writing a poem about the death of President Kennedy.

In this excerpt, Bray, who is African American, describes an adolescent experience that changed her forever: attending a new school in an all-white neighborhood. Bray was encouraged to attend the new school by the teachers in her old school who, recognizing her intelligence and ability, decided she needed more of a challenge. Bray's mother agreed with the decision because the children in Rosemary's old school kept picking on her because she liked to study.

Bray describes the events and experiences that led her to feeling "ashamed" of her circumstances: The opportunity to attend a better school in a better neighborhood forced her to realize, for the first time in her life, that her family was poor.

Vocabulary

antagonistic (paragraph 1)   to be unfriendly; to be against someone

kindled (1)   awakened; aroused

appalled (2)   shocked in an unhappy way

nonsectarian (5)   not connected to a religion

scrounged (5)   searched around for something

archrival (9)   serious competitor, even enemy

incredulous (10)   shocked

chaos (13)   total confusion

bar mitzvahed (16)   a sacred Jewish ceremony that signifies a boy's entry into manhood. Girls are bas mitzvahed.

dreidels (16)   four-sided tops with Hebrew letters, used during Chanukah

Purim and Yom Kippur (16)   Jewish holy days

conversion (18)   a major change, in this case, changing from one religion to another

dispensation (19)   permission

vestibule (21)   entry hall

sporadic (23)   from time to time

inhabited (23)   lived in

Suggestions for Free Writing

Before you read the excerpt, take about 10 minutes to free-write on the following topic:

Think about a time in your adolescence (between the ages of 10 and 14) when you felt different in some way from your peers. Explain whether this difference made you feel good or bad about yourself. Remember as many circumstances and details as possible, and describe exactly how you felt as a result of this difference.

One day when I came home from school, Mama and Daddy were talking in Daddy's room. For once they seemed more curious than antagonistic toward each other. Mama asked me how I felt about the idea of going to a new school. It would be far away from where we lived, and I would have to take a train to the North Side of Chicago by myself, she said. Right away, my ten-year-old's spirit of adventure was kindled. The idea of doing anything by myself was a small miracle. 1

It seemed that my mother had told our caseworker that we were all doing well in school, but that she was worried about me. The kids were still picking on me every day, and Mama still had to meet me after school. What's more, the nuns were just as concerned, but for different reasons. I needed a bigger challenge, according to my sixth-grade teacher, Sister Maria Sarto, one she felt I might get at another school with more money and resources. There were several such schools in Chicago, but the big requirement was a scholarship to pay for my going there. At least one of those places was a boarding school, which I was more than ready for. But neither of my parents was ready for that step. I was too young to be away from home, they said. My mother was especially appalled; in her mind, boarding school was where white people sent their children to get them out of the way. 2

So the caseworker had found out about this other school, the Francis W. Parker School, and had brought my mother the application form. She told Mama to fill out the application and send it back to the school. I looked at it and knew I would have to be the one to fill it out. It didn't take long to do, and a few weeks after we mailed it we were notified that I would have to take some kind of test before a decision could be made. I didn't mind that. Not long after, I found myself in a big room with a lot of kids, filling in those computer-scored blank ovals. I was too excited to pay real attention to how few black people were in the room. My mind was on getting to go to this school. It was something I could do without the constant presence of my siblings, without people making fun of me all the time, something that was mine alone. 3

On Holy Saturday, the day before Easter, a letter came in the mail from Parker. My mother let me open it; I had been accepted. I screamed 4 and ran through the house. My brothers and sister gawked; my parents grinned at each other in a rare show of united pleasure. What I didn't know for many years was that Sister Maria Sarto had called the school and spoken to the principal and some of the teachers about me. One of the teachers she spoke to that day would make a terrific difference in my life a few years later. But all I knew at the time was that I had done something that was an honor for the family.

Not long after, they sent a list of the clothes I would need; though the school was nonsectarian, I would still be wearing uniforms. But these were not the ugly blue-and-green plaid of the parochial school. These were quieter colors, solid navy blue and white, with light-blue blouses or knee socks allowed. Mama and I scrounged through thrift shops all summer, looking for skirts to cut down for me. For the first day of school, however, we found something special. It was a light-blue dress—a woman's dress—lavishly embroidered with flowers of every imaginable color and intertwined with leaves and stems of forest green. I thought it was the most perfect, pretty thing I ever saw. It even had a big skirt to swish when I twirled around in it. Mama bought it and cut it down for me to wear, tucking in the sides and waist with her old Singer pedal sewing machine. 5

On the morning of the first day of school, Mama went with me, and cautioned me to pay close attention. She would go with me the whole way this first time; after that, I had to go each day alone. I was eleven; it was thrilling. We walked to Forty-seventh Street and took the bus to the El. That part was familiar; I had been this way on trips downtown. Then we gave the attendant our transfers so she could punch and return them and climbed the long stairs to the elevated platform. Mama reminded me to always say "Return, please," to hold on to my transfer until I was on the Clark Street or Broadway bus. Transfers were good for an hour in Chicago; you could ride buses and trains in any order as often as you wanted, until your time ran out. That's why it was important to look at the time punched on the little transfer clock. The trip to school would take just about an hour, and bus drivers routinely gave you a little more time. 6

On the train, I stood at the little window up front, just as I would have if I'd been going anywhere with Mama, and watched as the tracks descended into the caverns under downtown Chicago. I counted the stops as I always did: Roosevelt Road, Harrison, Jackson and State, Madison-Monroe and State, Randolph and State. That was as far as I'd ever gone on the El until recently. The train took an enormous screeching turn; the sparks flew from the wheels of the train and sputtered out. Then we were pulling into the stations new to me: Grand and State; Chicago and State. Finally, Mama tapped me on the shoulder and told me our stop was next. Clark and Division was painted red; that was 7 how I would teach myself to remember where to get off the train until it became automatic. We went through the turnstiles, and walked up the stairs into the open fall air.

The sun was shining that day; the streets looked so clean you could eat from them. And in contrast to the handful of rugged, slightly rundown stores that occupied Forty-third and Forty-seventh Streets near our house, this intersection was overrun with stores: shoe shops and restaurants, a huge Woolworth's, a jewelry store. The street was full of people, not the slow procession of my neighbors headed for the store or the bus stop, but a steady, vigorous stream of people, going—it seemed—everywhere.

Mama directed me to walk across the street and stand at the bus stop. I could take a 22 or a 36 bus, and both of them would stop where I wanted to go. The school was at Clark and Webster, she said, and I could ask the driver to stop at Webster. Or I could get off at Belden, the next stop, and walk back a half-block. We rode past high-rise buildings in formation, and townhouses that looked like cleaned-up versions of our own building. Soon we rode past another private school, the Latin School, which I would learn later was Parker's archrival. The bus ride gave me my first glimpse of Lincoln Park, and I wondered where the famous zoo was to be found. It turned out to be in back of the school; the zoo's entrance was right across the street from the football field.

Soon my mother buzzed for the bus to stop, and we got off across the street from a low, sprawling brick structure, with lots of windows, a courtyard with trees, two playgrounds, and a huge playing field. The signs directed us to the front entrance, a set of stairs with a driveway in front and a low brick wall running the length of the property. As Mama and I came up the steps, I could hear the buzz of children's voices. When we reached the top and peered through the windows, I saw a huge space filled with children and teenagers. I was incredulous: there were hundreds of kids there, and every one of them, it seemed to me, was white.

No one had told me. They had talked about what a good school it was. They had talked about what a wonderful thing it would be for me to come here; they had talked about how many more interesting things I would be able to do here. Not one soul—not even my parents—had thought to mention a crucial detail. I would be going to school with white people, and anyone with an ounce of sense knew white people were dangerous.

I literally backed away from the door. "Mama, those people are white!" I couldn't believe she looked so unexcited. "They'll kill me!" She watched the same news I watched; she knew white people had thrown bricks at us in the demonstrations in Chicago years earlier. She knew as well as I did that white people sicced dogs on little boys in Selma and blew up churches in Birmingham while little girls were in Sunday school

8

9

10

11

12

and shot people in the back in Mississippi and nearby Cicero and spit on them everywhere. Now she wanted me to go to school with them? What could she and Daddy have been thinking about?

Mama took my hand and pulled me through the door. "Girl, these   13
kids ain't going to bother you. You're here to get an education." We walked inside to the near center of the hall. What looked like chaos had its own curious sense of order. What seemed to be a milling crowd was in fact a cluster of several grades, including my own. I was to be in Mrs. Reid's seventh-grade class. My mother found Mrs. Reid just in time; at eight A.M. the bell rang, and the crush of students began heading for stairs, some up, some down. I was headed down. I looked back helplessly at my mother. "I'll be up here," she said.

Inside the classroom, Mrs. Reid asked the new children to stand   14
with her. The other new kids were boys; at least one of them was handsome; all of them looked as though they belonged there. The teacher asked for volunteers, seasoned students to act as guides for the newcomers. When my turn came, only one hand went up. It was attached to a thin girl with curly brown hair and braces; her name was Monica. I had no idea at the time that she was already as unpopular as I would become. When homeroom was dismissed, she came up to me and grabbed my hand, offering to show me around. By the time I located my mother, Monica already was leading me off to the library. "Look Mama, I have a friend," I said to her.

For a very long time, Monica was my only friend. I was fine in the   15
classroom. The work was challenging, not hard, and there was always something interesting to do, a project you could make up for class. Monica and I both loved science, as it turned out. She and I both wanted to be doctors—not such a popular thing for eleven-year-old girls to want in the 1960s. But we were so weird, no one was surprised.

I was surprised at the number of kids in my class who were Jewish.   16
It might never have come up if it hadn't been for the fact that several of them were being confirmed, or bar mitzvahed. I had heard of confirmation; I'd been confirmed the previous year. But the solemn ceremony of the bar mitzvah was new to me. Monica wasn't going to be bas mitzvahed, but she was Jewish, too. I learned a lot that year about the High Holy Days and Jewish food (which it turned out my father knew all about from his abortive attempts at restaurants). I learned about dreidels and Purim (which I loved because it involved one of my favorite characters from the Bible, Esther) and Yom Kippur. I could appreciate the idea of having one day a year to confess every bad thing you'd done, as opposed to doing it continually, every Saturday afternoon, as Catholic kids did.

I also learned Jesus was a Jew. I cannot account for how it was that   17
I missed that minor detail, but I did. When Monica pointed out the logic of it—how he had to be a Jew or they would never have called him Rabbi

in certain parts of the New Testament—I was stunned. Monica and I were constantly having great debates over religion. We were much more preoccupied with it than with race. For a while, I kept trying to baptize her; I would wet my hands in the water fountain and chase her around the playground, reciting the words from the Baltimore Catechism: "I baptize you in the name of the Father, and of the Son, and of the Holy Ghost."

But after going to my classmates' bar mitzvahs and seeing the solemnity and beauty of the ceremony (and looking at the astounding gifts they received afterward), and after long religious discussions with Monica, I decided that I should be Jewish too. My parents had a fit. My father said: "What, being black isn't trouble enough; you want to be a Jew too?" I realize now that my desire had more to do with wanting to be like my best friend, with wanting to belong, than it did with any kind of conversion experience. But it took a particular incident to make it clear to me just how much I didn't belong. 18

It was the afternoon I went to play with Susie Levitt after school. She had asked me over to play earlier in the week. Because I was under strict orders to come home directly from school, going to her house required special dispensation from my parents, since I'd get home after dark. But Mama and Daddy seemed glad for once that I was making friends, and they'd agreed to let me go. 19

I knew the way to her house from the address: I passed within a block of where she lived each morning. I got off the bus a bit earlier than I usually did, and walked around the corner onto a street of immaculate brownstones. When I reached her address, a narrow, five-story house, I climbed the stairs and was momentarily confused. I couldn't figure out which apartment was hers; there was only one bell, with no message about how many rings would signal her. I took a chance and rang the bell once, figuring someone would direct me to where she lived. 20

A white woman in a uniform answered the door. When I told her I had come to see Susie, she opened the door wider and let me inside. I looked around for the mailboxes in the vestibule; there were none. I walked into the front room as Susie came downstairs. Something astounding dawned on me as we said hello: there were no apartments. The whole house was hers to live in. Susie asked if I wanted to see the house. I did. She took me through the parlor to the formal dining room and into the kitchen, where a black woman about my mother's age had her back to us. Susie asked me if I wanted a snack; I said no. The woman turned and smiled slightly at me and said hello. I said hello softly, then followed Susie out and upstairs. On the next level, another woman in uniform was ironing clothes as we passed. We walked up and up the elegant winding staircase until we reached the top floor, and Susie opened a door into what looked to me like Paradise. 21

In the life of every young girl, there is one fantasy. Some girls want the most beautifully dressed life-size doll. Others dream of a shining 22 prince to take them away one day to live as his wise and beautiful queen. My fantasy was small: one day, I would have my own room. I had never even given any thought to what would be in the room; I just knew that one day I would have a room that no one was in but me. Susie already had such a room, but she had more. The room contained the decor of a little girl's dreams. Everything in it was white and gold: the dresser, the mirror frame, the vanity and most of all, the four-poster canopy bed. White curtains floated across the top, sheltering the bed like clouds.

I wanted to know where her brothers and sister slept. She cheer- 23
fully showed me her siblings' rooms—none the room of my dreams, but each separate and apart. I don't remember what we did that afternoon. I only remember feeling numb and vague. All the way home I replayed the scenes at her house. By the time I got to Forty-seventh Street to take the bus home, the contrast was evident. The noise of the train, the smells of barbecue from the shack across the street, the sporadic blare of Motown in the record shop as customers checked to be sure the 45 they wanted to buy was the right one, the strolling people in late afternoon, all dark like me, all different from those who inhabited the world I'd left only forty-five minutes earlier. I was different, too.

I walked home from the bus stop, back down Ellis Avenue, past the 24
pansy growing in the cat lady's yard, past the blackberry bush, past Denise Young's fence. I turned on Forty-fifth Street, past the wisps of morning glory vines and the pods filled with next spring's seeds, across the alley to knock on the back door. Mama let me in and asked me if I'd had a good time. I said I had. What else could I say, when anything else would have worried her? Daddy wasn't home yet. I walked through to the front room and put down my school things, hung up my coat. My sister and brothers were playing, Mama was cooking. I walked back to the bathroom, painted a year earlier a brilliant emerald-green enamel that I now saw emphasized the cracking walls. I shut the latch tight before I sat down on the toilet and started to cry.

Being black was not the worst of it; I realized that afternoon that I 25
was poor, too. I would not have my own room, or a white-and-gold canopy bed. Suddenly it was clear—the way my blue skirts and white blouses looked and felt so different from the other girls'. The soft wool they wore did not come from Sears or Goldblatt's, but from Marshall Field or Saks Fifth Avenue. My blouses were not cotton, they were 100 percent drip-dry polyester. I didn't have penny loafers or Bass Weejuns. I had shoes from the 2-for-$5 store. I knew the facts of all these things long before; I had joined with my mother in planning around them. But this was the day I felt it—how different, how really different I was.

When I was cried out, I wiped my face over and over with cold 26
water until I could pass for normal. Fortunately, no one had paid much attention to how long I'd been in the bathroom. They assumed I had started reading something and lost track of time, as I always did. They

were wrong this time. Something in me had broken somehow, but I was determined that they wouldn't know. For them to know, it seemed to me, would mean they would feel bad. And I didn't want Mama or Daddy or anybody to feel bad. We couldn't help being poor. It wasn't anybody's fault. And if I hadn't started going to that school, I probably wouldn't even have known. But it was too late for me; I knew that now. And in the months that followed, except when I was with a couple of people like Monica, I grew more silent and unhappy in my awareness. Now I know the feeling for what it was. I was ashamed.

Questions for Reflection and Discussion

1. At the beginning of paragraph 22, Bray writes, "In the life of every young girl, there is one fantasy." Hers was to have her own room. Think back to when you were 11 or 12 years old. What was your fantasy?
2. Bray's parents and teachers decide to send her to a "better" school so that she can be challenged. During your junior and high school years, did you attend the "better" schools in your neighborhood or area, or did you attend the schools that were not considered "elite"? What impact did this have on your education? On your future? Do you wish you had attended other schools? Why?

Topics for Writing

1. Based on your own educational experiences, your knowledge of the importance of a good education, and your observations of your classmates and other students, write an essay in which you explain whether you would send your children to a "better" school, as Bray's parents did, or keep them in the neighborhood school. Provide as many reasons as possible for your decision. Begin each paragraph of your essay with one reason, and then be sure to provide background information, descriptions, details, examples, and explanations to support your opinion.
2. Return to the free write you completed before you read Bray's excerpt. Use the information there to write an essay in which you describe an adolescent (ages 10 to 14) event, an experience, or a circumstance in your life when you felt different (for example, because of your race, where you lived, your athletic ability, your scholastic ability, the way you dressed or spoke, where you came from, the way you behaved in class, the way you looked, your family's financial status). Be sure to answer the important who, what, where, when, why, and how questions. Then explain how being different made you feel. Again, be very specific so that your reader can fully understand the impact this difference had on you.

Reading 5–5

REVIVING OPHELIA (EXCERPT)

Mary Pipher

In this *excerpt* (an excerpt is part of a longer work) from a book entitled *Reviving Ophelia,* Dr. Mary Pipher, a psychologist who has worked with adolescent girls for more than 20 years, explains the issues and problems that adolescent girls face in the United States. In this excerpt from the third chapter, entitled "Developmental Issues: I'm Not Waving, I'm Drowning," she explains an adolescent girl's physical, emotional, thinking, academic, and social self.

When this book was published in 1994, it received great attention, helping parents, teachers, sociologists, and psychologists to better understand the pressures that society places on young girls. There have since been similar studies done on adolescent boys as well.

This excerpt is similar to the type of reading that would be assigned in a college-level sociology class, women's studies class, cultural issues class, or adolescent psychology class.

Vocabulary

reviving (title)   bringing back to life

Ophelia (title)   Ophelia is the adolescent girl in love with Hamlet in Shakespeare's play. As a girl, she was happy and free, but when she falls in love with Hamlet, she lives only for his approval.

crucible (paragraph 3)   temptation

articulate (5)   to speak clearly

serpentine (6)   winding; not straight or simple

ascertain (9)   figure out

imperative (12)   necessary; essential

Pyrrhic victory (16)   not a true victory because in the end the loss is greater than the gain

judged more holistically (19)   taking everything into consideration when judging

discrepancy (20)   difference

artifice (21)   to change or disguise

eschewed (24)   avoided

cryptic (25)   secretive; mysterious

unmodulated (27)   not controlled

frenetic (29)   having too much energy

lethargic (29)   not enough energy

cataclysmic (31)   a completely destructive disaster

tattered (33)   a bit damaged; battered and worn

vibrancy (33)   full of life; a love of life

formal operational thought (34)   the ability to reason through problems and issues logically

trite (38)   unimportant, even foolish

invulnerable (43)   unable to be hurt or damaged

discrepant information (46)   information that contradicts or means two different things

distorting reality (46)   viewing something in an unrealistic or inaccurate way

anorexic, anorexia (46)   an eating disorder that causes people to see themselves as heavier than they are; it can result in serious illness, even death

precipitous (55)   dangerously sudden

Suggestions for Free Writing

Before you read the excerpt, take about 10 minutes to free-write on the following topics:

Think back to junior high school or high school, and make a list of all of the problems and issues that boys face in junior high and high school. Then make a list of all the problems and issues that girls face in junior high and high school. Be as specific as possible—for example, pressure to get good grades, pressure to be popular, pressure to get into a good college, pressure from home, pressure to earn enough money to support themselves, pressure to avoid drugs, pressure to get on a sports team. After you finish making the two lists, read them over and decide which problems and issues *both* boys and girls face during adolescence.

Generally, puberty is defined as a biological process while adolescence is defined as the social and personal experience of that process. But even puberty is influenced by culture. Girls are menstruating much earlier now than during the colonial era, and even earlier than in the 1950s. There are many theories about why puberty comes earlier—changes in nutrition (girls get bigger at a younger age because they are better nourished), hormones added to beef and chicken (growth hormones that are known to affect humans may trigger early puberty) and electricity (bodies are programmed to enter puberty after exposure to a certain amount of light, which comes much earlier in a woman's lifetime in an age of electricity). The point is that girls enter adolescence earlier than they did forty years ago. Some girls menstruate at age nine.   1

Early puberty actually slows down many aspects of girls' development. Early development and the more difficult culture of the 1990s   2 increase the stress on adolescents. Girls who have recently learned to bake cookies and swan-dive aren't ready to handle offers for diet pills. Girls who are reading about Pippi Longstocking aren't ready for the sexual harassment they'll encounter in school. Girls who love to practice piano and visit their grandmothers aren't ready for the shunning by cliques. And at the same time girls must face events prematurely, they are encouraged by our culture to move away from parents and depend on friends for guidance. No wonder they suffer and make so many mistakes.

3　　Girls stay in adolescence longer now. In the fifties and sixties, most teens left home as soon as they graduated from high school, never to return. Increasingly in the 1980s and 1990s young adults do not want to leave home, or they leave home for a while and return to live with their parents in their twenties. Partly children stay because of economics, partly they stay because home seems a safe haven in an increasingly dangerous world. Now adolescence may begin around age ten and may last until around age twenty-two. It can take twelve years to make it through the crucible.

4　　There is an enormous gap between the surface structure of behaviors and the deep structure of meaning. Surface structure is what is visible to the naked eye—awkwardness, energy, anger, moodiness and restlessness. Deep structure is the internal work—the struggle to find a self, the attempt to integrate the past and present and to find a place in the larger culture. Surface behaviors convey little of the struggle within and in fact are often designed to obscure that struggle.

5　　By definition, the deep-structure questions are not articulated clearly to adults. Rather, the surface questions are coded to speak to larger issues. "Can I dye my hair purple?" may mean "Will you allow me to develop as a creative person?" "Can I watch R movies?" may mean "Am I someone who can handle sexual experiences?" "Can I go to a different church?" may mean "Do I have the freedom to explore my own spirituality?"

6　　The deep-structure questions are processed in a serpentine manner with friends. Endlessly girls discuss the smallest details of conversations and events—who wore what, who said what, did he smile at her, did she look mad when I did that? The surface is endlessly combed for information about the depths.

7　　This deep structure–surface structure split is one reason why girls experience so much failure in relationships. Communication is confused and confusing. Relationships between friends are so coded that misunderstandings abound. Parents who attend to the surface structure often miss the point.

8　　Because the deep structure work is so serious, the surface behavior is often tension-releasing, a way of dispelling internal energy that must escape somehow. This marked difference in behaviors reminds me of my first few years as a therapist. I spent long days being serious, talking about problems and analyzing situations. Then after work I craved goofing off with my kids, telling stupid jokes and watching W.C. Fields movies. The harder my day, the more I wanted comic relief. Teenage girls are doing therapy all day too, only it's inside their own heads. They need the time off whenever they can get it.

When I work with adolescent girls I try to understand what their   9
surface behavior is telling me about their deep-structure issues. I try to ascertain when their behavior is connected to their true selves and when it is the result of pressure to be a false self. Which thinking should I respect and nurture? Which should I challenge?

Physical Selves

The body is changing in size, shape and hormonal structure.   10
Just as pregnant women focus on their bodies, so adolescent girls focus on their changing bodies. They feel, look and move differently. These changes must be absorbed, the new body must become part of the self.

The preoccupation with bodies at this age cannot be overstated.   11
The body is a compelling mystery, a constant focus of attention. At thirteen, I thought more about my acne than I did about God or world peace. At thirteen, many girls spend more time in front of a mirror than they do on their studies. Small flaws become obsessions. Bad hair can ruin a day. A broken fingernail can feel tragic.

Generally girls have strong bodies when they enter puberty. But   12
these bodies soften and spread out in ways that our culture calls fat. Just at the point that their bodies are becoming rounder, girls are told that thin is beautiful, even imperative. Girls hate the required gym classes in which other girls talk about their fat thighs and stomachs. One girl told me of showering next to an eighty-five-pound dancer who was on a radical diet. For the first time in her life she looked at her body and was displeased. One client talked about wishing she could cut off the roll of fat around her waist. Another thought her behind was "hideous."

Geena was a chubby clarinet player who liked to read and play   13
chess. She was more interested in computers than makeup and in stuffed animals than designer clothes. She walked to her first day of junior high with her pencils sharpened and her notebooks neatly labeled. She was ready to learn Spanish and algebra and to audition for the school orchestra. She came home sullen and shaken. The boy who had his locker next to hers had smashed into her with his locker door and sneered, "Move your fat ass."

That night she told her mother, "I hate my looks. I need to go on   14
a diet."

Her mother thought, Is that what this boy saw? When he looked at   15
my musical, idealistic Geena, did he see only her behind?

Girls feel an enormous pressure to be beautiful and are aware of 16 constant evaluations of their appearance. In an art exhibit on the theme of women and appearance, Wendy Bantam put it this way: "Every day in the life of a woman is a walking Miss America Contest." Sadly, girls lose if they are either too plain or too pretty. Our cultural stereotypes of the beautiful include negative ideas about their brains—think of the blonde jokes. Girls who are too attractive are seen primarily as sex objects. Their appearance overdetermines their identity. They know that boys like to be seen with them, but doubt that they are liked for reasons other than their packaging. Being beautiful can be a Pyrrhic victory. The battle for popularity is won, but the war for respect as a whole person is lost.

Girls who are plain are left out of social life and miss the develop- 17 mental experiences they most need at this stage of their lives. They internalize our culture's scorn of the plain.

The luckiest girls are neither too plain nor too beautiful. They 18 will eventually date, and they'll be more likely to date boys who genuinely like them. They'll have an identity based on other factors, such as sense of humor, intelligence or strength of character. But they don't feel lucky in junior high. A college girl told me, "In junior high I wanted to kill myself because I was too tall. I could not conceive of happiness at that height." Another told of watching a cute blonde in her eighth-grade class flirt with boys. "The same boys who tripped over themselves to open doors for her would look away if I walked by."

Appearance was important when I was in junior high, but it's even 19 more important today. Girls who lived in smaller communities were judged more holistically—for their character, family background, behavior and talents. Now, when more girls live in cities full of strangers, they are judged exclusively by their appearance. Often the only information teenagers have about each other is how they look.

The right look has always mattered, but now it's harder to obtain. 20 Designer clothes, leather jackets, name-brand tennis shoes and expensive makeup shut more girls out of the competition. The standards of beauty are more stringent. Miss Americas have become taller and slimmer over the years. In 1951, Miss Sweden was 5 feet 7 inches tall and weighed 151 pounds. In 1983, Miss Sweden was 5 feet 9 inches tall and 109 pounds. While beautiful women are slimmer, average women are heavier than they were in the 1950s. Thus the discrepancy between the real and the ideal is greater. This discrepancy creates our plague of eating disorders.

What is culturally accepted as beautiful is achieved only with great 21 artifice—photo croppings, camera angles and composite bodies are necessary to get the pictures we now see of beautiful women. Even the stars cannot meet our cultural ideals without great cost. Dolly Parton dieted until she looked ill. Jamie Lee Curtis, who worked months to get in shape for the movie *Perfect,* felt her body was not right for the part. Jane Fonda and Princess Di have both had eating disorders.

I'm struck by how intense and damaging these issues are every 22 time I speak in a high school or college class. I ask, "How many of you know someone with an eating disorder?" Usually every hand goes up. After my talk girls come up to ask about their friends, their sisters or themselves. They all have horror stories of girls who are miserable because they don't quite meet our cultural ideals.

With early adolescence, girls surrender their relaxed attitudes 23 about their bodies and take up the burden of self-criticism. Just at the point their hips are becoming rounder and they are gaining fat cells, they see magazines and movies or hear remarks by peers that suggest to them that their bodies are all wrong. Many girls scorn their true bodies and work for a false body. They allow the culture to define who they should be. They diet, exercise compulsively and wear makeup and expensive clothes. Charlotte thought of her body as something other people would examine and judge. How her body appeared to others, not how it felt to her, was what mattered.

A girl who remains true to herself will accept her body as hers 24 and resist others' attempts to evaluate and define her by her appearance. She's much more likely to think of her body in terms of function than form. What does her body do for her? Lori, for example, was proud of her body's ability to dance and swim. Her self-esteem didn't revolve around her appearance. She eschewed diets and time spent in front of a mirror. Interestingly, even as her friends primped and dieted, they envied her her casual attitudes about beauty. Lori cared more about being than seeming. She was lucky because, as De Beauvoir writes, "to lose confidence in one's body is to lose confidence in oneself."

Emotional Selves

A friend once told me that the best way to understand teenagers 25 was to think of them as constantly on LSD. It was good advice. People on acid are intense, changeable, internal, often cryptic or uncommunicative and, of course, dealing with a different reality. That's all true for adolescent girls.

The emotional system is immature in early adolescence. 26 Emotions are extreme and changeable. Small events can trigger enormous reactions. A negative comment about appearance or a bad mark on a test can hurl a teenager into despair. Not only are feelings chaotic, but girls often lose perspective. Girls have tried to kill themselves because they were grounded for a weekend or didn't get asked to the prom.

Despair and anger are the hardest emotions to deal with, but other 27
emotions are equally intense. Just as sorrow is unmodulated, so is joy. A
snowstorm or a new dress can produce bliss. There's still a childlike
capacity to be swept away. One girl told me of wandering about in woods
reading poetry and feeling in touch with the central core of the universe. She was elated by the sunlight dappling the leaves, the smells of
wild plum blossoms, the blueness of the sky and the trills of mead-
owlarks. The feeling of the moment is all that exists.

I teach girls to rate their stress as a way to modulate their emotions. 28
I'll say, "If one is a broken shoestring and ten is a terminal brain tumor,
rate things that upset you on this one-to-ten scale." Then I'll ask, "What
would you rate your argument with your boyfriend today?" The girl will
say, "A fifteen."

The instability of feelings leads to unpredictable behavior in ado- 29
lescents. A wildly energetic teen will be frenetic one moment and
lethargic the next. A sentence or a look from a parent can start a crying
spell or World War III. A girl who is incredibly focused when it's time to
plan a skit for prom night is totally disorganized about her social studies
project due the same day.

It's hard for adults to keep up with the changes and intensity of 30
adolescent emotions. When Sara was in junior high I called her after
school. Some days she was full of laughter and confidence. ("School
rocks my world.") Other days she needed crisis intervention over the
phone. ("It sucks to be me.")

Girls' emotional immaturity makes it hard for them to hold on to 31
their true selves as they experience the incredible pressures of adolescence in the 1990s. They are whipped about by their emotions and
misled by them. At a developmental time when even small events are
overwhelming, big events such as date rape or a friend who tests positive
for the HIV virus can be cataclysmic.

Girls deal with intense emotions in ways that are true or false to the 32
self. A girl who operates out of her false self will be overwhelmed by her
emotional experiences and do what she can to stop having these painful
emotions. She may do this by denial of her feelings or by projection onto
others. Charlotte did this by running away, by using alcohol and drugs
and by losing herself in a relationship in which she thought only of her
boyfriend's feelings. When girls fail to acknowledge their own feelings,
they further the development of a false self. Only by staying connected
to their emotions and by slowly working through the turbulence can
young women emerge from adolescence strong and whole.

Lori is still remarkably stable emotionally. I predict that she may 33
have a rough time ahead, and that like most girls she may feel anxiety,
confusion and despair. But I suspect she will manage to acknowledge
these emotional experiences. She'll be able to rage, cry, talk and write
about her emotions. She'll process them and gradually sort them out.

Lori will emerge from adolescence somewhat tattered emotionally but intact. She will be an authentic person who owns all her emotional experiences. She'll possess what Alice Miller calls "vibrancy."

Thinking Selves

Most early adolescents are unable to think abstractly. The brightest are just moving into formal operational thought or the ability to think abstractly and flexibly. The immaturity of their thinking makes it difficult to reason with them. They read deep meaning into casual remarks and overanalyze glances.   34

The concreteness of girls' thinking can be seen in their need to categorize others. People are assigned to groups such as geeks, preps and jocks. One girl's categories included "deeper than thou," a derogatory term for the sophisticated artists at her school. Another divided the world into Christian and non-Christian, and another into alternative, non-alternative and wannabe alternative.   35

Teenage girls are extremists who see the world in black-and-white terms, missing shades of gray. Life is either marvelous or not worth living. School is either pure torment or is going fantastically. Other people are either great or horrible, and they themselves are wonderful or pathetic failures. One day a girl will refer to herself as "the goddess of social life" and the next day she'll regret that she's the "ultimate in nerdosity."   36

This fluctuation in sense of self would suggest severe disturbance in an adult, but in teenage girls it's common. Psychological tests, like the MMPI, need different norms for female adolescents. Their thoughts are chaotic and scrambled. Compared to stable adults, they all look crazy.   37

Girls also overgeneralize in their thinking from one incident to all cases. One affront means "I have no friends." One good grade means "I am an academic diva." Offhand remarks can be taken as a prophecy, an indictment or a diagnosis. One client decided to become a nurse because her uncle told her she would be a good one. When I was in eighth grade, my teacher returned my first poem with the word "trite" scribbled across the top of the page. I gave up my plans to be a writer for almost twenty years.   38

This tendency to overgeneralize makes it difficult to reason with adolescent girls. Because they know of one example, they'll argue, "Everyone else gets to stay out till two," or "Everyone I know gets a new car for their sixteenth birthday." They'll believe that because the girl next door gets a ride to school, every girl in the universe gets a ride to school. They aren't being manipulative as much as they earnestly believe that one case represents the whole.   39

Teenage girls have what one psychologist called the "imaginary audience syndrome." They think they are being watched by others who   40 are preoccupied with the smallest details of their lives. For example, a niece was most upset that her mother wanted to take binoculars to her soccer game. She told her mom, "All the other kids will know you are watching my every move." A friend told me how anxious her daughter was when she wore jeans and a sweatshirt to her daughter's school conference. A twelve-year-old told me how embarrassing it was to go to performances with her mother, who had a way of clapping with hands high in the air. Sometimes when her mother was particularly pleased, she shouted bravo. My client said, "I can't believe she does this. Everyone in the place knows she's a total dork."

Teenage girls engage in emotional reasoning, which is the belief   41 that if you feel something is true, it must be true. If a teenager feels like a nerd, she is a nerd. If she feels her parents are unfair, they are unfair. If she feels she'll get invited to homecoming, then she will be invited. There is limited ability to sort facts from feelings. Thinking is still magical in the sense that thinking something makes it so.

Young girls are egocentric in their thinking. That is, they are   42 unable to focus on anyone's experience but their own. Parents often experience this egocentrism as selfishness. But it's not a character flaw, only a developmental stage. Parents complain that their daughters do only a few chores and yet claim, "I do all the work around here." A mother reports that her daughter expects her to spend hours chauffeuring to save the daughter a few minutes of walking.

At one time I would have said that teenage girls think they are   43 invulnerable. And I could have cited many examples, such as girls refusing to wear seat belts or to deal with the possibilities of pregnancy. I still see glimpses of that sense of invulnerability. For example, one of my clients who volunteered at a rehabilitation center came in with stories of head-injured patients. One day, after a particularly sad story about a boy her age, I blurted out, "Well, at least now you are wearing your seat belt." She gave me a surprised look and said, "Not really. I won't get in a wreck."

But I do see this sense of invulnerability much less frequently. It is   44 shattered by trauma in the lives of girls or their friends. Most twelve-year-olds know they can be hurt. They read the papers and watch television. Psychiatrist Robert Coles writes that children in some parts of America are more frightened than children in Lebanon or Northern Ireland. Girls talk more about death, have more violent dreams, more spooky fantasies and more fears about the future. As one client put it, "With all these shootings, all the people will disappear."

It's important not to oversimplify this topic. Some children feel   45 much safer than others. Lori, for example, with her lovely neighborhood and stable family, feels much safer than Charlotte, with her history of trauma. Even traumatized children sometimes forget to be scared, while protected children have nightmares about being shot. But experience largely determines whether or not a girl feels invulnerable. Becoming conscious of the dangerous world can happen overnight or be a gradual process. The same girl can be of two minds depending on the week. One week she'll lock doors and worry aloud about danger, the next she'll believe that she can fight off any attacker. But generally, adolescents no longer feel invulnerable in the ways they did in my childhood, or even ten years ago.

Girls deal with painful thoughts, discrepant information and cognitive confusion in ways that are true or false to the self. The temptation is to shut down, to oversimplify, to avoid the hard work of examining and integrating experiences. Girls who operate from a false self often reduce the world to a more manageable place by distorting reality. Some girls join cults in which others do all their thinking for them. Some girls become anorexic and reduce all the complexity in life to just one issue—weight. 46

Some girls, like Charlotte, work hard not to think about their lives. They run from any kind of processing and seek out companions who are also on the run. They avoid parents who push them to consider what they are doing. Charlotte was heavily swayed by peers in her decision making. She was a sailboat with no centerboard, blowing whichever way the winds blew. She had no North Star to keep her focused on her own true needs. 47

Girls who stay connected to their true selves are also confused and sometimes overwhelmed. But they have made some commitment to understanding their lives. They think about their experiences. They do not give up on trying to resolve contradictions and make connections between events. They may seek out a parent, teacher or therapist to help them. They may read or write in a journal. They will make many mistakes and misinterpret much of reality, but girls with true selves make a commitment to process and understand their experiences. 48

Lori was particularly good at looking within herself to make decisions. She thought through issues and decided what was best for her. After that, she was relatively immune to peer pressure. She was steering, not drifting, determined to behave in ways that made sense to her. 49

Academic Selves

Schools have always treated girls and boys differently. What is new in the nineties is that we have much more documentation of this phenomenon. Public awareness of the discrimination is increasing. This is due in part to the American Association of University Women (AAUW), which released a study in 1992 entitled "How Schools Shortchange Girls." 50

In classes, boys are twice as likely to be seen as role models, five times as likely to receive teachers' attention and twelve times as likely to 51 speak up in class. In textbooks, one-seventh of all illustrations of children are of girls. Teachers chose many more classroom activities that appeal to boys than to girls. Girls are exposed to almost three times as many boy-centered stories as girl-centered stories. Boys tend to be portrayed as clever, brave, creative and resourceful, while girls are depicted as kind, dependent and docile. Girls read six times as many biographies of males as of females. Even in animal stories, the animals are twice as likely to be males. (I know of one teacher who, when she reads to her classes, routinely changes the sex of the characters in the stories so that girls will have stronger role models.)

Analysis of classroom videos shows that boys receive more classroom attention and detailed instruction than girls. They are called on more often than girls and are asked more abstract, open-ended and complex questions. Boys are more likely to be praised for academics and intellectual work, while girls are more likely to be praised for their clothing, behaving properly and obeying rules. Boys are likely to be criticized for their behavior, while girls are criticized for intellectual inadequacy. The message to boys tends to be: "You're smart, if you would just settle down and get to work." The message to girls is often: "Perhaps you're just not good at this. You've followed the rules and haven't succeeded." 52

Because with boys failure is attributed to external factors and success is attributed to ability, they keep their confidence, even with failure. With girls it's just the opposite. Because their success is attributed to good luck or hard work and failure to lack of ability, with every failure, girls' confidence is eroded. All this works in subtle ways to stop girls from wanting to be astronauts and brain surgeons. Girls can't say why they ditch their dreams, they just "mysteriously" lose interest. 53

Some girls do well in math and continue to like it, but many who were once good at math complain that they are stupid in math. Girl after girl tells me, "I'm not good in math." My observations suggest that girls have trouble with math because math requires exactly the qualities that many junior-high girls lack—confidence, trust in one's own judgment and the ability to tolerate frustration without becoming overwhelmed. Anxiety interferes with problem solving in math. A vicious circle develops—girls get anxious, which interferes with problem solving, and so they fail and are even more anxious and prone to self-doubt the next time around. 54

When boys have trouble with a math problem, they are more likely to think the problem is hard but stay with it. When girls have trouble, they think they are stupid and tend to give up. This difference in attribution speaks to girls' precipitous decline in math. Girls need to be encouraged to persevere in the face of difficulty, to calm down and believe in themselves. They need permission to take their time and to make many mistakes before solving the problem. They need to learn relaxation skills to deal with the math anxiety so many experience. 55

The AAUW study found that as children go through school, boys   56
do better and feel better about themselves and girls' self-esteem, opinions of their sex and scores on standardized achievement tests all
decline. Girls are more likely than boys to say that they are not smart
enough for their dream careers. They emerge from adolescence with a
diminished sense of their worth as individuals.

Gifted girls seem to suffer particularly with adolescence. Lois Murphy   57
found that they lose IQ points as they become feminized. In the 1920s
Psychologist Louis Terman studied gifted children in California. Among
the children, the seven best writers were girls and all the best artists were
girls, but by adulthood all the eminent artists and writers were men.

Junior high is when girls begin to fade academically. Partly this   58
comes from the very structure of the schools, which tend to be large and
impersonal. Girls, who tend to do better in relationship-based, cooperative learning situations, get lost academically in these settings. Partly it
comes from a shift girls make at this time from a focus on achievement
to a focus on affiliation. In junior high girls feel enormous pressure to be
popular. They learn that good grades can even interfere with popularity.
Lori learned to keep quiet about grades. She said, "Either way I lose. If I
make a good grade, they are mad. If I make a bad grade, they spread it
around that even I can screw up." Another girl said, "When I started
junior high I figured out that I'd have more friends if I focused on sports.
Smart girls were nerds." Another, who almost flunked seventh grade, told
me, "All I care about is my friends. Grades don't matter to me."

I saw a seventh-grader who was failing everything. I asked her why   59
and she said, "My friends and I decided that making good grades wasn't
cool." Her story has a happy ending, not because of my work, but
because the next year, in eighth grade, she and her friends had another
meeting and decided that it was now "cool" to make good grades. My
client's academic situation improved enormously.

This tendency for girls to hide their academic accomplishments is   60
an old one. Once on a date I was particularly untrue to myself. Denny
and I went to the A&W Root Beer Drive-In on Highway 81, and he asked
me what I would like. Even though I was famished I ordered only a small
Coke. (Nice girls didn't eat too much.) Then he asked about my six-
weeks grades. I had made As, but I said I had two Cs and was worried my
parents would be mad. I can still remember his look of visible relief.

As Charlotte got lost in junior high, her grades fell. Partly this was   61
because she didn't work, and partly it was because she lost the confidence
in herself that a student needs to tackle increasingly difficult material. She
expected to fail and gave up at the first sign of frustration. Lori, on the
other hand, liked challenges. She had found that by trusting herself and
working hard, she could succeed. She was aware that her good grades
didn't help her socially, but she wasn't willing to sacrifice her academic
career for the short-term goal of pleasing her easily threatened peers.

Questions for Reflection and Discussion

1. Based on your own experiences, your knowledge of the way girls act during adolescence, and your own observations, do you agree with Mary Pipher's findings about adolescent girls? With which findings do you most agree? Least agree? Does she speak for all girls or just a certain class or type of girls?
2. You've just read some evidence confirming the problems and issues faced by adolescent girls. Based on your own experiences, your knowledge of the way boys act during adolescence, and your own observations, what are some of the problems and issues faced by adolescent boys?

Topics for Writing

1. Pipher's description of the challenges and issues facing adolescent girls is not very encouraging. In fact, she makes it seem as if adolescent girlhood is a potentially unpleasant and dangerous time of life. Reread the excerpt and identify five major issues or problems faced by adolescent girls, according to Pipher. Then write an essay in which you agree or disagree that adolescent girls face those issues or problems, using your own experiences and observations as evidence. Be sure to name one problem or issue in the topic sentence of each of your paragraphs. Then, in the rest of the paragraph, give details, descriptions, examples, and evidence to support your ideas and opinions. Remember, it is perfectly okay for you to use Pipher's exact words, as long as you place them in quotation marks.
2. Return to the free write you completed before you read the excerpt from *Reviving Ophelia.* Use the information there to write an essay in which you describe the issues and problems that *both* adolescent girls and boys face as they grow up in today's society. Be sure to use the topic sentences of each of your paragraphs to identify the issue or problem. Then, in the rest of the paragraph, give details, descriptions, examples, and evidence to support your ideas and opinions.

Additional Writing Topics about Adolescence

1. The reading selections in this chapter offer a good overview of adolescence: the problems and challenges adolescents face in avoiding societal pressures, the importance of these years in terms of growth and development, the fears and concerns faced by adolescents. Review all of the selections in this chapter and choose the one with which you most agree, based on your own experiences. Then write an essay explaining how your experiences were similar to those described and explained in the reading selection.

2. Sometimes, experience is the best teacher. Return to the free write you completed at the beginning of this chapter, and use the information there to write an essay on the following topic: When you have children of your own, based on your own challenges, struggles, and behavior, what will you do to help them avoid the problems and pressures of adolescence? Be sure to explain your own experiences so that your reader will understand why you feel it is important for you to help your children avoid them, and explain *how* you will help your children avoid these problems and pressures.

Chapter
6

Parents and Guardians: What They Mean to Us

The reading selections in Chapter 5 contain many references to the people who raised us, and as several of those readings show, we seem to need our parents and guardians more during adolescence than we do during childhood. But, often, as we leave adolescence and enter adulthood, we are finally able to see our parents as real people. As we gain more independence, experience, and knowledge of the world, we are able to get enough distance from our parents and guardians to be able to look back and understand their strength, their wisdom, their energy, and their devotion to us. We are even able to understand their weaknesses. And as we grow older and move away from home to embark on careers and to start families of our own, we begin to realize how much we have been influenced by them and how much we have learned from them—not only from their words but from their actions as well.

All of the selections in this chapter are descriptions of parents or guardians written by adult children. Some are more complimentary than others, but all reflect the deep and permanent feelings we carry with us about the people who raised us. These selections contain more than descriptions, however; they tell stories: stories of a father's determination, of a mother's wisdom and beauty, of a father's reaction to racism, of a grandfather's ability to make his grandchildren laugh, of an uncle's willingness to give his nephew time and attention. These selections help us to see that, through stories, we can come to better know and understand the people we love, and it is through stories that we can help others to know and understand the people we love as well.

Hopefully, these selections will enable you to see your parents and guardians from a new perspective. Perhaps they will help you to understand why your parents or guardians acted as they did. Perhaps they will enable you to recall and record stories about the people who raised you–stories that will bring you, and them, pleasure and satisfaction. And finally, perhaps they will help you to decide what kind of parent you are or want to be.

Pre-reading Activity

Before you begin to read the selections in this chapter, take about 15 minutes to respond to the following free-writing topics. They will help you to recall the stories your parents and guardians have told you about themselves and their lives.

Parents, grandparents, and guardians are famous for telling wonderful stories that help us understand what life was like when they were growing up. Make a list of those stories; jot down as many details as possible about each story and decide which one you like best. Then decide if the story has a *moral* (a message). If so, what is it?

Parents, grandparents, and guardians are also famous for telling stories— repeatedly—to prove they had it much harder growing up than young people have it today—how far they had to walk to get to school; how many hours they had to work after school to support the family; how strict their parents were; how few material possessions they had. Make a list of the stories of this type you have heard over and over throughout your childhood, and jot down as many details as possible about each story. What was the *moral* (the message) of each story? Was there a particular time or event when these stories were told? For example, every time you asked to borrow the car, were you told a story of how your father had to walk to school? Or every time you asked for your allowance, were you told how hard your mother had to work and that she turned all her earnings over to run the household? Do you believe the stories, or do you think there is some exaggeration involved?

What stories will you tell (or do you tell) your own children to show that you had to make struggles and sacrifices during your childhood? What stories will you tell (or do you tell) to show your children how wonderful your childhood was?

Reading 6–1

AFTER LONG SILENCE (EXCERPT)
Helen Fremont

In the following excerpt, taken from a book-length memoir entitled *After Long Silence* by Helen Fremont, the author describes an event that occurred to her father in Poland long before she was born, shortly before World War II (during the war he barely survived six years as a prisoner in Siberia). Notice that the author provides little more than a description of her father's actions, but through these actions we are able to know much about what kind of person her father was.

Vocabulary

voluptuous (paragraph 1) full-bodied and attractive
relentlessly (5) without stopping; with enormous determination

Suggestions for Free Writing

Before you read this excerpt, take about 15 minutes to free-write on the following topic.

> Think of a story told to you by your parents, grandparents, uncles, aunts, or guardians that describes a happy, funny, or embarrassing moment or event in their lives. Write down as many details of the story as you can remember. Then write down what you discovered about the person's personality based on the story itself (for example, that he or she was intelligent, hardworking, stubborn, proud, humble, or kind).

At his music teacher's urging my father practiced with another   1
promising student, Katrina Czezynski, who accompanied him on the
piano. Katrina was a full-throttle blonde of dramatic proportions—
Polish, pink-cheeked, and voluptuous. Her boyfriend, Markus, a cocky
aqua-eyed sprinter, escorted her to her lessons. "Her boyfriend was a
very big deal," my father says dryly. "The regional track star, very popular,
and dumb as a brick.

Source: From *After Long Silence* by Helen Fremont. Copyright © 1999 by Helen Fremont. Reprinted by permission of Dell Publishing, a division of Random House, Inc.

"Actually," my father adds thoughtfully, "Katrina was no mental giant either." He tosses me a half smile and a shrug. "I was interested in her other qualities," he admits. 2

My father and Katrina began practicing duets together, and soon my father fell in love. He likes to blame it on Chopin. Every few weeks he and Katrina gave a recital in the little music hall at the foot of Trenowska Street. Her boyfriend, Markus, dutifully attended and dozed off in the back row, wedged into a folding chair, his huge head drooping like a sunflower on a stalk. At the end of the evening he sprang up, smiled broadly, and walked Katrina home through the park. 3

My father nestled his violin and bow in the worn leather case and followed the couple outside. Under a sputtering streetlamp, he watched his beloved Katrina recede into the darkness, enveloped in the arm of her boyfriend. My father turned and walked home, quietly vowing to win Katrina for himself. 4

It was early summer. My father had a plan. He began to train in secret in the field behind his house. He ran wind sprints and leapt imaginary hurdles, pumping his arms and springing from his toes as he'd seen sprinters do at the local track meets. He practiced shot put with a rock. He improvised a discus with a flat piece of iron. Day after day he trained relentlessly, like a machine. Gradually he lost his pudginess and improved his strength and speed. When school began in the fall, he continued his training in secret. 5

At the end of the fall season the regional championship track meet was held at the stadium overlooking the town. To everyone's amusement, my father entered his name in the one-hundred-meter dash and took his place at the starting line. Katrina's boyfriend, the local champion, strutted back and forth across the track, shaking the ropes of his long arms and legs. My father dropped to one knee, sweat beading his upper lip. He had never used starting blocks before, and he fiddled with them a little before getting the hang of it. His feet felt awkward pressed against the metal. The other runners stretched and approached the blocks, then crouched into position. 6

"Take your mark!"

The gun went off. 7

"I shot out like a cannonball!" my father says, grinning from ear to ear, his dentures soaking in a glass by the kitchen sink. "I beat him!" He chuckles. "Of course no one could believe it! I'd never been on an athletic team in my life! That poor fellow didn't know what had happened!" My father's face is gleeful. 8 9

And sure enough, not only did he win the race, but he also won the girl. Katrina dumped Markus and started dating my father. "That should have tipped me off," he adds a little ruefully. "She would do the same to me a few years later." 10

Questions for Reflection and Discussion

1. Reread paragraph 9 and discuss why you think Fremont makes a point of telling us that, during the time her father told her this story, his dentures were "soaking in a glass by the kitchen sink."
2. Decide on four or five *adjectives* (words that describe) that accurately reflect the father's character based on the story, paying particular attention to the last two lines of the excerpt.

Topics for Writing

1. Recall a time in your life when you did something that made you feel very good about yourself, or very proud, or very competent, or very kind. Write an essay describing what you did in great detail. Be certain to answer the important who, what, where, when, why, and how questions so that the event or incident is explained clearly to your readers. In your conclusion, give a full description of the way you felt and what you learned about yourself as a result of your actions.
2. Return to the free write you completed before you read Fremont's excerpt about her father. Use the information there to write an essay in which you retell a story that a parent, grandparent, aunt, uncle, or guardian has told you about something that occurred to him or her earlier in his or her life. Remember to give enough background information for your readers to be able to understand your relationship to the person and under what circumstances you have heard the story. In addition, be certain to answer the important who, what, where, why, when, and how questions so that the story makes sense to your readers. In your conclusion, *speculate* (try to figure out) why the person told you this story, and then decide what the story says about the person's personality.

Reading 6–2

COLORED PEOPLE (EXCERPT)
Henry Louis Gates, Jr.

The next reading is also an excerpt from a book-length memoir, *Colored People,* written by Henry Louis Gates, Jr., a highly respected scholar of African-American culture and history at Harvard University. Gates is using the word *colored* to show that he grew up during the period of time in the United States, before the civil rights movement, when blacks had few rights and were referred to as "colored." Although it was not appropriate to use the word then, it was a widely accepted practice. Of course, to use the word today to refer to African Americans would be perceived as a sign of ignorance and bigotry.

Vocabulary

muted (paragraph 3)   controlled
scorn (3)   showing great displeasure, even hatred
remonstration (4)   correction, objection, or complaint
dotingly (6)   with affection and attention
mordant (6)   sarcastic or sharp wit
eulogy (7)   a speech in praise of a dead person
mellifluously (20)   sweetly flowing
hypercorrection (20)   overcorrection that makes something incorrect
traipse (21)   walk
cowering (27)   curled up in fear
revelation (27)   discovery

Suggestions for Free Writing

Before you read the excerpt, take about 15 minutes to free-write on the following topic:

All parents or guardians teach us lessons about how to live our lives not only by their words but by their actions. Make a list of the most important lessons about life a parent or guardian believed in. Why do you think these lessons were important to him or her? Do you think it had something to do with the person's own experiences when he or she was a child? Will you (or do you) consider the same lessons important when (or as) you raise your own children? Why?

Source: From *Colored People* by Henry Louis Gates, Jr. Copyright © 1995 by Henry Louis Gates, Jr. Reprinted by permission of Alfred A. Knopf, a division of Random House, Inc.

I remember the first time I got angry at my older daughter, Maggie. Not the angry that a parent gets when he's tired, or irritable, or stressed. But *angry*, deep-down angry, angry like: Do I know this person I've helped bring into the world and have been living with for seven or eight years? We were driving along the highway that connects Piedmont to Cumberland, and I was going on about Mama, about how she had taught me to read and write in one day in the kitchen of our second house, down Rat Tail Road. ("You want to learn how to write?" was all she had asked me. And I had said yes, so she wrote out all the letters in printing and in script, and we made them together on our red kitchen table.) And about how elegant, graceful, and beautiful she was when I was growing up. 1

"Too bad she was never like that when *I* knew her," Maggie called from the back seat. 2

It was less the words than her tone, the muted scorn with which she said she had never seen my mother as beautiful, that knocked the wind out of me. My head fell toward my chest, stopped by the top of the steering wheel. I felt my eyes blinking as I searched for breath and searched for words. I wanted to yell at her, I wanted to stop the car and shake her little shoulders and smack her little butt, I wanted to thunder at her and demand that she apologize on her dead grandmother's grave. 3

Instead, tears filled my eyes as I said, "That was a terribly rude thing to say!" or some such bland parental remonstration. Then we all sat in silence as we drove on down to Cumberland, straight down Greene Street, right past the house that my great-grandparents bought in 1882, headed for the Country Club Shopping Mall by way of Hanson's drugstore, which still makes the best cherry smashes in the world. Passing the house where Daddy was raised, after his parents sold the farm at Patterson's Creek and moved the twenty or so miles into town, reminded me of Daddy's mother, Nan, or, more properly, Gertrude Helen Redman Gates. People used to talk about how beautiful she was—like a little china doll, they'd say—and she must have loved me, because she loved her seventh and youngest son, my daddy. And he worshiped her. Had I ever said anything like my Maggie just said in my car, I would have been dead, the late Skippy Gates. But I wouldn't have *said* what my daughter said, though I might have *thought* it. 4

And that's what I spent the time in the car on the way to get the cherry smashes thinking about. I was remembering how musty I thought Nan smelled, and how she had scraggly, yellowing gray hair, like a scarecrow with corn silk for its mane. 5

Then, anger melting into dizzy affection, I began to think, dotingly, about how mordant my Maggie's sense of timing had been, how deep her thoughts must be. How masterfully the blow had been delivered. How wrong I was to have been angry. 6

I found myself wishing, too, that Maggie could have seen my mother when she was young and Mama and I would go to a funeral and she'd stand up to read the dead person's eulogy. She made the ignorant and ugly sound like scholars and movie stars, turned the mean and evil into saints and angels. She knew what people had meant to be in their hearts, not what the world had forced them to become. She knew the ways in which working too hard for paltry wages could turn you mean and cold, could kill that thing that had made you laugh. She remembered the way you had hoped to be, not the way you actually were. And she always got it right, even if after the funeral Daddy would wonder aloud which sonofabitch had been put in that casket instead of that simple-assed nigger So-and-so. Mama'd always laugh at that: it meant that she had been real good. 7

One day, Mama and I were sitting at home, like we did almost every day. She used to get *McCall's* magazine for the sewing patterns. She'd gone to seamstress school in Atlantic City, and she could sew *anything*. But *McCall's* also provided me with cutout dolls, the Betsy McCall dolls. 8

(I enjoyed playing with paper dolls, just as I enjoyed playing with puppets and marionettes. My all-time favorite Christmas present was a Jerry Mahoney ventriloquist dummy and a tap-dancing black minstrel known as Dancing Dan the Colored Man. I wish we had kept that thing: you sang or spoke into a microphone, and Dancing Dan's legs and feet would go this way and that, propelled by a moving platform activated by the sound of your voice. 9

(It never occurred to me that it was racist; I just thought it odd that he was so very dark and that his lips were so big and so red.) 10

Anyway, Mama and I were at home one weekday, and she was sewing on her magnificent Singer sewing machine, and Betsy and I were getting down to some serious business in the middle of our kitchen floor. The phone rang. I remember that phone because we had one just like it in every house we lived in: a solid-black kitchen wall phone, with a rotary dial that wouldn't be hurried no matter how urgently you dragged your finger. 11

"What?" I heard Mama gasp. "Where?" 12

She slammed down the phone and ran to the television in the front room. (The poetry in our lives did not extend to the naming of our rooms.) She had turned to an afternoon program called *The Big Payoff*. Just as she flipped on the show, we saw a handwritten letter being scrolled up the screen. 13

The letter was all about Mama! 14

It turns out that Mama's brother Harry had written to the producers of the show, telling them about my mother. About how she had left school at the end of junior high and gone to work to support her family—especially to put four of her brothers through college—and how she sent them money regularly, and how they would send her their dirty 15 laundry and she would darn, wash, iron, and starch whatever appeared in those dark-brown semi-cardboard boxes that you had to tie closed with even darker-brown straps and send through the mail. And how for all these reasons, she should be selected as the winner of their write-in contest.

The phone started ringing off the hook, and all the colored people who were at home poured into Erin Street. Mama broke down and cried—and she almost never cried, not even at funerals. So I started to cry too, because I did not know what was going on. Hell, everybody else knew. "And colored too," Mr. Phil Cole, Daddy's best friend, mumbled to him later that night, after the celebrating was over and everyone else had filed out of our house. I bet they didn't know they were giving all this to a colored lady.   16

A week or two later, our kitchen floor was crowded with large cardboard boxes, brought by a delivery truck. I remember a gold evening dress, lots of earrings and necklaces, perfume and shoes, and a whole set of American Tourister luggage. I loved the color of that luggage, a deep luxurious tan. (The leather wore very well. I used the medium suitcase when I went off to Yale some fifteen years later.)   17

Mama *strutted* in those clothes. I couldn't believe that Uncle Harry had done this nice thing for Mama; he and his brothers had never done anything special for her before.   18

If only Maggie could have seen Mama when she'd stand up to read the minutes of the previous meeting of the PTA. Because in 1957, Mama was elected the first colored secretary of the PTA.   19

I used to get dressed up after dinner and walk down to the high school with Mama, over in the Orchard. I'd sit near the front so I'd get a good view, and then Betty Kimmel, the PTA president, would ask Mom to read the minutes. Mama, dressed to kill in that gold dress she'd won on *The Big Payoff*, would stand and read those minutes. It was poetry, pure poetry. She'd read each word beautifully, mellifluously, each syllable spoken roundly but without the hypercorrection of Negroes who make "again" rhyme with "rain."   20

Before Mama started reading the minutes, colored people never joined the PTA. But she was a leader. They still were scared, but they couldn't let Mama down. They "had to represent colored," as they'd say, and just get on with it. And so they'd dress up, too, the women, and traipse on over to the PTA, just to see Mama read her minutes, just to represent the race, just to let those white people know that we was around here too, just to be proud that one of us could do it.   21

No more beautiful woman existed than Mama—so it seemed to me when she read aloud her own careful script. She had shiny black sparkling eyes; a light inside would come on when she performed.   22

Stylish, stylish: all the men used to say that, standing on the bank corner while Mama and I walked by, heads held high, and acknowl-   23 edging the riffraff without being too interested or too rude about it. My mama *knew* she looked good.

As a child, I was secure in her knowledge of things, of how to *do* things and function in the world, of how to *be* in the world and command respect. In her courage I was safe. She was not afraid of dogs, like I was, not even Brownie, the Drains' spaniel, or Spotty, the Wilsons' crazy barker, or even Mugsy, the brindle who, standing on his two hind legs, had ripped open the shoulder of my flight jacket when I was eight.   24

But most important of all, for Piedmont and for me, she did not seem to fear white people.   25

She simply hated them, hated them with a passion she seldom disclosed.   26

There were rare occasions when I would look into her face and see a stranger. In 1959, when I was nine, Mike Wallace and CBS aired a documentary about Black Muslims. It was called "The Hate That Hate Produced," and these were just about the scariest black people I'd ever seen. Black people who talked right into the faces of white people, telling them off without even blinking. While I sat cowering in our living room, I happened to glance over at my mother. A certain radiance was slowly transforming her soft brown face, as she listened to Malcolm X naming the white man the Devil. "Amen," she said, quietly at first. "All right now," she continued, much more heatedly. All this time, and I hadn't known just how deeply my mother despised white people. It was like watching the Wicked Witch of the West emerge out of the transforming features of Dorothy. The revelation was both terrifying and thrilling.   27

The same thing would happen several years later when the Martin Luther King riots were shown on television. The first colored secretary of the Piedmont PTA watched the flames with dancing eyes.   28

But Mama was practical as well as proud. Her attitude was that she and Daddy would provide the best for us, so that no white person could put us down or keep us out for reasons of appearance, color aside. The rest was up to us, once we got in those white places. Like school, which desegregated without a peep in 1955, the year before I started first grade. Otherwise she didn't care to live in white neighborhoods or be around white people.   29

Questions for Reflection and Discussion

1. Race had an impact on almost every aspect of the lives of the Gates family. Reread the excerpt and find as many examples as you can of the role race played in the Gates family's day-to-day lives. Did race have any impact on your family life? In what way or ways?

2. Throughout this memoir, Gates keeps saying, "If only Maggie [his daughter] could have seen Mama when. . . ." Then he goes on to describe a time when his mother was beautiful or brave or happy or strong. Think back over your parents' or guardians' lives, and identify moments or incidents that occurred that were especially impressive, moments that you will always remember and that you will want to share with your own children.

Topics for Writing

1. In paragraph 7, Gates describes his mother's wonderful ability to read a eulogy. In paragraph 8, he describes her excellent ability as a seamstress, saying she "could sew *anything*." In paragraph 9 he describes her ability to read the minutes of the PTA meetings as "poetry, pure poetry." In paragraph 23, he explains that she was stylish, that she "*knew* she looked good." And in paragraph 24, Gates recognizes her greatest talent: "In her courage I was safe," he writes.

   Think about the talents and skills that one of your parents or guardians possesses or possessed, and write an essay describing those talents and skills in great detail. Devote each of the paragraphs in your essay to one particular skill, being sure to explain and describe it fully by providing details and examples. Or, if you prefer to concentrate on one talent or skill, use your entire essay to describe and explain it. Be sure to give various examples of how often and when you saw the skill or talent being used, the effect it had on others, and the advantages and benefits of the skill or talent. In your conclusion, explain the effect this talent or skill had on you.

2. Perhaps the most important lesson Gates's mother taught him was not to fear white people. As he says in the last paragraph, "Her attitude was that she and Daddy would provide the best for us, so that no white person could put us down or keep us out for reasons of appearance, color aside. The rest was up to us, once we got in those white places."

   Return to the free write you completed before you read the excerpt, and use the information there to describe and explain the most important lesson your parents or guardians taught you. Be sure to give enough background information and to answer the important who, what, where, when, why, and how questions so that the reader can fully understand exactly what the lesson was, when and how often it was taught and repeated, and why it was so important. In your conclusion, explain whether this will be the same lesson you will teach your children. If not, explain why it will not be, and then explain what the most important lesson you will teach your children will be.

Reading 6–3

THE MOTHER TONGUE

Veronica Chambers

The next selection is an essay written by Veronica Chambers that describes the effect learning Spanish—her mother's native language—had on her relationship with her mother and on the way she feels about her heritage. You will notice that the Spanish words are *italicized* (the print is slanted), making it easy for readers to recognize and identify foreign words and phrases as they read.

Vocabulary

plátanos (paragraph 1)   bananas

flawless (1)   perfect

Flatbush (2) a neighborhood in Brooklyn, N.Y., with a large African-American population

Angela Davis Chambers (2)   radical African-American feminist who often got in trouble with the law for fighting for the rights of African Americans

cultural icons (3)   heroes in a particular culture or country

Renaissance man (3)   a man with many talents and abilities rather than just one

campiness (10)   so goofy it's almost good

comprises (11)   makes up, consists of

Suggestions for Free Writing

Before you read this essay, take about 15 minutes to free-write on the following topic:

Think about the language used in your home and among your family members and compare it to the language used outside your home. Do your parents, grandparents, aunts, uncles, or guardians speak a language other than English? What impact did this or does this have on you? Did you learn the language? Are you comfortable with another language being used in your home? Did its use cause any problems?

Source: "The Mother Tongue" by Veronica Chambers, *Brooklyn Bridge*, Vol. 1 #10. Reprinted by permission of Brooklyn Bridge.

If English was the language spoken in your home and by your family members, then think about the way your family members communicated with each other. Were there certain expressions, phrases, or words that were used only inside your home? Were there favorite expressions used over and over? What were they? Were there things said that bothered or upset you? Were there things said that pleased you or made you feel very comfortable and secure? When you were a child, was there a prayer or expression or series of words that were repeated each night before you went to sleep? Was there a lot of talking in your home when you were growing up, or was it a "quiet" house? Who did most of the talking? Was dinnertime when the family got together and talked about the day? At breakfast? Another time? With whom did you talk the most in your home as you were growing up? Do you sometimes catch yourself sounding like one of your parents or guardians when you speak?

She's a *plátanos*-frying, Malta Dukesa-drinking, salsa-dancing 1 *mamacita*—my dark-skinned Panamanian mother. She came to this country when she was 24—her sense of culture intact, her Spanish flawless. Even to this day, more than 20 years since she left her home country and became an American citizen, my mother still calls herself Panamanian, checks "Latina" on the census form.

For me, having dark skin and growing up in Flatbush in the '70s 2 meant that I was black—period. Maybe if we had spoken Spanish more often at home, I would have drifted to the pockets of Latina girls in the school yard. But my mother and father, who is also from Panama, were movement-oriented—they named my brother Malcolm X Chambers, and came this close to naming me Angela Davis Chambers. Black history and the civil-rights movement were the things we discussed and read. Panamanian culture was more about the food we ate, the music we played, the language my mother spoke when she didn't want Americans to understand.

I knew next to nothing about Panamanian history, leaders or cul- 3 tural icons, the exception being Ruben Blades, whom my mother discussed in the awestruck tones that American women used to discuss JFK. I knew that Blades had a law degree from Harvard and was also an actor and a musician. He was the ultimate Renaissance man to my mom, and because I copied her in everything I did, he was my hero too. I learned very quickly to pronounce his name *Blah*-dez and not *Blay*-des like the razor blades.

I learned Spanish at home like a dog learns English, and under- 4 stood mostly commands: "*Callate la boca!*" ("Shut your mouth!"). Or "*Baja la cabeza!*" ("Drop your head!") when my mother was braiding my hair and I kept looking up to see my favorite show on TV. My father's mentality was simple: "You're in America. Speak English." It wasn't until my parents were divorced, when I was 10, that my mother tried to teach Malcolm and me to speak Spanish.

But she was a terrible language teacher. She had no sense of the 5 structure of the language and answered every one of our questions with

"That's just the way it is." We couldn't grasp, for example, why we were supposed to say "*Toma café*"—literally, "He takes coffee"—instead of "He drinks coffee." A few short weeks later my mother gave up and we were all relieved.

Still, I was intent on learning my mother's language. At Ditmas Junior High School, I had to petition the principal so I could take Spanish because all the other kids in the gifted program were taking French. Apparently, to the powers that be, French was considered more cultured, and Spanish more basic, less intellectual. I didn't care. For two years, I dove into the language, matching what little I knew from home with all that I learned at school. 6

I never asked my mother for help with my homework; she never asked me about my lessons. But one day when I was in the ninth grade, I felt confident enough to start speaking Spanish with my mother, and it's been that way ever since. 7

My brother never learned Spanish and doesn't speak it to this day; the language became a bond that I shared with my mother. In the ongoing battle of sibling rivalry, I felt that speaking Spanish made me more culturally aware than Malcolm. 8

Learning my mother's tongue brought me even closer to my Latina heritage, but mostly it brought me closer to my mother herself. When I was little, she used to watch astrologer Walter Mercado and *telenovela* soap operas on the Spanish language stations. I would sit impatiently as she translated Mercado's horoscope for me for the coming week and tried to explain what was going on in the latest installment of *La Tragedia de Lisette*. 9

After I learned Spanish, I watched these programs with my mother—not needing translations, poking fun at the campiness of Spanish-language TV. My mother and I would talk to each other in Spanish at our jobs or anywhere we needed some semblance of privacy to dish. When I had only spoken English, I had been the daughter, the little girl. As I began to learn Spanish, I became something more—a *hermanita*, a sister-friend, a Panamanian homegirl who could hang with the rest of them. 10

My mother has few close friends who are African-Americans. Her friends are mostly Caribbean—both English-speaking and Spanish-speaking. For me, the exact opposite is true. African-American culture is the one that I grew up in; it comprises the majority of the books I've read and the music I listen to. I think this shows just how American I am—that I define myself, and that others define me, by the color of my skin and the kinkiness of my hair. 11

But the other day, a friend left a voice-mail message for me. He called me a "secret Latina-at-large." The message made me ridiculously happy. I saved it and played it again and again. He had hit on a perfect description for me. 12

Ever since I was a little girl, I have wanted to be exactly like my 13
mom. In one of my most vivid memories, I am seven or eight and my
parents are having a party. Salsa music is blaring and the refrain,
Whappin,' Colon? Hola, Panama, is bouncing off the walls because there
is so much bass. My mother is dancing and laughing. She sees me
standing off in a corner, so she pulls me into the circle of grown-ups and
tries to teach me how to dance to the music. Her hips are electric. She
puts her hands on my sides and she says, "Move these," and I start
shaking my hipbones like my life depends on it.

Now I am a grown woman, and I have hips and booty to spare. 14
Sometimes I throw down with the hip-hop tunes, but every once in a
while, I like to salsa. I am definitely African-American and African-iden-
tified. But I speak Spanish and read Spanish, and while I'll never be the
super Latina that my Panamanian mother is, that's okay. Being a secret
Latina-at-large is more than enough for me.

Questions for Reflection and Discussion

1. In paragraph 13, Chambers says that ever since she was a little girl, she has
   always wanted to be exactly like her mom. Did you or do you feel that way
   about one of your parents or guardians? Why?
2. In paragraph 12, Chambers notes that her friend's message in which he
   calls her a "secret Latina-at-large" pleased her so much that she "saved it
   and played it again and again." Think of an expression someone used to
   you or about you, or of a compliment you received that pleased you, and
   decide why it had that effect on you.

Topics for Writing

1. In this writing assignment, you do not have to write an essay. Instead, create
   a dialogue between two members of your family. You can be one of the
   family members, but you don't have to be—it can be between your parents,
   between a parent and one of your siblings, between a grandparent and a
   parent. This dialogue can be made up, but it should be based on the kinds
   of conversations that actually occur in your home.

   You can begin this writing exercise with a brief introduction,
   explaining to your reader who is speaking to whom, and where, when, and
   why the conversation is taking place. The rest of your writing exercise
   should consist almost entirely of dialogue between these two people. This
   dialogue should reflect the way language is used in your home, and as a
   result of reading this dialogue, your reader should be able to understand
   the kind of relationship that exists between these two family members.
   Remember to place quotation marks at the beginning and end of each line

of dialogue, and remember to start a new paragraph each time another person starts speaking.

2. Return to the free write you completed before you read Chambers' essay, and use the information there to write an essay about the way language is used in your home—in other words, the way your family members use language as they speak to each other. In order to make it easier for you to organize this essay, you may want to devote each of the paragraphs of your essay to one family member, describing the way he or she speaks: tone of voice, facial expressions, hand gestures, body posture, the way he or she talks on the phone, repeated phrases or favorite expressions, anything that helps the reader to almost "hear" that person talking. In your conclusion, explain whether your speaking habits are the same or different than those of your family members.

Reading 6–4

LESSON

Forrest Hamer

The next selection is a poem entitled "Lesson," written by Forrest Hamer, an African-American psychologist who teaches at the University of California, Berkeley. In this poem, Hamer describes a car trip he took with his family. This was not a vacation or pleasure trip: Hamer's father was driving his wife and children from their home in Texas to North Carolina, where they would stay while he went to fight in Vietnam.

Vocabulary

Ft. Hood (paragraph 1)   a military base in Texas

Klan (1)   the Ku Klux Klan, an organization of white racists whose members harassed, beat, and killed blacks, particularly in the South before and during the civil rights movement

Suggestions for Free Writing

Before you read the poem, take about 15 minutes to free write on the following topics:

Consider a time in your life when you needed a parent or guardian to help or protect you from someone: a teacher, a bully, a stranger, an older sibling, a gang or group of people, or when you needed a parent or guardian to protect you from something: the dark, a monster in the closet, a doctor's appointment, an event or occurrence happening in school or in your neighborhood. Recall as many details as possible and decide if your parent or guardian did a good job in protecting you. If he or she did not do a good job, explain why. Was it because the person didn't try hard enough, because he or she wanted you to handle it on your own, or because the situation was beyond his or her control?

It was 1963 or 4, summer, 1
and my father was driving our family
from Ft. Hood to North Carolina in our 56 Buick.
We'd been hearing about Klan attacks, and we knew
Mississippi to be more dangerous than usual.

Source: "Lesson" by Forrest Hamer from *Call and Response.* Copyright © 1995 Alice James Books. Reprinted by permission.

Dark lay hanging from trees the way moss did,
and when it moaned light against the windows
that night, my father pulled off the road to sleep.

Noises   2
that usually woke me from rest afraid of monsters
kept my father awake that night, too,
and I lay in the quiet noticing him listen, learning
that he might not be able always to protect us

from everything and the creatures besides,   3
perhaps not even from the fury suddenly loud
through my body about this trip from Texas
to settle us home before he would go away

to a place no place in the world   4
he named Viet Nam. A boy needs a father
with him, I kept thinking, fixed against noise
from the dark.

Questions for Reflection and Discussion

1. Each word in a poem is essential to the meaning of the entire poem. For example, the last line of stanza 3 and the first line of stanza 4 read: "he would go away to a place no place in the world he named Viet Nam." Examine these lines very carefully. Why do you think the poet uses the phrase "to a place no place in the world"? What does that tell you? And why do you think the poet says that his father "named" it Viet Nam rather than just saying "a place named Viet Nam"?
2. Find the lines in the poem in which the poet notices that his father is also afraid. Think of a time when you have seen a parent or guardian afraid of something. How did it make you feel?

Topics for Writing

1. Although you will probably not be asked to write poetry in college (unless you take a creative writing course), writing poetry provides us with the opportunity to explore and express our feelings by choosing just the right words and phrases to reflect our experiences, feelings, and emotions. Forrest Hamer describes the intense and painful experience of realizing that his father would not always be there to protect him (as he says in the last line of the poem: "a boy needs a father with him"). Think of a time in your life when you had an equally intense experience

(either pleasurable or painful) with a parent or guardian, and write a poem explaining the experience and the effect it had on you.

2. Return to the free write you completed before you read the poem, and use the information there to write an essay describing and explaining an incident, event, or time in your life (or more than one if you want to) when you needed a parent or guardian to protect you from someone or something. Explain how you were protected, or how you were not protected, and why. Be sure to answer the important who, what, where, when, why, and how questions so that your reader can fully understand the circumstances and situation. In your conclusion, explain the impact this event or incident had on your relationship to your parent or guardian.

Reading 6–5

UNDERGROUND DADS

Wil Haygood

The next selection, written by Wil Haygood, explains what it is like to grow up without a father. In this essay, he explains that although it would have been nice to have a "good, warm father," the other men in his life did a fine job because they were so "warm, honest, and big-hearted."

Vocabulary

gaping hole (paragraph 1)   huge hole
raucous (4)   noisy and loud
work ethic (5)   an understanding of the need to work hard
incessantly (6)   without stopping
mystical (7)   magical, not easy to understand

Suggestions for Free Writing

Before you read the essay, take about 15 minutes to free-write on the following topic:

> Think about the people in your life—other than your parents or guardians—who are important to you and who have had a good influence on you. Choose one of these people and write as much as you can about your relationship with the person, including examples of things you have done together, places you have gone together, favors the person has done for you, situations you've been in, advice the person has given you, and conversations you have had.

For years, while growing up, I shamelessly told my playmates that I 1
didn't have a father. In my neighborhood, where men went to work with lunch pails, my friends thought there was a gaping hole in my household. My father never came to the park with me to toss a softball, never came to see me in any of my school plays. I'd explain to friends, with the simplicity of explaining to someone that there are, in some woods, no deer, that I just had no father. My friends looked at me and squinted. My mother and father had divorced shortly after my birth. As the years rolled by, however, I did not have the chance to turn into the pitiful little black boy who had

been abandoned by his father. There was a reason: other men showed up. They were warm, honest (at least as far as my eyes could see) and big-hearted. They were the good black men in the shadows, the men who taught me right from wrong, who taught me how to behave, who told me, by their very actions, that they expected me to do good things in life.

There are heartbreaking statistics tossed about regarding single-parent black households these days, about children growing up father-less. Those statistics must be considered. But how do you count the other men, the ones who show up—with perfect timing, with a kind of soft-stepping loveliness—to give a hand, to take a boy to watch airplanes lift off, to show a young boy the beauty of planting tomatoes in the ground and to tell a child that all of life is not misery? 2

In my life, there was Jerry, who hauled junk. He had a lean body and a sweet smile. He walked like a cowboy, all bowlegged, swinging his shoulders. It was almost a strut. The sound of his pickup truck rumbling down our alley in Columbus, Ohio, could raise me from sleep. 3

When he wasn't hauling junk, Jerry fixed things. More than once, he fixed my red bicycle. The gears were always slipping; the chain could turn into a tangled mess. Hearing pain in my voice, Jerry would instruct me to leave my bike on our front porch. In our neighborhood, in the 60's, no one would steal your bike from your porch. Jerry promised me he'd pick it up, and he always did. He never lied to me, and he cau-tioned me not to tell lies. He was, off and on, my mother's boyfriend. At raucous family gatherings, he'd pull me aside and explain to me the importance of honesty, of doing what one promised to do. 4

And there was Jimmy, my grandfather, who all his life paid his bills the day they arrived: that was a mighty lesson in itself—it taught me a work ethic. He held two jobs, and there were times when he allowed me to accompany him on his night job, when he cleaned a Greek restaurant on the north side of Columbus. Often he'd mop the place twice, as if trying to win some award. He frightened me too. It was not because he was mean. It was because he had exacting standards, and there were times when I didn't measure up to those standards. He didn't like short-cutters. His instructions, on anything, were to be carried out to the letter. He believed in independence, doing as much for yourself as you possibly could. It should not have surprised me when, one morning while having stomach pains, he chose not to wait for a taxi and instead walked the mile to the local hospital, where he died a week later of stomach cancer. 5

My uncles provided plenty of good background music when I was coming of age. Uncle Henry took me fishing. He'd phone the night before. "Be ready. Seven o'clock." I'd trail him through woods—as a son does a father—until we found our fishing hole. We'd sit for hours. He taught me patience and an appreciation of the outdoors, of nature. He talked, incessantly, of family—his family, my family, the family of friends. The man had a reverence for family. I knew to listen. 6

I think these underground fathers simply appear, decade to 7
decade, flowing through the generations. Hardly everywhere, and
hardly, to be sure, in enough places, but there. As mystical, sometimes,
as fate when fate is sweet.

Sometimes I think that all these men who have swept in and out of 8
my life still couldn't replace a good, warm father. But inasmuch as I've
never known a good, warm father, the men who entered my life, who
taught me right from wrong, who did things they were not asked to do,
have become unforgettable. I know of the cold statistics out there. And
yet, the mountain of father-son literature does not haunt me. I've known
good black men.

Questions for Reflection and Discussion

1. In paragraph 1, Wil Haygood notes that he "did not have the chance to
turn into the pitiful little black boy who has been abandoned by his father."
In our society and culture, are children who do not have two parents
viewed as "pitiful" or somehow deprived? Why?
2. Make a list of the things you think fathers can do better than mothers with
and for their children, then compare lists with your classmates and a) see
if they match, and b) decide which of the things mothers could do as well
as fathers.

Topics for Writing

1. Wil Haygood talks about having a man in his life who fixed his bike, a man
in his life who taught him the importance of honesty and keeping
promises, a man in his life who taught him about the importance of work
and of paying bills on time, a man who took him fishing and taught him
the value and beauty of nature. Based on these examples, and on your relationship with one or both of your parents or guardians, write an essay in
which you describe, explain, and give examples of the kinds of activities
you will engage in (or do engage in) with your children and the kind of
lessons you will teach them (or do teach them) in order to let them know
they are wanted and loved. In order to make it easier for you to organize
your essay, you could devote each of your body paragraphs to one activity
or lesson. In your conclusion, explain what you hope the effect of partici-
pating in these activities with your children will have on them.
2. Return to the free write you completed before you read Haygood's essay
and use the information contained there to write an essay similar to
Haygood's. Explain, describe, and give examples of the beneficial relationship you had with the person about whom you wrote in your free write.
In your conclusion, explain what you have learned about yourself, about
life, or about the importance of relationships or friendships as a result of
your relationship with the person.

Reading 6–6

WORDS LEFT UNSPOKEN

Leah Hager Cohen

In this chapter-length excerpt, taken from a book entitled *Train Go Sorry*, Leah Hager Cohen writes about the extraordinary relationship her grandfather (Sam Cohen) and her father (Oscar Cohen) had with each other, and about the extraordinary relationship she had with each of them. Cohen's grandfather was deaf, and Cohen's father, who was hearing, was the principal of the Lexington School for the Deaf in Queens, N.Y.

However, this isn't merely description and explanation: The information contained in this chapter was obtained not only as a result of the author's memories of her grandfather and father but also through careful research and interviews—the kind of research and interviews you would be expected to conduct in a college-level class in sociology, psychology, anthropology, or ethnic studies. Although doing research is challenging, writing it up into an essay that reads smoothly and clearly is even more challenging. Notice the way the author weaves together the various types of information—memory, interviews, and research—in such a way that the reader can just sit back and enjoy the story of Sam Cohen's remarkable life.

Vocabulary

honed granite (paragraph 1) polished stone
swathed (1) wrapped
abrasive (1) rough, scratchy
chiding (2) correcting or making negative comments
expulsion (2) made to leave
percussive (2) vibrating sounds
implausible (4) hard to believe or understand
impassive (4) without life or expression
mimicked (5) made fun of
splayed (6) spread out
ampler (7) larger; having more room

closed captioning (7) words appearing on the bottom of a TV screen for the benefit of deaf people

lithe (8) graceful, moving with great ease

conduits (8) carriers

czarist pogroms (9) massacres of groups of people, ordered and led by the czar (ruler)

name-sign (10) Deaf people have short easy signs used to identify themselves and others in order to save the time it takes to finger-spell each letter of a name. The sign usually reflects some aspect of the person's appearance or personality.

Kinetoscope (11) a machine for reproducing a picture with moving figures

gait (12) walk

plethora (14) many; an overabundance

catacomb (14) underground tunnels

TTY (15) a teletypewriter/telephone that prints words, used by deaf people to communicate with each other

solicitude (15) paying close attention

paleontologist (15) one who studies animal fossils

complaisantly (18) cooperating; going along with

chagrin (19) annoyance

protruded (22) stuck out

reconstructed (23) rebuilt

invariably (33) without fail

affiliate (33) to be connected to something

peruse (34) look at

slovenly (37) sloppy

benevolence (35) goodness

sic (38) Latin for "as is," meaning that the spelling or grammatical error (layed instead of laid) existed in the original document

septuagenarians (44) people who are seventy years old

notorious (45) famous for doing something bad

sustenance (45) support, nourishment

cataracts (48) growths on the eyeballs that, unless removed, eventually cause blindness

apprised (53) informed

unabashed (53) openly, without hiding

queasy (54) uneasy; nervous

incomprehensible (55) impossible to understand

perilously (56) dangerously

intelligibly (61) understandably, in a way that he could be understood by others

placatingly (68) trying to satisfy someone's needs or to please someone in order to avoid trouble

awry (69) wrong; not as it is supposed to be

chronology (69) telling something in the order in which it happened

indomitable (70) unfailing

Suggestions for Free Writing

Before you read the chapter, take about 15 minutes to free-write on the following topic:

> Think of someone in your life whom you are fond of or close to, but about whose background you know very little. First, jot down all of the things you know about this person—from his or her personality traits to information about his or her life (place of birth, education, family background, career, hobbies, interests, talents, challenges in life, successes in life). Then make a list of questions about this person that you would like to have answered.

My earliest memories of Sam Cohen are of his chin, which I 1
remember as fiercely hard and pointy. Not pointy, my mother says, jutting; Grandpa had a strong, jutting chin. But against my very young face it felt like a chunk of honed granite swathed in stiff white bristles. Whenever we visited, he would lift us grandchildren up, most frequently by the elbows, and nuzzle our cheeks vigorously. This abrasive ritual greeting was our primary means of communication. In all my life, I never heard him speak a word I could understand.

Sometimes he used his voice to get our attention. It made a shape- 2
less, gusty sound, like a pair of bellows sending up sparks and soot in a blacksmith shop. And he made sounds when he was eating, sounds that, originating from other quarters, would have drawn chiding or expulsion from the table. He smacked his lips and sucked his teeth; his chewing was moist and percussive; he released deep, hushed moans from the back of his throat, like a dreaming dog. And he burped out loud. Sometimes it was all Reba, Andy [the author's brother and sister], and I could do not to catch one another's eyes and fall into giggles.

Our grandfather played games with us, the more physical the 3
better. He loved that hand game: he would extend his, palms up, and we would hover ours, palms down, above his, and lower them, lower, lower, until they were just nesting, and *slap!* he'd have sandwiched one of our hands, trapping it between his. When we reversed, I could never even graze his, so fast would he snatch them away, like big white fish.

He played three-card monte with us, arranging the cards neatly 4
between his long fingers, showing us once the jack of diamonds smirking, red and gold, underneath. And then, with motions as swift and implausible as a Saturday morning cartoon chase, his hands darted and faked and blurred and the cards lay still, face down and impassive. When we guessed the jack's position correctly, it was only luck. When we guessed wrong, he would laugh—a fond, gravelly sound—and pick up the cards and begin again.

He mimicked the way I ate. He compressed his mouth into dainty 5
proportions as he nibbled air and carefully licked his lips and chewed

tiny, precise bites, his teeth clicking, his eyelashes batting as he gazed shyly from under them. He could walk exactly like Charlie Chaplin and make nickels disappear, just vanish, from both his fists and up his sleeves; we never found them, no matter how we crawled over him, searching. All of this without any words.

He and my grandmother lived in the Bronx, in the same apartment my father and Uncle Max had grown up in. It was on Knox Place, near Mosholu Parkway, a three-room apartment below street level. The kitchen was a tight squeeze of a place, especially with my grandmother bending over the oven, blocking the passage as she checked baked apples or stuffed cabbage, my grandfather sitting with splayed knees at the dinette. It was easy to get each other's attention in there; a stamped foot sent vibrations clearly over the short distance, and an outstretched arm had a good chance of connecting with the other party. 6

The living room was ampler and dimmer, with abundant floor and table lamps to accommodate signed conversation. Little windows set up high revealed the legs of passersby. And down below, burrowed in black leather chairs in front of the television, we children learned to love physical comedy. Long before the days of closed captioning, we listened to our grandfather laugh out loud at the snowy black-and-white antics of Abbott and Costello, Laurel and Hardy, the Three Stooges. 7

During the time that I knew him, I saw his hairline shrink back and his eyes grow remote behind pairs of progressively thicker glasses. His athlete's bones shed some of their grace and nimbleness; they began curving in on themselves as he stood, arms folded across his sunken chest. Even his long, thin smile seemed to recede deeper between his nose and his prominent chin. But his hands remained lithe, vital. As he teased and argued and chatted and joked, they were the instruments of his mind, the conduits of his thoughts. 8

As far as anyone knows, Samuel Kolominsky was born deaf (according to the Lexington records, his parents "failed to take note until child was about one and a half years old"). His birthplace was Russia, somewhere near Kiev. Lexington records say he was born in 1908; my grandmother says it was 1907. He was a child when his family fled the czarist pogroms. Lexington records have him immigrating in 1913, at age five; my grandmother says he came to this country when he was three. Officials at Ellis Island altered the family name, writing down Cohen, but they did not detect his deafness, so Sam sailed on across the last ribbon of water to America. 9

His name-sign at home: *Daddy.* His name-sign with friends: the thumb and index finger, perched just above the temple, rub against each other like grasshopper legs. One old friend attributes this to Sam's hair, which was blond and thick and wavy. Another says it derived from his habit of twisting a lock between his fingers. 10

Lexington records have him living variously at Clara, Moore, 11
Siegel, Tehema, and Thirty-eighth streets in Brooklyn and on Avenue C
in Manhattan. I knew him on Knox Place, and much later on Thieriot
Avenue, in the Bronx. Wherever he lived, he loved to walk, the neighborhoods revolving silently like pictures in a Kinetoscope, unfurling
themselves in full color around him.

Shortly before he died, when I was thirteen, we found ourselves 12
walking home from a coffee shop together on a warm night. My family
had spent the day visiting my grandparents at their apartment. My
grandmother and the rest of the family were walking half a block ahead;
I hung back and made myself take my grandfather's hand. We didn't
look at each other. His hand was warm and dry. His gait was uneven
then, a long slow beat on the right, catch-up on the left. I measured my
steps to his. It was dark except for the hazy pink cones of light cast by
streetlamps. I found his rhythm, and breathed in it. That was the longest
conversation we ever had.

He died before I was really able to converse in sign. I have never 13
seen his handwriting. I once saw his teeth, in a glass, on the bathroom
windowsill. Now everything seems like a clue.

One afternoon, after the last yellow buses had lumbered away from 14
school [the Lexington School for the Deaf], I went with my father down
to the basement. He sorted among his plethora of keys while we
descended the stairs, finally jangling out the master as we approached
the heavy brown doors to Lexington's storage room, an impressive if
forbidding catacomb of huge proportions. Great sections of the win-
dowless room were fenced into compartments very much resembling
penal holding tanks; these enclaves contained spare equipment and
ancient records belonging to the different departments. My father
unlocked the gate of the largest one. Thin light shone murkily from dan-
gling fixtures, and the pale, wet odor of mildew encouraged us to work
quickly.

Picking my way through cardboard boxes, film projectors, and 15
sheets of particleboard, I nearly tumbled into a familiar figure: our old
TTY, donated to the school when our family acquired a newer, portable
model. The original stood at waist level, a stout gray metal beast with a
keyboard that had clacked and collected oily clumps of dust. My grandmother, when visiting us, would demand an old toothbrush and, with
the rapt solicitude of a paleontologist, clean between the keys. She still
possessed one of these old models; she called hers the Monster.

Up ahead, my father stood before the high banks of file cabinets. 16
We suspected them of being wildly out of order; I was prepared to spend
the afternoon down here, inhaling particles of mold and sifting through
drawers of brittle documents. My father had asked one of the maintenance workers whether we could borrow a work light to prop above the
files; he had intended to wait with me only until the light was delivered,

but the spirit of the search had cast a spell, and now, in spite of himself, he scanned the rows of cabinets. Hands on hips, shoulders rounded over scooped chest, his posture mirrored his father's. After a moment he embarked on the middle aisle. I trailed after him doubtfully. There were perhaps forty cabinets, not all of them labeled.

I can't say why I sank to my knees just where I did. I suppose my 17 father had paused, thereby blocking me from going further. I suppose that because he was tall, I assumed the task of inspecting the lower drawers. I suppose it was as simple and meaningless as that.

I knelt and pulled out the drawer directly in front of me, stuck my 18 fingers a third of the way in, and parted a couple of thick brown folders. I had landed in a batch of Cohens. "Dad . . ." I picked through them gingerly; even so, flakes of discolored paper fluttered to the bottom of the drawer. "Dad, I think . . ." I passed Charlotte and Joseph, Lester and Millie, Rachel and Ray and Rebecca, and there, quite complaisantly, followed Samuel. "Dad."

I held the folder out to him. Somewhat to my chagrin, he did not 19 say, "Go ahead, look," but accepted it from me. I stood on tiptoes behind his shoulder.

The first thing inside was a note, typed on a relatively fresh white 20 index card. "This is it," my father murmured, reading the card. "This is Grandpa's." The note read:

1/12/79   21

This new file was made up since
Mr. Samuel Cohen's original file was
destroyed in a fire that occurred in
the old school at Lexington Ave. &
68th St., Manhattan.

Paperclipped to the note was a long brown envelope. My father 22 shook out its contents: one wallet-size photograph of a boy in late adolescence. "This is it," my father repeated. The boy wore a heavy dark sweater over a white shirt, the left shoulder of which bulged messily against his collar. His hands were clasped just below the chest, and his chin and neck were thrust forward so that his Adam's apple protruded above the knot of his tie. His hair was slicked back in a glossy wave. His lips were just parting. The pockets of skin below his eyes were gathered in mirth; he looked slightly up, as though he were gazing at the photographer rather than the lens.

I knew about the fire that destroyed the original file; my father had 23 warned me not to expect much of this reconstructed one, if we even located it. But the folder was gratifyingly thick. We took it upstairs to examine in better light.

On the way to my father's office, we met a maintenance worker 24 wheeling a garbage can down the hall.

"Do you still need that light, Dr. Cohen?" he asked. 25

"No. No thanks, Fernando. We got it." My father held up the   26
brown folder, showing what the "it" was, then, almost shyly, extended it.
"This is the file of someone who was a student at Lexington in 1916," he
explained as Fernando gently, quizzically opened the cover. "The
student's name was Sam Cohen," he went on, pausing to let the connection take hold. "My father."

"Your father was a student at this school?"   27

"Yes."   28

"Then he don't hear?"   29

"No, he was deaf."   30

Fernando and my father beheld each other for a moment and   31
smiled. Then Fernando handed back the folder. "Okay, see you later," he
said, and went on dragging the big garbage can on wheels down the hall.

On the wall behind my father's desk hangs an old photograph,   32
creased and cracked and now pressed under glass. In the photograph,
eleven men kneel or stand in the dark athletic uniforms of the Hebrew
Association of the Deaf, their hands clasped behind their backs, chins
tucked in, chests out. On the floor in the center rests a basketball on
which is inscribed "1937–1938 Champions." The young man standing
second from the right, trying to look serious, is Sam Cohen.

When visitors come to my father's office for the first time, he will   33
invariably point out the photograph. Often he will invite people to step
behind his desk for a close look at the faces. Sometimes he will ask them
to guess which man is his father. I have seen him display the picture to
a deaf leader visiting from Moscow, a couple of black women pilots
giving a presentation for Black History Month, the ambassador from
Grenada, the deaf president of Gallaudet University, and a frightened
high school student who was sent to his office for in-school suspension.
He uses this photograph like a passport. With hearing people, it
becomes a point of reference. With deaf people, it is a port of entry,
proof of affiliate membership.

It was back to this office that we brought Sam Cohen's file, and it   34
was here, thanks to the fact that my father's calendar was crammed with
prior commitments, that I had the opportunity to peruse its contents
alone. I read slowly, handling each spotty, crumbling document with
care. They rustled and whispered as I turned them over, laid them softly
down: the crackling onionskin, the mossy carbon copies, the yellowed
memos scrawled with a fountain pen, their old-fashioned flourishes and
curlicues gone a parched brown.

In 1916, Lexington was known as the Institution for the Improved   35
Instruction of Deaf-Mutes, or, more familiarly, as the Deaf-and-Dumb
Institution. Those words appear on nearly every page in the folder,
weighing heavily, like lead sinkers lashed again and again to his name:
Deaf-Mute Sam, Deaf-and-Dumb Sam, making him the responsibility of
the authorities, turning him over to the institution. One set of papers

makes him a state pupil, "to be educated and supported . . . at the expense of the county of Kings." Several other papers, signed by Sam's father (also named Oscar), authorize the institution doctors to examine the child, remove his adenoids and his tonsils, inoculate him, give him glasses. Most of these permissions consist simply of a signature, but the one that includes a brief note may well reveal the core of my great-grandparents' attitudes toward the role of the authorities regarding their deaf son. In hasty, looping script, my great-grandfather wrote, "I am satisfied that you are going to do the right thing for him. and oblige yours truly Oscar Cohen." The grim lead weights, son and all, dropped neatly out of sight.

In 1928, after twelve years of school, Sam graduated and moved back home to Brooklyn. Within months his father was appealing to Lexington for help, writing, "Sam tried very hard to find work, but it was impossible. He had no trade as your school did not teach him a trade. We do not know what to do. We are all upset. He is a boy of twenty-one years old and is nearly a man and has to earn a living." 36

Mr. Harris Taylor, the principal of the Institution for the Improved Instruction of Deaf-Mutes, responded defensively that although everyone at the school was extremely fond of Sam, "he was one of those boys who wasted an enormous amount of time," and "we have never been able to make a worker of him, and unless he learns to work harder he will have trouble." He cited specifically Sam's poor speech and language skills, as well as his slovenly work in the sign-painting and printing departments. Then, with mighty benevolence, Mr. Taylor wrote that the twenty-one-year-old Sam was "a good boy," and assured my great-grandparents that "in any failure or in any trouble that may arise, you may count upon our sympathy, because everyone is a friend to Sam." 37

Indeed, the same day he wrote that letter, the principal advised Sam, via Western Union, "May have job for you. Come here tomorrow morning at eleven." Further correspondence in the file testifies to the school's continued attempts to help Sam find a job, as well as to the apparent lack of success of these efforts. The following February, my great-grandfather again wrote to the principal on his son's behalf: "During the time he has been out of school (he has been out a year now) he has only worked for two months at sign-painting for $12.00 a week. Then he was layed [sic] off. Since then he has gone out to look for work every day and can't seem to find any because of his being handicapped, it seems. Perhaps it is in the power of your Institution to help Sam find work? If so will you please let me know?" 38

I picture my great-grandfather as a sturdy man bundled in a thick overcoat and fur hat, plodding through snow to post the letter, his great bushy eyebrows bunched with worry. And I picture the principal as a clean-shaven man in a brown suit, a goodhearted man who had abandoned other, more comfortable careers to help deaf-mutes improve 39 their unfortunate lot; I picture him reading the letter at his desk, perhaps rubbing a hand across his smooth jaw, sighing.

But in all the letters, the telegrams, the documents, the medical records, I couldn't locate Sam himself. I didn't know how to picture my grandfather in any of this, until one day when my Uncle Max was visiting. I had taken the bulky brown folder home to study more carefully, and Max sat at the kitchen table, jiggling his knee and leafing through it. He came to his grandfather's letter, read it, and snorted. [40]

"Pop went out to look for work every day, my ass," barked Max, tugging at the corner of his blond mustache. The skin under his eyes creased faintly in a private grin. "He was out playing ball." [41]

The final picture slid into place. Now I could complete the image: my great-grandfather dropping his letter anxiously into the box; Mr. Harris Taylor shaking his head behind a big polished desk; and my grandfather, Sam, on the court, away from language lessons and hearing employers and jobs where he couldn't talk with anyone, just Sam on the court, flying up and down the asphalt, his heart and lungs and limbs all engaged in what they did best. [42]

The spring Sam turned seventy, we sent out dozens and dozens of birthday party invitations, hand-lettered by my mother and watercolored by me. We cleaned our whole house—the dust mice under the armchair, the peanut shells in the hearth, the dog-nose smudges on the windowpanes over the couch. We bought two six-foot submarine sandwiches, at which Reba, Andy, and I marveled; still in their amber cellophane wrappers, they spread importantly down the entire length of the dining room table. And all along the one-mile route from the Tappan Zee Bridge to our house, we thumbtacked markers to telephone posts, colored balloons with signs reading SAM. [43]

It was not our family's custom to throw large birthday parties, even for septuagenarians, but something greater was being celebrated this year. My grandfather had finally been elected into the Hall of Fame of the New York State Athletic Association for the Deaf. This was his life's dream, the one he had given up hoping for nearly two decades earlier. [44]

Shortly after his marriage, Sam had landed a job cutting terry cloth for women's bathrobes. This remained his occupation throughout his life. A member of the International Ladies' Garment Workers Union, he provided the sole income for his family—his wife, Fannie, and their two hearing sons. Each morning he rode the elevated train along Jerome Avenue to work; he punched a clock and cut cloth all day with heavy shears; at night he returned home so tired that he was notorious for sleeping past his stop on the train. It was a fine job for a deaf man in the middle of the twentieth century, and with these hours of his life he provided sustenance for his family. [45]

But Sam lived for his moments on the court. He had always loved   46
basketball. In grammar school, he played it alone in the rain and snow
during lunch recess and after school in the Lexington courtyard. At
home during the summers, when his parents imposed limits on his
playing, he would toss his sneakers and shorts from the window of their
sixth-floor apartment and tell his mother he was going out to buy a newspaper, then return hours later, most often without the paper.

As an adult his life continued to revolve around basketball, and   47
around the Union League, one of the oldest deaf clubs in the country.
Every Thursday night my grandfather would go to the Ansonia Hotel
in Manhattan, where the club members met to play cards and talk. He
attended so devoutly that on Knox Place, Thursday was fingerspelled
U-L; my father likes to say that he grew up believing the days of the
week were Sunday, Monday, Tuesday, Wednesday, UL, Friday, and
Saturday.

Sam played basketball for the Union League, the Lexington   48
Boys, the Hebrew Association of the Deaf, the Pelicans, and other deaf
teams. He was the only deaf player on two semiprofessional teams, the
Philadelphia Spas and the Castle Hill Beach Club. He coached and
played basketball until 1959. When he stopped, my father, just out of
high school, wrote a letter to the American Athletic Association of the
Deaf (AAAD), the first of many letters he would write on his father's
behalf. It explained that Sam, then fifty-two years old, had developed
cataracts and was awaiting an operation; moreover, the factory where
he had been employed for twenty-five years had shut down, so he was
out of work as well. "For the eighteen years of my life," my father
wrote,

> I have regarded my father as a happy, jovial person who seems to enjoy life   49
> more than any person possibly could. During these past five weeks I have
> seen him turn into a depressed, despondent individual. On the outside he
> still acts the same but on the inside there has been a change that only one
> as close to him as myself could notice.
>
> Just yesterday while looking through some papers I found the   50
> letter that you sent to him in 1956 concerning his nomination to the
> AAAD Hall of Fame. Knowing my Father as I do I realized that he most
> likely forgot all about answering your letter, as his main interest is par-
> ticipating in sports events and not the publicity or notoriety involved.
>
> So now I can tell you the purpose of this letter. I thought of any pos-   51
> sibility that might have a chance of cheering him up a little and I thought
> that if there was a chance of him making the Hall of Fame this would be
> a terrific lift. I am not asking for any charity nor do I want you to feel sorry
> for my Father for he is not a man to feel sorry for but a man to envy
> because of his great talents. I know how good an athlete he was and still is
> because he taught me everything I know about basketball and I have a few
> trophies to show for the learning he has given me. I would like to say again
> that my Father does not know anything about this letter, if he did he would
> probably beat the daylights out of me because of the tremendous amount
> of pride instilled in him.

My father signed his name in neat black script, sealed and stamped   52
the envelope, and then I imagine him tramping through the snow to the
mailbox, following the ghost-prints of his dead grandfather. The letter
went unanswered, yielding no results, and Sam never knew what his son
had done. It was eighteen years before Sam's nomination resurfaced
and he was finally inducted into the Hall of Fame. He received news of
the honor just four months shy of his seventieth birthday.

The day of the party, my grandfather appeared mildly bewildered   53
when he first emerged from one of the rear doors of the car that friends
had driven up from the Bronx. All of his friends and relatives clustered
expectantly in our yard, holding hunks of submarine sandwich and beer
and cake, grinning at him while he blinked uncertainly back. (Later we
learned that my grandmother, in a cunning effort to prevent him from
seeing the posters along the roadside, had snatched his glasses from his
face as soon as the car left the exit ramp, on the pretext that they were
shamefully filthy, and proceeded to scrub them vigorously with her skirt
for the next mile, effectively keeping the party a surprise.) When my
grandfather was finally apprised of the occasion for this gathering, his
thin, wide mouth opened in unabashed appreciation, and he went
around most of the afternoon beaming, his eyes glittering behind clean,
clean lenses.

Late in the afternoon someone bounced a basketball out of the toy   54
box in our garage. We didn't have a hoop, but one was mounted on the
Rotellis' garage, next door, so we all gathered at the edge of their
driveway and my grandfather took the ball out to what seemed like half-
court. I had no faith at all that he would make it—him at seventy years
old, with hair as white as birchbark and teeth that came out at night—
and it made me queasy to think of him missing, today of all days. We
watched in silence as he gently coiled his frame, his hands a smooth
socket for the ball, then sprang his body open and let the sphere arc
above us. It sank through the net, steady and definite. In this arena he
never missed.

Three years later, in July, we held his funeral gathering at Max's   55
house in Brewster. People drove up from Mount Hebron Cemetery in
Queens and walked through the house depositing armloads of food, pot
roast and kugels and soups and challah and pickles and olives and pas-
tries and fruit baskets and nuts and chocolates, and then they continued
out to the back lawn, where the acre of neatly trimmed grass rolled to
the edge of the woods. The grownups reclined in plastic chairs and
metal chaises, the women plucking damply at the necks of their dark
blouses. We children kicked off our good, uncomfortable shoes and
stepped bare-foot over bees in the clover. We got sick on too much fruit
and chocolate and sat in the grass, eavesdropping on the hearing people
and watching the deaf people sign to one another; all of it seemed
equally incomprehensible.

After a while I retreated into the cool, wood-smelling shade of the   56
living room and stood looking through the square panes of the sliding
doors. Uncle Max had wept at the service, but my father had not cried
at all. I saw him now through the polished glass, moving about on the
lawn, his shoulders rounded beneath his white shirt, a forgotten drink
suspended perilously from his fingers. He nodded while someone
signed to him. I had not been able to speak to him all day; I felt a little
bit afraid of him, his iron sadness, his awful grace.

Some hearing children of deaf parents say that they had to assume   57
parental roles when they were young, that they had to function as inter-
preters, caregivers, providers, instructors. They talk about growing up
under the crushing weight of these responsibilities.

My father has never had much use for essays and articles   58
expounding on this subject. He is quick to point out that *he* never supported the family, *he* didn't buy the groceries, *he* didn't feed the family
or take care of the apartment—that it was his parents who tended him,
who nurtured him emotionally, who were the rock.

Watching him on the lawn that day, his broad shoulders so bent,   59
his muscles gripping in a kind of mineral stillness, I both craved and
dreaded to witness some slippage, some chipping or crumbling. It would
be ten years before this happened, before I heard my father's voice
thicken and break, before I heard the full story of my grandfather's
death.

On Saturday afternoon, July 25, 1981, Sam and Fannie had been   60
heading to the Union League when Sam, walking a few steps behind
Fannie, collapsed. Someone touched Fannie's arm; she turned and saw
a crowd gathered around her husband. He lay crumpled on the bright
sidewalk; blood came from his head. Police came, then an ambulance.
He was taken to the Cabrini Medical Center on East Nineteenth Street
and admitted to the Cardiac Care Unit.

When my father arrived at the hospital that afternoon, he   61
explained to the CCU staff, nurses, and physicians that Sam was pro-
foundly deaf and could not speak intelligibly. He emphasized the importance of having someone who was able to communicate in American
Sign Language so that Sam could know what was happening to him and
so the hospital staff could obtain information about symptoms and
medical history and responses to their questions. My father said that he
would serve as an interpreter. He gave the hospital his telephone
numbers at home and at work. He said he would come to the hospital
immediately whenever he was called.

On Sunday at three P.M. he tried to visit his father, but he was barred   62
by the worker at the front desk, who informed him that because of doctors'
rounds he could not visit at that time. My father explained that he wished
to be present during doctors' rounds to serve as an interpreter during the

examination. The worker replied that the hospital had an interpreter program for the deaf and that my father's services were not needed. She refused to let him in. Later my father learned that no interpreter had been available; the Cabrini interpreter did not work on weekends.

That night my father called the CCU to inquire about Sam's con-   63
dition. The nurse on duty said the doctor was not there. My father asked for the doctor please to return his call on Sunday night at home. No one returned the call.

On Monday morning at nine, my father called the CCU again and   64
was told that Sam had improved, that a heart attack had been ruled out, and that he had been moved from the CCU to the fifteenth floor. My father called Fannie on the TTY to give her the good news.

Fannie arrived at Cabrini at 11:15 A.M. to visit her husband.   65
Requesting a visitor's pass, she was told that Mr. Cohen was not a patient. After she insisted that he was, the person at the desk made some phone calls and then directed her to the fifteenth floor. No one tried to call for an interpreter. On the fifteenth floor she was directed to a waiting room. Because the nurse could not communicate with her, Fannie did not understand what she was waiting for. Finally a resident who spoke with an Indian accent, which was extremely difficult to lip-read, came and described in technical terms that Mr. Cohen had not survived the second of two cardiac arrests that had occurred at about eight that morning. Fannie did not know what "cardiac arrest" meant, nor could she understand the resident's speech very well. But when he shook his head, she understood.

In a state of shock and confusion, she was sent to the hospital   66
lobby. The doctor called my father at work. Dazed, frozen, behind a tightly stretched skin of silence, Fannie waited for him. But it was Max who arrived first. When she saw him striding jauntily up the passage toward her, unaware of his father's death, the blond ends of his mustache curved in greeting, Fannie dissolved, her sobs breaking against the lobby walls.

In the days afterward, there were many questions. Why had no   67
interpreter been present to help Sam understand why he was being moved from the CCU on Sunday night? Why had no interpreter been present during the crises on Monday morning, to give Sam the doctors' instructions or tell the doctors what he might have been trying to communicate? Why had no interpreter been present at any of the examinations, after my father had offered this necessary service and been told that Cabrini would provide it? What possible explanation could the hospital have for preventing my father from serving as an interpreter during the doctors' rounds on Sunday afternoon? And why had no interpreter been present to deliver the news to Fannie of her husband's death?

My father wrote to the medical center administrators requesting   68
answers to these questions. Months passed; it was November before he

got a response. It acknowledged no fault but concluded placatingly, "You can be assured that we have reinforced our staff training programs in our continuing effort to communicate with our hearing impaired patients. . . . I want you to know that your persistence in pursuing this matter will impact favorably on other hearing impaired patients treated at the Cabrini Medical Center."

As a child, I was only partially conscious that something had gone awry, that something wrong and bad had happened beyond the fact of death itself. Years later, I asked my father to tell me the story. He obliged, reliving its chronology, and I finally witnessed the crack for which I had searched in vain a decade earlier. The craggy planes of his face darkened and shifted; something staggered painfully in his throat. For a moment I saw him fold softly into grief. I saw him miss my grandfather.

And I wondered at his vision of Sam, so clearly one of indomitable strength. When I go looking for Sam, it seems I come up only with papers, sheaves of dry correspondence about him and for him but never by him. If he was a rock, he has long since gone to dust, and any fossils left behind were left by others, just as the ink on the pages has been left by others, by Oscar his father and Oscar his son. Sam's own motions— the words of his hands, the path of his body as it worked the court—are traceless; once realized and finished, they left no mark.

69

70

Questions for Reflection and Discussion

1. Do you think that Sam Cohen perceived his deafness as a problem or a disability? Why?
2. Think of one of your own grandparents or another older person in your life. What information would you need about that person to write an essay similar to the one Cohen wrote about her grandfather?

Topics for Writing

1. Choose someone with a physical or mental disability and interview him or her to find out what it is like living with a disability. Before the interview, make a list of questions you want to ask, but be prepared to ask other questions if the opportunity or need arises. After the interview, write an essay describing what life is like for that person, paying special attention to the way the person copes with his or her disability and the way other people react to the disability.
2. Return to the free write you completed before you read this chapter. Use the information there to begin a research project that will result in a fully developed essay about an older person in your life, similar to the essay Leah Hager Cohen wrote about her grandfather.

As you begin this research project, continue to develop the list of questions you started to compile (put together) in your free write. You should have about five to ten questions. Next to each question, write the source to which you will go to find the answer—interviews with the person and/or other family members and friends, reading family papers and letters, researching the history of the period in which the person was born, or your own memory.

After you have gathered as much information as possible about the person and answered as many questions as possible in the time period given to you by your instructor, write an essay about the person that is complete, interesting, and informative.

Additional Writing Topics
about What Our Parents (Guardians) Mean to Us

The reading selections in this chapter contain honest, complete, and interesting information and insights about parents and guardians. They show the great influence parents and guardians have on us, and they show as well the gratitude most of us feel for the way our parents and guardians have raised and cared for us. These writers recalled, with extraordinary detail, the traits, habits, practices, and actions of the people who raised them. If these works had not been written, it is possible that the information contained in them would have been lost. In almost every case, the article or essay was part of a larger work, a larger record of the parent's or guardian's life.

This is an opportunity for you to create your own record of your parents or guardians, and you can do it in one of several forms or styles. Read the options below, and choose the style or form that best suits you. Be sure to save what you write; perhaps some day you can read it to your own children so they can know about someone who had an extraordinary influence and impact on your life.

1. In the excerpt from *Colored People*, Henry Louis Gates, Jr., tells how his mother was selected as the winner of the write-in contest on the television show *The Big Payoff*, based on a letter about her accomplishments written by her brother, Harry. Imagine that you want to nominate one of your parents or guardians to be selected to win the prizes on a show like *The Big Payoff*. Write a letter describing this person's accomplishments in great detail, being sure to give examples to prove that he or she actually possesses the qualities you name and describe.
2. Find out the date on which one of your grandparents (preferably the oldest) was born. Go to the library and find a newspaper that was printed on that date. Then describe, in your own words, the story that made the headlines on that day.
3. As the author of "Underground Dads" explained, growing up with only one parent doesn't have to be a terrible thing. If you grew up with only one

parent, write an essay in which you describe and explain that you were not deprived of the things you needed to become a successful and happy adult. Be as specific as possible in explaining the way your single parent or guardian provided the necessities—and extras—that made your life successful, safe, and happy. In fact, you may even want to describe some of the advantages of growing up in a single-parent household.

4. There is no one correct way to be a parent; in fact, all of the parents and guardians described in the readings were very different. Write an essay in which you describe the methods your parents used to raise you that you think were particularly effective. *Or* write an essay in which you describe the methods they used that you think were *not* effective.

5. Write a letter thanking your parents or guardians for all that they did for you; you must be specific and give clear details and examples. Don't just say, "Thanks for being there when I needed you," or "You were like a best friend to me." Such phrases, without support, sound like greeting-card slogans. Be specific, supporting each of the things you say your parents or guardians did for you with clearly and fully explained examples.

Chapter
7

Class and Race in Our Society: Are We Really Created Equal?

Most of us hope that we can learn, work, and raise our families in a society that does not judge us because of race or class or economic status. However, it does not always work out that way. Some of the selections from previous chapters give an indication of this.

In Chapter 1, Langston Hughes writes in his poem, "Theme for English B," that as an African American writing to a white professor, it is a fact that "sometimes perhaps you don't want to be a part of me. Nor do I often want to be a part of you."

In Chapter 2, Sandra Cisneros, who is Latina, notes that her parents were unable to afford the kind of toys (Barbie Doll outfits and Ken dolls) she wanted.

In Chapter 3, James McBride describes the struggle his mother endured and the long hours she worked to support her children after her husband died.

In Chapter 4, we are told that Wendy Williams is called a "trailer girl" by the wealthier students in her school, and she is further humiliated when they make fun of her thrift shop, mismatched clothes.

In Chapter 5, Rosemary Bray describes how attending a private school outside of her neighborhood made her realize "how really different [she] was." It was an experience that left her "silent and unhappy," and for the first time in her life, she felt "ashamed."

In Chapter 6, Henry Louis Gates describes the way being black affected so many aspects of his childhood. Although he was very young, he was still able to understand that discrimination and racism had resulted in his mother hating white people "with a passion she seldom disclosed." And in the same chapter, Leah Hager Cohen explains that her deaf grandfather died alone and frightened because no one on the hospital staff bothered to find a sign language interpreter to help him understand what was happening to him.

Perhaps there can never be such a thing as a perfectly equal or fair society; there will always be differences among us, and those differences will sometimes be used to separate, and to hurt. But we cannot ignore one crucial fact: The writers seem to be sharing their experiences not only to tell us of the hardships they faced but to inspire us by helping us to see that they survived and endured and succeeded in overcoming the obstacles that seemed so overwhelming to them in childhood.

And it is very possible that Wendy Williams will not live in a trailer all of her life. We are told at the end of the article that she decided to take the advanced math class and is beginning to show an interest in attending college. Perhaps someday she will have a real house, matching clothes, and money for extras. And it is very possible that Wendy will become an inspiration for others. Perhaps she will write her own article or book explaining the way she succeeded—through education and perseverance and hard work.

Pre-reading Activity

Before you begin to read the selections in this chapter, take about 15 minutes to respond to these free-writing topics. They will help you to understand the way that we view ourselves and others in our society based on what we have, where we live, the way we speak and dress, and what we or our parents do for a living.

Think about your present economic status (and your family's economic status), your race, and where you live. How do these three factors affect the way you are perceived by others in your neighborhood, school, or town? Do these three factors place you on the "wrong side of the tracks"? On the "right side"? In other words, would you be considered a "have" or a "have-not"? Is there racial and cultural diversity in your neighborhood? Do members of different races and ethnic groups mix and socialize? Or do they stay together?

When you were in high school, did the way you dress or the kind of car you drove (or even whether you had a car) have an impact on the way other students viewed you? Explain. Did your financial status have an impact on the way teachers and administrators viewed you? Explain. Were the wealthy students in your high school admired? Envied? Resented? Was there racial and cultural diversity in your high school? Were the members of different races and cultures comfortable with each other? Did they mix and socialize? Or did they stay together? Explain.

Reading 7–1

SHOCKING VISITS TO THE REAL WORLD

Monique P. Yazigi

In the following selection, "Shocking Visits to the Real World," the author describes the "difficulty" very wealthy young adults from New York City and the surrounding suburbs (most of whom have inherited or will inherit huge fortunes from their parents or grandparents) have in keeping a job. The problem isn't that they aren't qualified; it's that working interferes with their ability to shop, party, and take vacations! Psychologists and child experts have come up with a term to describe these rich people—*affluenza*, a play on the word *flu*, and a play on the word *affluence*, which means rich.

Vocabulary

touting (paragraph 3)   talking about; showing off

Agnes B. and Chanel (5)   famous fashion designers; their clothes are very expensive

endowed trust funds (12)   funds that are guaranteed for life

post-debutantes (12)   at about the age of 20, a debutante "comes out" in society at a series of fancy balls attended by other rich and well-connected society people.

Claridge's (12)   a famous hotel in London

Ibiza (12)   an "in" vacation spot

a Merchant & Ivory month (12)   Merchant and Ivory are a team who produce films that depict India or England or other countries as they were when wealthy people traveled abroad to relax and to view the "natives."

bastion of male privilege (13)   a bastion is a place that is secure, a fortress. In this case, a place where wealthy men can go to relax and be with others like themselves

defer (14)   delay, put off

Prada and Armani (15)   famous fashion designers; their clothes are very expensive

Renaissance mosaic (25)   a mosaic is made of tiny pieces of tile of many different colors; an art form that was often used during the Renaissance (1300–1600)

paradox (25)   a contradiction

conceded (27)   admitted; gave in

Baccarat bubble (29)   a clever expression on the part of the author to reflect privilege: Baccarat is a brand of very expensive crystal, similar to Tiffany or Steuben

ingrained (29)   built-in

Paris couture shows (31)   every season, fashion designers hold extravagant shows in Paris to show their latest lines of clothes; very wealthy people attend to choose their wardrobe

stifle (33)   limit; prevent from growing

Source: "Shocking Visits to the Real World" by Monique P. Yazigi, *The New York Times,* February 20, 2000. Copyright 2000 by the New York Times Co. Reprinted by permission.

disincentive (36)   An incentive encourages; a disincentive discourages.
hampered (38)   held back; prevented
introspection (48)   to examine one's own behavior and motives

Suggestions for Free Writing

Before you read the article, take about 15 minutes to free-write on the following topics:

> Imagine that you had all the money you would ever need. Decide how your life would change as a result, and make three lists in answer to the following questions: (1) What would you start doing that you don't do now? (2) What would you stop doing that you have to do now? (3)What would you continue to do? Now look over the three lists, and decide to which degree money would change your life, using the following categories: (1) It would completely change. (2) It would change somewhat. (3) It would not change at all. Finally, based on your lists, decide if you would like the kind of person you would become if you had all the money you would ever need.

Starting in the management training program at Chase Manhattan Bank didn't turn out exactly the way one 29-year-old Upper East Sider expected.   1

In the five years since she'd graduated from college, she had been supported in Manhattan by her family and spent her days addressing envelopes for charity parties.   2

But suddenly, among her friends, it was no longer acceptable for young adults not to work. All the glittering Park Avenue princesses were touting their serious day jobs. It was chic to have a career. The young woman asked her father, a prominent financier, to help find her a position. Daddy, as she refers to him, talked to golfing friends at the Round Hill country club in Greenwich, Conn., and within two weeks she was in at the bank.   3

The chicness wore off fast.   4

When she started, in March 1998, supervisors informed her of the dress code: replace those puffy Agnès B. skirts and Chanel flats with dark suits, stockings and classic pumps with one-inch heels. She complied, though she found stockings "especially middle class." She was told to limit personal calls, and so she made her party plans after work. She obeyed what she called the bank's "silly" rules, but then summer approached and she informed her supervisor that her family traditionally took a three-month vacation in the south of France.   5

She was told she could have one week off.   6

"One week?" said the woman (whose fear of ridicule led her to ask for anonymity). "That was so ridiculous. That's not even enough time to shop."   7

When she returned to the office three months later, in mid-September, she found, not surprisingly, that she was out of a job.   8

"The entire experience was a shock," the woman said the other   9
day. "I had never been around that many middle-class people all in one
room. It was dreadful. They were mean and jealous and expected me to
miss out on all our family fun."

Pity the adult children of the modern leisure class.   10

Well, O.K., don't pity them—but at least try to see it their way for   11
a moment.

Raised with unlimited charge-card privileges and BMW's for   12
their 16th birthdays, they knew early on that they would not have to
work for a living. Their parents bought them apartments when they
turned 21 and endowed trust funds to provide for cash flow. The post-
debutantes thought nothing of flying to London for a party in a suite
at Claridge's, or to a disco on Ibiza, or drifting through India for a
Merchant & Ivory month.

But now it has become socially unacceptable not to work, no   13
matter how much money your parents have. Young women dread being
stuck with the label "socialite," or worse, as middle-aged 1980's-vintage
"ladies who lunch." It is the same for men. Just a generation ago, about
half the members of the Racquet & Tennis Club, the Park Avenue
bastion of male privilege, listed "gentleman" or "sportsman" as their
occupations, members say; now, there are precious few who fit those
descriptions. And most of them hide it.

And yet, despite the fashion for careers, many children of   14
extreme privilege can't seem to hack it. They lack the drive and the discipline of their hungrier peers. They get frustrated easily when confronted with setbacks, and grow angry at the need to defer immediate
pleasures. They job-hop, throw tantrums and have a tough time
relating to people who come from different backgrounds (and almost
everybody does).

"A lot of the kids I grew up with are still stuck doing the same   15
things they were doing in high school—partying every night, not
working terribly hard, traveling a lot," said Noel Ashman, 29, an owner
of the nightclub Veruka, where many of his former private-school
buddies congregate. "They are dressed in Prada and Armani now and
don't really worry about how they're going to wake up for work the next
morning."

Many have tried working, he said, "but when it gets difficult, they   16
won't stick it out because they don't have to."

Tara Peters, 28, an artist, attended private schools in Manhattan   17
and, after college, moved to Paris for six years, before returning to New
York. "It's unacceptable to say you don't work," she said. "Work is a definition on how you spend your time. If you don't work, and you don't
have to work, you eventually look like a dummy who lunches."

Anthony Buhl, 30, who grew up in New York and Switzerland, has briefly held jobs as a temp at a stock brokerage in Boston and as a trainee at a brokerage in London. He left, he said, when he became bored. Most recently he worked for an uncle on building sites in Palm Beach. That, too, he found tedious.   18

"I liked it in the beginning, but it got a little boring, repetitive," he said hesitantly. "I didn't like the people. There was nothing wrong with them, but there are a lot of rednecks down there."   19

He added: "I got tired of Palm Beach. It got dull."   20

Mr. Buhl returned to New York, where he has many friends who are supported by their families. They call themselves artists, he said, or hop from job to job. "Some of my friends are brats," he said. "Some are just looking for new and exciting experiences."   21

Mr. Buhl's father, Henry Buhl, a retired mutual fund manager and philanthropist, laments that all three of his grown children lack career ambitions. "None of them seem to have any work ethic," he said. A second son, 35, has had three jobs in a year and lives to crew on sailboats. His daughter, 36, lives in Portugal.   22

They have many contemporaries in the same position. "This is a flighty group from New York and Switzerland," Henry Buhl said, "I won't mention names, but there are so many kids of rich people who are given too much money and too much freedom and are 'cool' and haven't been handled properly."   23

To force his own children to take responsibility, Mr. Buhl said, he stopped giving them money a few years ago, but they have independent incomes from their grandparents. The family patriarch, Louis Mendelssohn, was a wealthy architect and builder in Detroit.   24

The elder Mr. Buhl, who said he did not come into family money until later in life, worked his way up on Wall Street. Today he lives in a 4,500-square-foot loft in SoHo, with a dome over the entry painted to look like a Renaissance mosaic. It is no small paradox that Mr. Buhl is the founder of the SoHo Partnership, which helps homeless people find jobs as well as housing. Participants are paid $6 an hour to clean the streets while being trained to dress and speak well in interviews to win jobs.   25

Mr. Buhl said his program has helped more than 200 people find employment since 1992, but he has been unable to help his own children. "My kids should be in the program, but they are not hopeless enough," he said. "You have to be desperate to make my program work."   26

He conceded that he bears some responsibility for his children's aimlessness. "I guess I shouldn't have given them such a high life," he said.   27

It's hard, no doubt, to work up much sympathy for this segment of the trust-fund set, especially when so many others in their age group are working 70-hour weeks on the lower rungs of law firms or banks or as   28

Internet entrepreneurs. They manage to delay gratification on their climb to the top, which also teaches lessons in dealing with people, both superiors and subordinates, from diverse backgrounds.

At least one 27-year-old woman who grew up in a wealthy and socially prominent family, on the other hand, never stayed long enough in a sales job she took, at a corporation in Midtown, to experience the world outside her Baccarat bubble. If she had, she might have lost what seems to be an ingrained snobbery. 29

"I was talking to people who took four trains from God knows where to get to work, who didn't understand that my job did not come first," said the woman, who did not want to be named. "Certainly it didn't, for $37,000 a year." 30

Her immediate manager, she recounted, rolled her eyes when she came in late, grunted when she took three-hour networking lunches and finally put her foot down when she wanted to take an unpaid vacation to go to the Paris couture shows. After 18 months, she quit. She now works for her family, helping to invest its fortune. She goes to a family office when she is so inclined, where the employees, all on the family payroll, can't boss her around. 31

Such cases may seem extreme, easy to tsk-tsk over; but a sense of entitlement coupled with a lack of discipline is also a growing problem for young people from less lofty strata, some psychotherapists and child experts say. The term "affluenza" has been popularized by one therapist, Jessie H. O'Neill of Milwaukee, to describe how values are distorted by too much money. Merrill Lynch offers advisers who help clients teach their children the responsibilities that come with wealth. 32

Dr. Pamela Sicher, a psychiatrist in private practice on the Upper East Side, said: "We have more and more children that are having trouble finding personal reasons to work hard at their own goals. Many feel that they will passively inherit, if not money, a work life, and this type of thing tends to stifle creativity and drive." 33

She added, "A lack of focus, a lack of direction and a lack of drive is a problem that has increased in frequency among the young 20-somethings and 30-somethings, who are now going to therapists." 34

Robert C. Elliott, an executive vice president at the Bessemer Trust Company, which manages trusts for many old-line families (minimum fund: $5 million), said the latest wave of the newly wealthy is learning from past mistakes in giving money to children. 35

"Parents are recognizing the potential problem and delaying the time when their children would actually receive money in order to not have it serve as a disincentive," he said. 36

After their children's educations are paid for, he said, parents now typically "buy a house, give them money to start a business, but don't let them get their hands on the big money." These children come into their 37 legacy in stages, at the ages of 30, 35 or 40, and some parents even require offspring to pass drug tests.

"The work ethic is hampered by access to money at too young an age," Mr. Elliott said. "It's hard for someone who has several million dollars, which produces income of over $100,000 or so, to be interested in a job that pays $40,000." 38

"Ultimately they become less committed to their career than their peers, which obviously produces less success in their career and ultimately less satisfaction with their lives." 39

And trust funds have a habit of running out, especially in the second or third generation. 40

Bobby Kravitz admitted that he grew up as a spoiled brat in and around New York. His artist mother, Brenda Kravitz, and his father, Philip L. Kravitz, the owner of a very profitable insurance brokerage, had homes in New Jersey and off Sutton Place in Manhattan. 41

"I basically had whatever I wanted," Mr. Kravitz said. That included, during Christmas vacations in Palm Beach, his own room at the Breakers hotel with a stocked bar, which made him popular with the junior social set there. When he was 19, he had his own Manhattan condominium. "Basically, I was so unruly my parents thought it would be easier for me to have my own apartment," he said. "You know, so I wouldn't mess up the pillows." 42

He partied through college (he attended several) and kept on partying all the way into his 30's. When he left school, he took a job at his father's company, Kalvin Miller International, a large insurance brokerage. When his father sold it, the new owners politely told him, he recalled, that he would always have a job there but that since he didn't work hard he would not advance far. 43

"I was full of arrogance and conceit and felt there were plenty of opportunities for me," Mr. Kravitz said. "I didn't show up in the office when I was supposed to. I was very unruly." 44

He was clubbing nightly. He recalled thinking that the norms that guided most people's careers and behavior didn't apply, thanks to the great cushion that wealth provided. "There's a degree of snobbery," he said. "You say to yourself, 'I'm different from everyone else.' You say, 'I'm better than everyone else.'" 45

He added: "Especially in the New York scene, there is such tremendous affluence, and you're surrounded by so many affluent friends, you kind of think you'll always be taken care of. You feel you have all this privilege, and it's almost a right of passage that you will succeed. You think that everything will come magically and easily." 46

Between ages 23 and 28, Mr. Kravitz held four jobs. He quit three and was fired from one. At one point, he moved to London to try developing real estate, but was discouraged and returned home. 47

In moments of introspection, he recognized that he was deeply 48 unhappy with his inability to sustain a career, or even a long-term relationship. He saw how the heavy use of drugs and alcohol among his set was an attempt, as he put it, "to medicate these awful feelings."

Mr. Kravitz became depressed over his lack of direction, and con- 49 sidered suicide. "My life just stopped working the way it was," he said. "I had no clue about how to focus on work. I saw my life standing still while friends were getting married, were getting promoted at work."

Out of worry for his son, his father, who died last year, had him go 50 work at another company he owned, Global Risk Management, which audits workers' compensation insurance. "I had to grow up and I had to learn how to work and have responsibility," Mr. Kravitz said. He married, and he says he now goes to an office all day, almost every day. At 33, he says he has turned his life around.

"The people who really matter, the people who I respect," he said, 51 "I've earned their respect now."

Questions for Reflection and Discussion

1. Do you think the young adults described in Monique Yazigi's article are happy and satisfied with their lives? Explain.
2. If you had as much money as the people described in the article do, how would you make sure your children did not grow up to be spoiled and unable to hold a job?

Topics for Writing

1. In paragraph 10, the author says, somewhat sarcastically, "pity the adult children of the modern leisure class." However, there really *are* reasons why they should be pitied. Based on the information and evidence given in the article, write an essay in which you describe the reasons why they should be pitied. In order to make it easier for you to organize your essay, you could devote each paragraph to one of the reasons why these young adults should be pitied.
2. Return to the free write you completed before you read the article, and use the information there to write an essay describing how your life would change if you suddenly found yourself with all the money you would ever need. In order to make it easier for you to organize your essay, you could devote each paragraph to one of the ways your life would change. Remember to explain the way your life is now so your readers can see what will be different. Be sure to begin your paragraph with a topic sentence, and then provide your readers with all of the explanations, details, descriptions, and examples needed to fully understand your meaning.

BETTER BEHAVE, CHILD; MS. FENSTERMAKER IS WATCHING YOU

Peter Waldman

The next selection, an article published in *The Wall Street Journal*, describes the process used to decide which children will be accepted into the kindergarten class in one of San Francisco's most competitive private elementary schools. For the children who are applying, the competition to "make it" starts early—at four years old, to be exact.

Vocabulary

interlude (paragraph 3)   short conversation or interaction between two people
espionage (4)   spying
culminates (4)   ends
demystify (5)   take the mystery or confusion out of
bewilders (5)   confuses
growing legions (5)   large numbers
pseudonyms (5)   made up names to protect the privacy of the person being written about
coveted (6)   highly desired
reputedly (7) something that has been heard but is not known for certain
the lion's share (10)   the largest share
transitioned (13)   shifted from one activity to another
hunker down (22)   hide out

Suggestions for Free Writing

Before you read the article, take about 15 minutes to free-write on the following topics:

Think about an occasion in your life when you had to or wanted to impress someone or a group of people: a job interview, a school function, a date, someone important, the family of your girlfriend or boyfriend, giving a speech, a sports team, a sorority or other group, admission to a school. Or think about an occasion where you had to perform at your best: a sports event, acting, delivering a speech, writing. What were some of the things you thought about? How did you prepare? What were some of the things you worried about? What were some of the things you felt most confident about? What did you do during the occasion or event itself? Were you successful or unsuccessful? If you had it to do over, what would you do differently? What would you do the same?

SAN FRANCISCO—Candice licks a gob of cream cheese from the   1
crust of her sandwich, curls it in a ball on the tip of her tongue and sticks it out at classmate Lauren.

Unimpressed, Lauren shoves an orange wedge into her own   2
mouth and lodges the peel between her teeth and lips like a gorilla.

Not exactly the charming interlude most parents would choose with   3
their four-year-old's educational future on the line, but it will have to do. Cecile Fenstermaker, admissions director of San Francisco Day School, watches the action from behind a two-way mirror mounted inside the preschoolers' classroom, evaluating if these tots have what it takes for entry into one of San Francisco's most competitive private schools.

The kiddy espionage, or "site visit," in Ms. Fenstermaker's words, is   4
one of the final acts in a secretive ritual that began last fall with parent interviews and culminates this Friday with the mailing of about 60 acceptances, 30 or 40 wait-list letters, and 150 or so rejections for the San Francisco Day School Class of 2009.

To help demystify an ordeal that bewilders growing legions of young   5
families applying to private schools each year, Ms. Fenstermaker agreed to open the process to a Wall Street Journal reporter. (By agreement with the school, the children's names in this article are pseudonyms.)

Candice and Lauren are running neck and neck for a coveted   6
kindergarten spot at San Francisco Day, both having earned high marks during screening sessions held at the school's campus in January. But, on paper at least, the girls are too similar: white, upper-middle class, solid but not superstars. Only one of them will get in, Ms. Fenstermaker says. So the admissions director turns up at their preschool on a rainy March morning, to see for herself how the two candidates, and three less-promising applicants, handle themselves on their own turf.

At snack time, their teacher asks Candice and Lauren how many   7
kids are at their table. Lauren says four, which is true. Candice says five, counting the boy who has just darted off to look at a book on the carpet. For the next several minutes, the girls eat quietly, flashing the occasional food face at one another, while the teacher contends with another little boy who has reputedly been having family problems at home.

"Site visits are a really important piece of the whole puzzle of   8
making good kindergarten matches," says Ms. Fenstermaker, who spies on kindergarten applicants at about 20 preschools every year, unbeknownst to most of their parents. "I like to see the kids where they feel most comfortable."

For elite private schools like San Francisco Day, this year's applica-   9
tion frenzy has been the worst ever, not just here in Internet-bloated San

Francisco, but across America. Betsy Haugh, head of admissions at the Latin School of Chicago, has seen 30% more applications to its prekindergarten program this year compared to last. Why? "A lot more people can afford private schools now than 10 years ago," she explains.

But that makes it a lot harder to get in. This year, San Francisco   10
Day, which offers grades K–8, intends to accept 18 siblings of its current students to its kindergarten class. It will also take 22 "people of color" in accordance with a policy set by its board of trustees. That leaves just 20 or so slots for the lion's share of its 253 kindergarten applicants.

Of those, the school has identified six candidates whose families,   11
says Head of School Jim Telander, "can help the school in the long run"—meaning they are really rich. Those kids are pretty much in. That narrows the field to roughly 14 slots. (The school accepts 60 applicants for its 44 kindergarten places, knowing some will choose other schools.)

Ms. Fenstermaker likens her job to cooking up a grand feast—   12
blending ethnicity, personality type, parental background and income, so all the "flavors" balance. "You don't serve seafood as an entree if you're serving it as an appetizer," she says.

That means there's no room on the menu for both Candice and   13
Lauren. Both girls impressed Ms. Fenstermaker's staff at the January screenings, designed to test developmental readiness. They followed directions well and "transitioned" nicely between activities. The screeners noted Lauren's "good attitude"; Candice showed "self-confi-dence" by asking for more beads to complete a necklace project.

Neither girl stood out—sometimes a virtue in itself. Ms.   14
Fenstermaker says Candice and Lauren fall into the "healthy middle" category of applicants, "anchor" kids who provide needed ballast in a highly charged classroom. "Sometimes there's too much emphasis on finding the 'perfect child,' " Ms. Fenstermaker says.

Both girls come from solid families—also vital, the admissions   15
officer says. In addition to good kids, San Francisco Day looks for parents who will give time and energy to the school, plus money. Parents who can contribute unusual skills are particularly hot. "We have chefs and makeup artists," Ms. Fenstermaker says.

Lauren's parents shot themselves in the foot by neglecting to book   16
an interview with Ms. Fenstermaker last fall. She never met them. In contrast, she liked Candice's parents when they met, and found them eager to get involved.

That's a big plus for Candice, as Ms. Fenstermaker takes her posi-   17
tion behind the two-way mirror. There are no big surprises, but the admissions officer notices Candice is more withdrawn than she remem-bers her. She sits passively during circle time, while Lauren jumps up to pin a rainy-day pictograph on the weather chart. On the play-ground, Candice cruises solo on a tricycle; Lauren joins several kids in a wagon train.

Later, the preschool's director raves about Lauren's parents, and 18
says she isn't sure if San Francisco Day is Candice's parents' first choice,
giving Ms. Fenstermaker pause. She leaves the preschool resolved to reread Lauren's file and to reconsider Candice's "to see if we need a solid,
mature, retiring type."

The next day, her mind's made up: Candice is in, Lauren is wait- 19
listed for a spot if another "anchor"-type kid declines to matriculate. (In
addition to its normal wait list, San Francisco Day keeps a "political wait
list," Ms. Fenstermaker says, for kids it doesn't want but whose families
mustered influential friends to write letters on their behalf.)

"Candice is a girl with solid skills and nice parents," she explains. 20
"She'll fit right in here."

The final hurdle is money. Ms. Fenstermaker's last task is to meet 21
with the head of the school, Mr. Telander, and the school's business
manager to go over financial-aid numbers for applicants who have
requested help. Sometimes they make last-minute adjustments to the
class for financial reasons.

Then, once the letters go out Friday, Ms. Fenstermaker intends to 22
hunker down in her office with the door closed for at least a week, to
escape the cloying parents.

"Come Wednesday," she says, "it's a madhouse." 23

Questions for Reflection and Discussion

1. Think about the racial and ethnic makeup of the classes in your elementary school. Did it reflect the kind of diversity the San Francisco Day School
   is trying to achieve? What do you think Ms. Fenstermaker means when she
   says in paragraph 12, "You don't serve seafood as an entree if you're serving
   it as an appetizer."
2. Do you think the children who are applying for admission to San Francisco
   Day School are being admitted based on their qualifications, or are they
   being admitted for another reason or reasons? Make a list of the reasons why
   you would (or do) send your children to a private school. Make a list of the
   reasons why you would not (or do not) send your children to a private school.

Topics for Writing

1. When you become a parent, (or if you are already a parent), what factors
   will you (or did you) consider as you decide(d) which elementary school
   to send your child or children to. (Use the information from the lists you
   made in answering question 2 above to help you write this essay.) In order
   to make it easier to organize your essay, you could devote each of your
   paragraphs to one factor you will consider, followed by explanations, examples, details, and descriptions.

2. Return to the free write you completed before you read the article. Use the information there to write an essay in which you describe a time in your life when you had to impress someone or prove that you were capable of doing something. Be as specific as possible, answering the important who, what, where, when, why, and how questions so that your readers can fully understand your experience. In your conclusion, be certain to explain whether you were successful, and what impact your success, or lack of success, had on you.

Reading 7–3

SLUM LORDS

John Updike

The next selection is a poem entitled "Slum Lords," written by John Updike, a highly regarded American writer. In this poem, he addresses a recent phenomenon that is occurring all over the United States: People are getting so rich because of investments in the stock market or because of the success of Internet ventures that they can afford to buy houses in very expensive and desirable neighborhoods, and then tear the houses down to build ones that are larger and more showy.

Vocabulary

Tombstone (line 10)   a town in Arizona that boomed when silver was discovered there but that quickly became a ghost town after the supply of silver ran out

essence (11)   the real meaning

Suggestions for Free Writing

Before you read the poem, take about 15 minutes to free-write on the following topics:

Think about the neighborhood and the town or city in which you live. Are there different sections located there? Are the neighborhoods divided into "good" and "bad" sections? What makes a neighborhood good? What makes a neighborhood bad? Do all the rich people in your area live in one neighborhood or section of town? Do all the poor people in your area live in one neighborhood or section of town? Is your neighborhood, town, or city integrated, or do people of the same race or ethnic background tend to live in the same area? Are there advantages to this? Are there disadvantages?

The superrich make lousy neighbors—	1
they buy a house and tear it down	2
and build another, twice as big, and leave.	3
They're never there; they own so many	4
other houses, each demands a visit.	5
Entire neighborhoods called fashionable,	6

Source: "Slum Lords" by John Updike. Copyright 1998 John Updike. Reprinted by permission of the author.

bustling with servants and masters, such as	7
Louisburg Square in Boston or Bel Air in L.A.,	8
are districts now like Wall Street after dark	9
or Tombstone once the silver boom went bust.	10
The essence of the superrich is absence.	11
They're always demonstrating they can afford	12
to be somewhere else. Don't let them in.	13
Their money is a kind of poverty.	14

Questions for Reflection and Discussion

1. Describe, in your own words, what you think John Updike means by the last two lines of his poem: "Don't let them in. Their money is a kind of poverty." In particular, what does he mean when he says that their money is a kind of poverty? Is this a contradiction? What *kind* of poverty is it? What is it depriving the neighborhood of?
2. If you could move into the most expensive neighborhood or section of your town, what would be the advantages? What would be the disadvantages?

Topics for Writing

1. Although you will probably not be asked to write poetry in college (unless you take a creative writing course), writing poetry enables us to examine our feelings and thoughts by experimenting with the way we put words together. We do not have to obey the traditional rules of grammar and punctuation; we can just choose the words that say exactly what we mean and combine them in new and unexpected ways. (For example, Updike "spreads" one sentence over the first three lines of his poem.)

   Write a poem in which you describe either the apartment or house you live in now, or your dream apartment or house, being certain to use very specific examples so your readers can actually "see" the house. Or write a poem in which you compare your real home to your dream home.
2. Return to the free write you completed before you read the poem, and use the information there to write an essay in which you compare and contrast the best and worst neighborhoods in your town. A very effective way to write a compare and contrast essay is to make a list of the categories you can compare (similarities) and contrast (differences) and devote one paragraph to each category, explaining the similarities and differences and giving specific examples.

Reading 7–4

FIRST THEY CHANGED MY NAME . . .
Caffilene Allen

The next selection is an essay written by Caffilene Allen and published in *Ms.* magazine. Allen describes the way that language set her apart from mainstream society: Her mother spoke English with a dialect that was common in the Tennessee hill area, and Caffilene's teachers, who spoke standard English, "had a very low opinion of her [mother's] speech and [way of] life." Thus, the author grew up with the confusion, embarrassment, and pain caused when one's parents are viewed by others as different or deficient.

Vocabulary

intriguing (paragraph 2)   interesting
clannish (3)   to stick to one's own kind
incomprehensible (3)   impossible to understand
phonetically (4)   to spell a word the way it sounds
briar (5)   a shrub or bush
reclaim (7)   get back
loomed (7)   threatened
a fundamentalist culture (15)   usually a religious culture in which everything is interpreted simply, with no room for discussion or interpretation
benevolent (15)   good
adamantly (16)   with great persistence; feeling strongly about something
slothlike (17)   like a sloth; lazy
inkling (17)   a small amount of information
Feenanzie (18)   the actual name of the TV show was "Bonanza."
temper (19)   soften
reconcile (20)   bring together

Suggestions for Free Writing

Before you read this essay, take about 15 minutes to free-write on the following topics:

Recall a time when you felt ashamed of a member of your family because of the way he or she looks, speaks, or acts. Explain why you felt that way. Recall a time when you felt pride in a member of your family because of the way he or she looks,

Source: "First They Changed My Name . . .": by Caffilene Allen, as it appeared in *Ms.* magazine, January/February, 1994.

speaks, or acts. Explain why you felt that way. Do you ever feel different or isolated from your parents or guardians because you dress, act, and speak in ways that are more accepted in our culture than they do? Explain. Have you ever had to explain why your parents or guardians do something or speak in a certain way to your friends or to others? How did you feel? Did you feel pride? Embarrassment? Annoyance?

Although I was born in 1951, I grew up speaking the English of an earlier century—a fact I was reminded of one Sunday afternoon at my mother's rest home. A nurse drew me aside and, blushing a little, said uncertainly, "Your mother says Esther has been 'progging' again."   1

Quickly, I put her mind at ease. How well I knew what progging meant. It had been the cause of all my spankings as a young child. Progging was the act of going through belongings that were not yours, digging into clothes drawers, purses, anything that contained intriguing items in its mysterious depths.   2

Though words like "progging" seemed strange to the nurse, the rest home was not more than 12 miles from Tumbling Creek, Tennessee, the town where I grew up. What we called "old" English was the only language that I knew until I was six years old, when I was dragged, wailing and sobbing, onto the school bus. In school, I soon discovered that the lack of communication links from Tumbling Creek to the outside world, as well as the clannish nature of the people who lived there, had allowed two separate cultures, divided by centuries, to exist within miles of each other. At the school, I heard such unfamiliar words as "church," "couch," "living room," "Christ," and "isn't." At home, we used "meetinghouse," "divanette," "front room," "the Good Man," and "ain't." I had vague memories of some of those strange words being spoken occasionally, but whoever had used them had been immediately accused of trying to be like the "town-doogers" (town dwellers). That these were the terms my teachers wanted me to use was incomprehensible.   3

Perhaps my confusion helps to explain why I was surprisingly meek when my teachers took it upon themselves to change my name, thinking that I had misspelled it. They were probably not too far from the truth. Coming from English, Scottish, Irish, and German stock that never left the Tennessee hill area, I inherited a linguistic pattern that was mostly oral and did not include the "th" sound. My mother was most likely trying to give me the good Irish name of Kathleen, but pronounced the "th" with an "f" sound and then spelled it phonetically for the nurse. All went well until I got to the first grade, where my teacher first decided that my name must be Caffie Lene but then settled on Kathleen. She told me I had to start writing it that way. My mother had no objection: whatever the God-Teacher said must be done—even if it meant changing my name.   4

In the second grade, my teacher told me that it was a law that everyone had to have a middle name, and that I should choose one for myself, so she could put it on my permanent record. I was delighted. Here was my chance to be Barbara Allen, the focus of an English ballad in which the heroine rejects "sweet William," supposedly causing his death. When they both eventually die of broken hearts, a rose grows from William's grave and a briar from Barbara Allen's. Why I wished to become the namesake of such a person is something that I have never wanted to examine too closely, but I was absolutely thrilled when my teacher wrote Kathleen Barbara Allen on my permanent record.

If I had known how much frustration would result from these changes, I would have been less thrilled. I soon discovered that Kathleen was one of the most common names in school, and that I was doomed to almost always have a number added after my name to distinguish me from the others with the same name. By the sixth grade I had developed a somewhat oversensitive approach to life, and began to notice that I was never Kathy #1 but always Kathy #2 or #3. I still had enough of my mother's awe for teachers that I was never able to express my displeasure to them.

I was given the chance to reclaim my name when, as a senior in high school, I was required to produce a birth certificate in order to graduate. By that time, I had almost forgotten about Caffilene, so I was very surprised to see the name on my birth certificate. My teachers were even more surprised, since the ones who had changed my name were long gone. A new problem loomed: I was one name on the school records and another on my birth certificate—therefore, I couldn't graduate. It took several teachers and a great deal of trouble to convince the bureaucracy I should be allowed to graduate.

Changing my name had a profound effect on my sense of identity, but my teachers had an equally long-lasting impact on my relationship with my mother, who believed that if the teacher said it was right, it was so. Having only a third-grade education obtained in a one-room country schoolhouse, she had the same reverence for school-teachers as she had for the mysterious government, which kept her and her five children alive by sending a monthly Social Security check after my father was killed in the copper mines when I was 16 months old. To her, the government and the teachers were the keepers of some noble and powerful system upon which our survival and well-being depended, and we would be nothing less than ungrateful fools if we questioned their sterling wisdom. My four older brothers and sisters seemed to catch on sooner than I did: if my mother ever found out that the teachers she revered had a low opinion of her way of speech and life, she would be deeply hurt. For her peace of mind, my siblings learned to behave and speak one way at school and another way at home, whereas I would bound home, armed with linguistic rules that created a lifelong conflict between my mother and me. My first demand was that she allow me to call her Mommy rather than Miney (actually, her name was de Sara de Mina de Magdalene Pless Allen, but we couldn't get all of that out).

"What for?" was her reply. None of her ancestors had ever done such a thing.   9

"Because the teacher said I wasn't showing proper respect."   10

She became even more puzzled. "What does that mean?"   11

I had to admit that I didn't know. "But she said I was supposed to call you Mommy, and so I'm going to."   12

Well, the God-Teacher had said it, so it had to be.   13

She had an easier time with my second question. After I learned to read about Dick and Jane, I soon realized that everyone—even Jane— was sometimes referred to as "he." Having a strictly literal approach to life, I couldn't understand. When I asked my teachers why only the male pronoun was used, they laughed at me, so I took my question home to my mother. Readily, she replied with the only answer that a good Baptist could give, and one which she sincerely believed: "Because men are better than women." I soon learned to stop asking my mother questions.   14

By the fourth grade I had become increasingly ashamed of my mother and almost came to despise her for her manner and speech. One evening at the supper table when she was speaking improper English, chewing with her mouth open, and propping her elbows on the table, I found myself staring in open disgust. Suddenly, she stopped speaking in mid-sentence and glared at me, her face turning purple. By now, I was familiar enough with this scene to know what was going to happen next. Sure enough, I escaped from my seat just in time to miss being hit by the fork that she threw at my eyes. "Stop looking at me like I was a freak!" she screamed. Later, after the dishes were washed and put away, I went into the kitchen to get a glass of water. Through the screen door, I saw my mother sitting on the back steps, watching the sun go down behind the Blue Ridge Mountains. Her shoulders were shaking with silent sobs. For the first time, I sensed the depth of her isolation and despair; I also got my first inkling that she was not the one who was in the wrong. An intelligent, beautiful woman raised in a fundamentalist culture that assured her that she was nothing simply because she was a woman, she now was confronted with the scorn, brought home to her by her daughter, of those whom she had once revered as her benevolent protectors. Now she was sure that she was truly worthless.   15

Even though that moment gave me some understanding of my mother, it did not give me enough to change my ways totally. I continued to try to convince her that she needed to speak and act more like the people in town. I didn't have much success by myself, but I eventually got help from a rather surprising source. My mother had adamantly refused to get a telephone or a car, which were becoming more and more common in Tumbling Creek by the mid-1960s, so it was an incred-   16 ible surprise to me when, one day when I was in the seventh grade, she brought home a television. Never in my life, not before or since, have I felt such a sense of wonder as when the television was first turned on in our house and people showed up on the screen in my living room who were fit to watch and listen to. Suddenly, the mountains seemed a little less lonely and my mother a little less mean.

By this time, I was pretty much considered an oddity by everyone 17 who knew me. Since I always ate first, with the men rather than with the women, who had to wait until the men were finished before they could even sit down at the table, I became a third sex; people would say, "the men, the women, and Kathy." My love for books and writing seemed especially odd and somewhat slothlike to those working in the fields and the house morning, noon, and night in order to survive (which seemed to include everyone except me). And more than once, students in my class had been sent to the principal's office for calling me a nigger-lover. (No one in Tumbling Creek or Copperhill had ever met a person of color, but racism existed there, and my support of the civil rights movement increased my isolation.) But there, on the television, were people who gave me some inkling of another world out there where I might find others with ideas like mine. Peter, Paul, and Mary showed up singing "Blowing in the Wind" at a civil rights march. One afternoon, while my mother and I were watching *Who Do You Trust?*, newscasters interrupted to report a confrontation between Governor George Wallace and a black student trying to enter the University of Alabama. My spirits rose. Although at first they all seemed to be losing, at least there were people out there fighting for the same things that I thought were right.

I picked up "correct" pronunciation and grammar from TV, as well 18 as an accent that gradually replaced my east Tennessee twang. My mother, on the other hand, changed the words to suit her own style of speech. Once, she told me that her favorite TV show was "Feenanzie." When I told her there was no such show, she retorted that there certainly was: "It's the one that has Hoss Cartwright and Little Joe and advertises Chevrolets."

Nevertheless, my mother did let television temper her cultural 19 approach to life. She stopped trying to compliment my friends by telling them they were "just as fat as a little pig." She learned to stop asking the kids I brought home if they wanted a "dope," which meant a soft drink in Tumbling Creek. Most important, through TV, she learned to understand me and the ways that I had already adopted, and so television made life a little easier for both of us.

Many years have gone by. I grew up and left Tumbling Creek, as my 20 teachers and my mother always knew I would. But even now, thinking back on those times and conflicts, I find my emotions toward my mother and my teachers still bound up in the same love-hate web most of us reserve for our families only. In a way, my teachers were my family. They were the first to encourage my love for learning, to find scholarships for me, to bring me books to read during the long, lonely summer months, to encourage my writing, to express their belief that I could even make a living as a writer. But at the same time, they taught me to hate my culture, to despise people who had a different linguistic approach to life, even if one of those people was my mother. After many long years, I have managed finally to reconcile to some extent my world with my mother's. Regaining a sense of pride in my Appalachian heritage and an appreciation for who my mother was as a person was one of the hardest and most valuable tasks of my adult life.

Questions for Reflection and Discussion

1. Caffilene Allen's mother held her teachers in such regard that Allen refers to them as "the God-Teachers." Why do you think Caffilene Allen's mother held her children's teachers in such high regard? Did your parents or guardians feel this way about your teachers?
2. Allen was different than her family and neighbors in several very important ways: She liked to read, she supported the civil rights movement, she didn't understand why all people were referred to as "he" (a practice that is no longer acceptable because such language is considered sexist), she insisted on eating with the men rather than waiting to eat with the women, she was often ashamed of her mother's speech and manners. What would you do and how would you feel if one of your children was very different than you and the other members of your family and cultural group?

Topics for Writing

1. Recall a time when you got in trouble in school (either elementary or high school) and one or both of your parents or guardians had to meet with the teacher, principal, coach, or other school administrator. Write an essay in which you explain and describe precisely what happened and whether your parents sided with you or the school representative. In your conclusion, explain whether you feel your parents did the right thing, in supporting you or in supporting the school administration.
2. Return to the free write you completed before you read Caffilene Allen's essay. Use the information there to write an essay in which you describe a time or occasion when you felt either great pride or great embarrassment about the behavior of one of your family members. Be sure to answer the important who, what, where, why, when, and how questions so that your readers can fully understand what happened. In your conclusion, explain if you still feel great pride or embarrassment, or if the passage of time has enabled you to see the incident or event in a different way.

WHEN GOD BLINKS

Rick Bragg

The next selection is a chapter from a book-length memoir entitled *All Over but the Shoutin'* by Rick Bragg, in which he praises his mother for her courage and determination in raising his brother and him under terribly poor conditions, both before and after his father died. In this chapter, Bragg recalls many aspects of his childhood, all of which help the reader to realize that the poverty he and his family endured affected every aspect of his childhood— and left lasting scars.

Vocabulary

idyllically (paragraph 2)   as if everything were perfect or ideal

stood sentry (2)   guarded

Faulkner (4)   William Faulkner, a very famous southern writer (1897–1962) who often wrote about poor people and conditions

sinister (5)   evil

commodity cheese (11)   huge chunks of cheese given free to poor people

caste system (15)   a system that divides people based on their class or wealth

the Snopeses . . . and the Forresters (18)   country folk who were uneducated and down to earth

eccentric (21)   someone with odd habits; unusual

bawdy limericks (21)   off-color words

limericks (21)   rhyming lines or phrases; a short or informal poem, usually funny

ornery (22)   grouchy; stubborn

enthralled (26)   fascinated

Suggestions for Free Writing

Before you read this chapter from Bragg's memoir, take about 15 minutes to free-write on the following topics:

Human beings want and need to feel a sense of belonging. Many of us feel this sense of belonging in our families, but some of us feel it with our friends, the people we go to school with, the people we work with, or the people we play

Source: "When God Blinks" from *All Over but the Shoutin'* by Rick Bragg. Copyright 1997 by Rick Bragg. Reprinted by permission of Pantheon Books, a division of Random House, Inc.

sports with. Describe the people with whom you feel a close sense of belonging because you can trust them and they can trust you, because you enjoy being with them, and because you have much in common.

We were raised, my brothers and me, to believe God is watching over us. The day we left our grandma standing in the driveway for that massive, hateful house on a hill, I guess He had something in His eye. Maybe it was Vietnam. Maybe it was Selma. Either way, as my daddy's Buick rumbled between the low mountain ridges and crossed into Cherokee County from Calhoun, we were on our own. I was six years old.

1

I will forever remember my first look at that house. It stood like a monument on the hill, smack-dab in the middle of a little farming community called, idyllically, Spring Garden. It was high and white, a two-story farmhouse with big, square columns in front, too big to reach around. There was a massive gray barn, and a smokehouse, and off in the distance, a string of shacks. The house stood sentry over fields of cotton and corn, and was ringed with live oak trees, trees that had outlived generations of men. There was an apple orchard and a pasture and acres and acres of empty, lonely pines.

2

He had told Momma he had a good job, but to rent this house, we thought, he would have to be a county commissioner, at least. For all our lives we had lived in tiny mill houses or in relatives' homes, places so small that people sit with their knees touching and their arms tucked in tight at their sides, the way prisoners sit when they are fresh out of jail. This, we thought, as the car rolled toward it on the blacktop, was a mansion.

3

But as the car pulled closer and turned up the long driveway, I saw that it was no mansion, only the corpse of one. I saw peeling paint and missing boards, and looking back on it now I know that my father must have rented it for a song, because it was a house no one else would have. We would have said it was straight out of Faulkner, if we had known who Faulkner was. The bathroom, like the one we had back at our grandma's little house, was out back, down a dirt trail, bordered by ragweed.

4

Inside, where the wallpaper hung like dead skin, a great mahogany staircase stretched up to a sinister, deserted second floor, a floor that we never used, one that remained covered in a fine gray powder of dust, like old graveyard dirt, the whole time we lived there. Even now, I can close my eyes and see the footprints in it, left by someone a week before, a month, years.

5

The house was almost empty. There was a bed in one room where Sam and I slept with our little brother, Mark, who was still just a baby, and a bed in another room for them. I remember a couch and a chair in the living room and a kitchen table, and nothing else, just space. It had a fireplace and a wood heater, which is fine when you have something to burn, and electric lights that only worked in a few rooms. The

6

floor had so many cracks that the wind reached up to tickle your ankles, like cold, invisible fingers reaching out of the ground. I jumped the first time I felt it, and my daddy laughed.

I believe now that if I would have listened very carefully, I could   7
have heard my mother's heart break and tinkle down in pieces on the warped floor. She did not say anything, of course. She never said anything. It was just one more broken promise, one more sharp slap to her pride. But if that was all she had to endure, she could.

I was afraid of that house. Sam was afraid. I think even she was   8
afraid. For the first month I slept with my head covered up, but there was no hiding from the monster in that old house. It was quiet at first, but it was only resting. It was with us just as sure as if it had been locked into one of those closets in the abandoned second floor.

For a little while, I believe, we were something very like a family. My   9
momma cleaned up the ground floor of the old house, stuck our baby pictures on the wall with Scotch tape and put a few plastic flowers on the empty shelves. For weeks, our daddy woke up early and went off to work at Merrill's body shop, carrying a lunch box full of bologna sandwiches and a Little Debbie snack cake. He came back home smelling of dust and paint, not whiskey, and on Fridays he cashed his check and put money in my momma's hand for groceries before going to get drunk. We had not one bottle of milk in the refrigerator but two. One pure white—what we call "sweet" milk—and one chocolate. We could drink as much milk as we wanted. The milkman came back for the half-gallon bottles, and left more. I thought it was free.

Our daddy came home almost every evening and we sat around a   10
table and ate supper. I can remember him holding three-year-old Mark on his lap, trying to get him to eat off his plate, remember how the food got in his hair and his son's hair, how my momma would run over, wiping, fussing, and my daddy laughing and laughing and laughing. It was nice, like I said, to hear that deep voice laugh.

I remember him sitting in the living room with a cigarette in his   11
thin fingers, talking about living, about life. He talked of life beyond cotton fields and Goodwill stores and commodity cheese.

I guess he was trying, to be a daddy, a husband. But even at six   12
years old I knew not to count on him, believe in him. I walked around him like he was a sleeping dog, afraid every minute that he would wake up and bite me. But the weeks turned into months, and still the demons in him were quiet, till the summer vanished into fall and the giant oaks around that giant house began to burn with orange, yellow and red.

Sam and I grew less and less afraid of the house. We climbed the   13
stairs and slid down the bannister until Momma hollered at us to quit or she would whup us, which was an empty threat if ever there was one. We

even dragged her up there, herself, one day, when Daddy was gone. She laughed like a schoolgirl.

But I never got completely over my fear of that second floor, so empty, like a family of ghosts lived over our heads. I would imagine they were chasing me as I flung myself on the bannister and slid down to safety, down to my momma and my brothers and the smell of baking cornbread and boiling beans and the sound of the Gospel Hour drifting from the plastic radio. 14

It was about that time I had my first taste of education in the Alabama public school system. We went to school at Spring Garden, where, in the first grade, I fell in love with a little girl named Janice. Janice Something. But the first grade was divided into a rigid caste system by the ancient teacher, and I was placed clear across the room from her. They named the sections of the divided classroom after birds. She was a Cardinal, one of the children of the well-to-do who studied from nice books with bright pictures, and I was a Jaybird, one of the poor or just plain dumb children who got what was left after the good books were passed out. Our lessons were simplistic, and I could always read. I memorized the simple reader, and the teacher was so impressed she let me read with the Cardinals one day. I did not miss a word, but the next day I was back with the Jaybirds. The teacher—and I will always, always remember this—told me I would be much more comfortable with my own kind. I was six, but even at six you understand what it means to be told you are not good enough to sit with the well-scrubbed. 15

Her name is lost in my head. She was an aristocrat, a white-haired woman with skin like a wadded-up paper bag that she had smeared red lipstick on and dusted with white powder. I did not know it then, but I was getting my first taste of the gentry, the old-money white Southerners who ran things, who treated the rest of the South like beggars with muddy feet who were about to track up their white shag carpeting. She drove a big car with fender skirts, probably a Cadillac, and wore glasses shaped like cat's eyes. 16

On Sunday evenings, we visited my daddy's people, strangers to me then, strangers to me now. But for one slender ripple in time I had a second family, a people unlike my momma's people. These were people, the menfolk anyway, without any governors on their lives, not even the law. They drove the dirt roads drunk, the trunks of their cars loaded down with bootleg liquor and unstamped Old Milwaukee beer, the springs squealing, the bumpers striking sparks on the rocks, the men driving with one hand and alternately lighting cigarettes and fiddling with the AM radio with the other, searching for anything by Johnny Horton. 17

They fought each other like cats in a sack, existing—hell no, living—somewhere between the Snopeses of Faulkner's imagination and the Forresters of *The Yearling*. It is a point of fact that the whole male con- 18 tingent of the family got into a brawl in town—"they wasn't fightin' nobody else, just each other," my momma said—and, as a family, went to jail. One cousin by marriage—and I am not making this up—refused to wear shoes, even in winter. They were constantly bailing each other out of jail, not for anything bad, merely for refusing to march in step with the twentieth century. If they had been machines instead of men, they would have had just one speed, wide-open, and they would have run at it until they blew themselves apart. I guess, in a way, they did. They are all dead now, not from age, but misuse.

Against my will, I grew fond of them. I would have liked to have known them better. 19

What I know I learned from those Sunday evenings, when we visited 20 my granddaddy Bobby and granny Velma Bragg's house to eat a meal that took hours to cook and a solid thirty minutes just to put on the table. I remember fine fried chicken, and mashed potatoes piled high with a small lake of butter in the middle, and cracklin' cornbread, and butter beans with a white chunk of fat pork floating like a raft in the middle, and sweet tea poured from gallon pickle jars. They lived in a big, rambling farmhouse, paid for with money from Bobby's steady job at the cotton mill, and they had a short, fat dog named Boots who was about 150 in dog years and moved stiffly around the yard, blind as a concrete block.

Bobby Bragg, a white-haired little man, was what we would now 21 call an eccentric. He still had a horse and wagon, and it was not too uncommon then to see Bobby riding around the mill village in his long underwear, drunk as a lord, alternately singing and cussing and— it must be said—shouting out bawdy limericks to mill workers and church ladies.

The town's police officers seldom bothered the ornery old man, 22 mainly because arresting him would would have left them not only with an unmanned horse and wagon but Bobby himself, and everyone with even a lick of sense knew Bobby would cut you as soon as look at you.

I was amazed by him. His hip bone was prone to come out of joint 23 and when it happened he would not go to a doctor or do anything else that was remotely sensible, but he would limp and cuss and drink and limp and cuss and drink until all he could do was lie on the bed and cuss and drink. Until, one day, my granny Bragg had enough. She reached down and got his bad leg by the foot, and commenced to jerking and twisting and jerking and twisting until his hip bone popped back into place with a sound like, well, a pop, and he was cured.

When sober, he often dressed for dinner, not in a suit but in a fresh 24 pair of overalls, and a white button-down shirt that was stiff as a board with starch. "Clean as a pin," Momma said. Of the bad things that can be said about my granddaddy, no one could ever say he did not have a certain style. (It is widely believed in my family that a good many of my peculiarities, I most certainly got from him.)

My granny Velma Bragg was a sad-eyed little woman who looked   25
very much like the part Cherokee she was, a sweet-natured woman with
great patience who hovered over the men when they drank whiskey at a
beautiful dining room table, trying to wipe up what they split before it
ate away the varnish. I remember she was always kind, always gentle,
especially to my momma. I guess, in a way, she had an idea what was in
store for her. Momma and Granny Bragg still talk, every week. Survivors,
both of them.

After supper the men went one way and the women went another.   26
The old man, Bobby, would hold court on the porch, surrounded by his
sons. The men drank—Lord, how they could drink—from endless cans
of beer or from a jug when they had one. They even talked about
drinking as they drank, and smoked Camels down to the barest nub
before flipping them out in the dirt of the yard. When I close my eyes I
can still see the trail of orange sparks it made. My momma often would
holler for me to come inside, but I was enthralled. These men were what
my momma's kinfolk called sinners, and it seemed to me like sinning
was a lot of fun.

Listening to them, I learned much of of what a boy should know,   27
of cars, pistols, heavy machinery, shotguns and love, all of which, these
men apparently believed, can be operated stone drunk. I learned that
fighting drunk is better than sober because a clear-headed man hurts
more when hit. I learned that it is okay to pull a knife while fighting
drunk as long as you are cautious not to cut off your own head.

I learned that whiskey will cure anything from a toothache to   28
double pneumonia, if you drink enough. (Once when I was bad sick
with flu, they even gave it to me. They heated it in a pan, being careful
not to let it get anywhere close to an open flame, and poured it over
honey in a coffee cup. Then someone, my granny probably, squeezed a
lemon into it. I drank it down in four gulps, took two steps, a hop, a skip
and a staggering leap and passed dead out on the floor. From what I
heard later, everyone except my momma thought it was pretty amusing.
I cannot say it cleared up any congestion, but it made my head hurt so
bad that I did not notice it so much.)

They talked about the mill. They talked about dogs. They talked   29
about fistfights and bootleggers and, a little, about war, but not my
daddy's war. They talked about the new war, Vietnam, but my daddy
never joined in, that I remember. He drank, smoked his cigarettes.
Once, I recall, he came off the porch and walked off into the night for
a long time. I remember it because Momma came outside, some time
later, ready to go, and we had to search for him. We found him in the
car, just sitting, smoking.

Now and then, the men talked of what they called "the nigger   30
trouble," but I could not attach any significance to that. We had no
contact with black people beyond a wave, now and then, from a car or

from the side of a road. I was not of a world where there were maids, cooks or servants. When they picked in the cotton field beside white pickers, like my momma, they kept to themselves. There were no black people in my school, and at that time no black person had ever been in my house or in my yard. So how, I wondered, could there be trouble between us? They lived in their world, and we lived in our world. It became gradually clear, as I sat there listening, watching the orange comets of their cigarettes arch across the dark, what the trouble was about.

They were sick and tired of living in their world. They wanted to   31
live in our world, too.

Questions for Reflection and Discussion

1. Bragg still remembers being told by a teacher that he would be more comfortable with his "own kind." "I was six," he says, "but even at six you understand what it means to be told you are not good enough to sit with the well-scrubbed." Did your elementary school teachers treat all of their students equally, or did they group or divide or separate students? On what did they base their decisions?

2. Although Bragg's father's family was very poor, he describes them (paragraphs 17–29) in a very positive and loving way, almost as if it was their peculiar habits that made them wonderful. Do you have relatives or friends whose unusual or peculiar habits or lifestyles make them seem wonderful to you?

Topics for Writing

1. In paragraphs 15 and 16, Bragg describes the humiliation he felt when a teacher made him return to the lower reading group, although he could do the work in the higher reading group. Write an essay in which you recall when a teacher treated you or another student (or students) unfairly because of your race, gender, ethnic background, social class, or economic status. Or recall a time when a teacher stood up for your rights or the rights of another student when you or the other student were being treated unfairly because of race, gender, ethnic background, social class, or economic status.

2. In paragraph 19, Bragg says he wished that he could have gotten to know his father's family better because he felt a sense of belonging with his "father's people." And in paragraphs 17 to 29, he describes them in great and loving detail.

Return to the free write you completed before you read Bragg's chapter. Use the information there to write an essay about a group of people (family, friends, co-workers, people with whom you go to school or play sports) with whom you feel a sense of belonging. Explain the kind of relationship you have: why you feel comfort, trust, and confidence when you are with these people; what you contribute to the relationship; what you gain from the relationship; what you learn from the relationship; how you feel because of the relationship; how you grow and change because of the relationship. Be sure to give enough background information, and answer the important who, what, where, when, why, and how questions so that the reader understands the relationship fully.

Reading 7–6

SHENANDOAH'S SECRET HISTORY

Audrey J. Horning

The next selection, entitled "Shenandoah's Secret History," explains the way city planners in Virginia during the1930s decided that a group of people who lived in the southern Appalachian Mountains should be forced to move from their homes and farms to make way for Shenandoah National Park. No one asked the people if they wanted to move, and no one stood up for the rights of these people. In fact, the city planners decided the move would be good for these people because they were nothing more than uncivilized "backward mountaineers."

Recently, archaeologists conducted a study of these people and their way of life (including interviews with some of the people who were forced to move), and they discovered that the 500 families who were relocated against their will were not backward at all; instead, they were living in an interesting, thriving, successful community before the "experts" came along and changed their lives forever.

This article is similar to the type of reading that would be assigned in a college-level archaeology class (the digging up and studying of sites where a group of people lived in order to understand the way they lived), an anthropology class (the study of groups of people), or a history class.

In paragraphs 3 and 24 and 25, you will find some words in brackets. This means that the authors inserted words into a quoted passage in order to make the meaning clearer to the reader.

Vocabulary

barter (paragraph 1)   a system of trading, using goods rather than money

disparate (2)   different; unlike each other

visionaries (2)   people who have great plans

unlettered folk (3)   people who are unable to read or write

earmarked (4)   intended

eschewed (4)   avoided

reconcile (6)   bring together; make sense of

nondescript (6)   impossible to recognize

Source: "Shenandoah's SECRET History," by Audrey J. Horning, *Archaeology Magazine*, Vol. 53, No. 1, Jan./Feb. 2000. Copyright © 2000 by The Archaeological Institute of America. Reprinted by permission.

deciduous forests (7)   trees that lose their leaves in fall
vestiges (7)   traces
burgeoning (7)   growing
inevitable (8)   bound to happen
stultifying (8)   to cause to appear stupid
flawed (9)   not done correctly
gingerly (9)   carefully
venomous (9)   poisonous
eking out an existence (9)   barely making a living
precariously (10)   uncertainly, insecurely
artifacts (10)   an archaeologist's term meaning evidence of human existence
systematic surface collection (11)   an archaeological method of collecting material
tangible (11)   real
delineating (12)   showing; marking
forest regeneration (13)   forest regrowth
nonchalantly (14)   casually
discrepancies (14)   differences
semi-subterranean (16)   halfway below ground
dismantled (17)   taken apart
bottomland (20)   the richest and most fertile farmland
charismatic (21)   having great charm and personal appeal
belying (22)   proving something is not true
anathema (23)   hated
moral imperative (24)   required to do something because it is believed to be right
codified (25)   organized
genealogical (25)   the study of families by generation
ethnographic research (25)   research done by going into the "field" to talk to and observe the people being studied
precluded (25)   prevented
egalitarian (27)   equal and fair
utopia (27)   a place where everything is perfect
replete (27)   complete
flotsam (28)   washed up; useless
meticulously (28)   very carefully and neatly

Suggestions for Free Writing

Before you read the article, take about 15 minutes to free-write on the following topics:

The apartment or house in which we live has a lot to do with our comfort, well-being, and happiness, but so does the neighborhood in which we live. Think about your neighborhood, and make two lists (with about ten items on each list). The first list should contain all of the elements you like about your neighborhood, and the second list should contain all of the elements you do not like about your neighborhood.

In one of the most progressive and productive countries in the world, and in that section of the country which has had its civilization and wealth longest, we find an area where the people are still living the frontier life of the backwoods, where the civilization is that of the eighteenth century, where people speak the English of Shakespeare's time, where the large majority of the inhabitants have never seen a steamboat or a railroad, where money is as scarce as in colonial days, and all trade is barter. These conditions are to be found throughout the broad belt of the Southern Appalachians.

1

Such were the conditions found in northwestern Virginia by geographer Ellen Churchill Semple in 1901. Thirty-two years later, a disparate collection of visionaries seeking the ideal location for an eastern national park found that little had changed in Virginia's Blue Ridge. Sociologist Mandel Sherman and journalist Thomas Henry had just published *Hollow Folk*, a study of the inhabitants of what in December 1935 would officially become Shenandoah National Park; they penned this astonished observation:

2

> Here, hidden in deep mountain pockets, dwell families of unlettered folk, of almost pure Anglo-Saxon stock, sheltered in tiny, mud-plastered log cabins and supported by a primitive agriculture. One of these settlements [Corbin Hollow] has no community government, no organized religion, little social organization wider than that of the family and clan, and only traces of organized industry. The ragged children, until 1928, never had seen the flag or heard of the Lord's Prayer; the community is almost completely cut off from the current of American life. It is not of the twentieth century.

3

Beginning in the 1920s, the Commonwealth of Virginia had set about acquiring what would eventually total 196,000 acres in northwestern Virginia for the new national park, which would feature the 97-mile-long, ridge-top Skyline Drive (now 105 miles) and address the recreational needs of millions of Depression-weary Americans living within a day's drive. Although the lands earmarked for the new park were covered with homes and farms, there was little public outcry when inhabitants of the nearly 5,000 individual land tracts were expelled, their lands presented to the federal government. After all, the Blue Ridge dwellers were not only different from the mainstream of American society, but, according to one contemporary journalist, their existence in the dark hollows represented "about the limit of destitution at which human life could be sustained." Park promoters and government officials publicized the fact that "these people will be moved to more civilized regions of agriculture and industry." The creation of the national park propelled these backward mountaineers into a world they had pre-

4

viously eschewed. Or had they?

Sixty years after the establishment of Shenandoah National Park, archaeological investigation has revealed that pre-park life in the Blue Ridge wasn't as uncivilized as was long reported. Designed to inventory the material remains of the park's more recent human past, the Survey of Rural Mountain Settlement project focused specifically on Nicholson, Corbin, and Weakley Hollows on the eastern slopes of the Blue Ridge, formerly home to three communities with eighteenth-century roots. Conducted by a small team of archaeologists from the Colonial Williamsburg Foundation on behalf of the National Park Service, the study complemented two decades of archaeological research into the park's prehistory. At least 460 people were forced to abandon their homes in the three hollows when the park was created, taking their place among the 500 or so families who were displaced park-wide. These three hollows, located in the shadow of granite-topped Old Rag Mountain, made for an ideal case study.

Although structures throughout the park were razed and burned by Civilian Conservation Corps recruits—young men drafted into the New Deal make-work program who were charged with restoring nature to the new park—selected homes in Nicholson Hollow were spared the torch. Log houses were permitted to decay under a policy of benign neglect, a nod to the park's human history. Most of these have long since succumbed to falling trees or violent weather, their chestnut logs tumbling to the ground to decay into a rich hardwood humus. We have recorded the architecture that has survived into the 1990s. We also read transcripts and listened to more than 200 hours of taped interviews with former residents, recorded over the past 25 years. We interviewed those still living nearby, some of whom accompanied us on an emotional journey back to the site of their old homesteads, struggling to reconcile the present forested landscape with the open fields of their youth, the nondescript piles of stone with their proud houses. Although the federally funded Resettlement Administration had at the time set up seven communities outside of the park for displaced park residents, many chose to resettle on small holdings near park boundaries.

Today's hikers along the shady trails through the park's dense deciduous forests are likely treading on tracks that once bore traffic between homes and farms. Pausing for a sip at a clear, cold spring, the careful observer may note how the water's flow is carefully channeled and contained within a rock-lined box. Occasional ceramic sherds or glass fragments stare up at the thirsty adventurer, in mute testimony to past delicacies once stored in the cool, dark spring. Vestiges of apple and peach orchards attract the park's burgeoning bear population, while the numerous white-tailed deer dine on the daffodils and day lilies marking old flower beds, as well as on the extensive new-growth forests that blanket former cornfields.

By systematically walking the 2,500 hilly acres in Nicholson, 8
Corbin, and Weakley hollows and by analyzing aerial photographs, historic maps, and property records, our team has recorded 88 settlement sites. Residents displaced in the 1930s were descendants of a diverse mix of settlers moving south and west in the mid-eighteenth century. English, Welsh, Scots-Irish, Irish, German, and African-American settlers colonized the hills that had been inhabited by Native Americans for at least 10,000 years. From this ethnic stew a strong local identity would emerge, based upon kinship, geography, and shared economies. The archaeological record, however, reveals that this local Blue Ridge identity was not the inevitable result of isolation or the stultifying impact of the "dark interior valleys" described by Sherman and Henry.

From the first day of the survey in the three hollows it was obvious 9
that some observations about the region were flawed. The often-grueling nature of the fieldwork—packing heavy survey equipment up miles of steep and rocky mountain paths, gingerly wading through icy cold rivers, and suffering innumerable tick bites, recurrent cases of poison ivy, and not infrequent hair-raising encounters with the venomous copperheads and timber rattlers that den in collapsed chimneys—heightened our sense of being outsiders, as belabored in the writings of the 1930s. So nothing was more jarring than stumbling across the remains of a Model T along roads no longer traveled. Automobiles, Coke bottles, Bakelite (hard plastic) toys, cologne, hair tonic, and hot-sauce bottles, even a half-torn 1931 cellulose card calendar featuring the artwork of Maxfield Parrish, all shattered the accepted image of backward hillbillies eking out an existence that was "completely cut off from the current of American life." The recovery of a small, metal ray gun from the rubble of farmer Wesley Corbin's three-room log house in lower Corbin Hollow speaks to a keen awareness of twentieth-century popular culture, if not of imaginary twenty-first-century conflicts. Thomas Henry asked in a 1936 article, "Can the distance between Henry VIII and Franklin D. Roosevelt" ever be bridged by the mountain folk? To us in the field, the answer was already clear: Yes.

Even the site of one down-and-out family's home in upper Corbin 10
Hollow—where a tiny log cabin had perched precariously upon a foundation of uneven, unmortared loose rocks—yielded artifacts demonstrating clear interaction with mainstream American society: mismatched ceramics including one bearing the logo of the Washington, D.C., Ritz Carlton Hotel; a number of toys; 78 RPM record fragments; costume jewelry; dry-cell batteries; and a variety of containers for commercial food products, pharmaceutical remedies, bonded liquor, and soft drinks.

The systematic surface collection of 14 sites in the hollows 11
unearthed tangible material evidence to demonstrate that these people—in contrast to their presentation in *Hollow Folk*—wore shoes,

cured their sore throats not only with a home remedy made from cherry tree bark, but with patent medicines sold in a variety of bottles and vials. They were as likely to purchase bonded liquor as homegrown products, ate their meals on a variety of imported and domestic tablewares, were entertained by the radio and the phonograph, and slept in fancy brass beds as well as on cheap metal cots. They served beverages in containers ranging from tin cans, enameled tin-ware cups, even a "borrowed" tin pitcher from the nearby ridge-top Skyland Resort, to the cut-glass wine goblets now lazily reflecting the sunlight in the overgrown front yard of the former Oscar Sisk home deep in Weakley Hollow.

While Mrs. Bailey Nicholson may have willingly donned her old-timey bonnet to pose for Farm Security Administration photographer Arthur Rothstein in the doorway of her Corbin Mountain home in 1935, she joined her family in dining off the fashionably decorated Japanese porcelain found in the debris of her once-tidy four-room log-and-frame house. The "hollow folk" of the immediate pre-park period clearly had access to the same types of goods that are found on archaeological sites of their era throughout the United States—many no doubt originating from the Sears and Roebuck Company catalog. Of course, some hollow residents were able to afford more than their neighbors. All of them made choices based upon economy, need, and desire, but clearly not constrained by geography nor by their "cultural retardation," as suggested by the 1930s sociologists. Overall, the material record from the hollows underscores an active involvement in American consumer culture, delineating an evolution in individual household economies for the late nineteenth and early twentieth centuries.   12

We recorded 88 sites in measured architectural drawings and black-and-white, color, and digital imagery and surface collected or excavated 14 domestic sites in the three hollows. We mapped each site's location using GPS (Global Positioning System) technology, and even employed GPS to find sites recorded on historic maps but lost through forest regeneration. And we documented lingering architectural traces: the vestiges of stone chimneys and foundations where dwellings, churches, schools, gristmills, sawmills, and distilleries once stood.   13

In 1932, visiting journalist Joan Hampton from the *Baltimore Sun* commented upon the quality of architecture in the Old Rag Mountain vicinity: 14

> The rustic charm of the Shenandoah cabins is very very rustic. Most of them are made of roughly hewn logs; the chinks are filled, somewhat nonchalantly, with mud, and the interior, in happy instances, is whitewashed. Since one rarely encounters a straight line or a true angle in the walls or ceilings, there are likely to be conspicuous discrepancies between wall and doors or window frames. No matter, says the mountaineer, and fills up the space with mud.   15

Hampton clearly did not venture far enough into Weakley Hollow to observe the stately three-story frame, stone, and brick dwelling occu-   16 pied by the Haywood Nicholson family on a 432-acre tract owned by local resident Hettie Hudson. Nor could she have visited the five-room, double-end chimney frame dwelling of James Oscar Sisk, flanked by three well-built semi-subterranean storage buildings and accompanied by a barn, the ruins of a nineteenth-century sawmill, and seven other out-buildings. Up slope from the Sisk farm was a series of modest log and frame houses owned at the time of the park's creation by William Weakley and his sons. Further down the hollow, the site of George Weakley's former home was surface collected by our team in 1996. Notable objects recovered include an ornate Art Deco pocket-watch face and the handle from a military silverware set dated 1917—neatly contradicting Sherman and Henry's 1933 contention that "neither the recent World War nor the Civil War meant anything to the hollow folk." On that score, county records never examined by Sherman and Henry indicate active military enrollment from the hollows.

As in any rural community, the quality of housing and the size of landholdings varied. In Nicholson Hollow, twentieth-century farms ranged from the five acres held by George Corbin to the 237-acre farm of Thomas Nicholson. Although several of his Corbin Hollow neighbors were propertyless, J. E. Jenkins owned 29 acres in the base of the hollow. Back down in Weakley Hollow, Tera Weakley owned only a single acre on the steep northern slope of Old Rag Mountain, where a log dwelling, henhouse, and peach orchard were perched. Although these well-hidden structures were the only ones in Weakley Hollow that were not dismantled by the CCC, precious little survives to be recorded. The 16-by-18-foot chestnut log house has fallen from its stone foundation, its 8-by-18-foot frame addition has rotted away, and only two rock piers now hint at the location of a front porch. The 12-by-16-foot henhouse, also of chestnut logs with hand-rived vertical sheathing, was crushed by a falling tree when Hurricane Fran roared through the Old Rag Valley in 1996. [17]

Analysis of the archaeological, documentary, and oral historical data from the hollows has revealed a rich and complex local history, one that was not isolated, but ever-changing in response to local, regional, and national conditions. In Weakley Hollow, a tangle of trees and dense undergrowth now lines a popular trail up Old Rag Mountain through the former village of Old Rag, which once boasted a post office, two stores, two churches, a cemetery, and a school. On a broad, flat terrace in the center of the village, excavation of Old Rag's oldest home—built in 1750, according to local lore-unearthed fragments of eighteenth-century creamware and pipestems. Sites along the abandoned Old Rag Road through Weakley Hollow, a road with eighteenth-century origins, attest to the nineteenth- and twentieth-century development of sawmills, gristmills, distilleries, and smithies. The road itself once led outside of the present park boundaries to villages at either end of the Old Rag Valley. [18]

Nicholson Hollow's farm-based economy relied on interaction   19
with the manufacturing pursuits of its Weakley Hollow neighbors.
Extensive terracing and stabilization of the banks of the swift-moving
Hughes River affirm a long-term vision of land maintenance.
Nineteenth-century census returns indicate that Nicholson Hollow
farmers were producing for a market as well as for subsistence. Grain
grown in the hollow was marketed via the local mills and shipped
throughout the state. Corn and orchard products were distilled into
whiskey and brandy for the regional market. Three substantial nineteenth-century distilleries have been located in the hollows, along with a
series of (well-hidden!) illicit, Prohibition-era stills.

By the early twentieth century, competition over bottomland in the   20
hollow resulted in the establishment of smaller farms further up the
slopes on increasingly marginal land. Nicholson Hollow residents like
George Corbin often sought day labor outside of the hollow for needed
cash income.

Depression-era poverty was a fact in the Blue Ridge, as it was   21
throughout the country. Steep and rocky Corbin Hollow was clearly the
hardest hit in the park area. Ironically, the economic difficulties of
Corbin Hollow were not bred by cultural isolation. Residents had abandoned farming in favor of wage labor at the Skyland Resort, serving as
builders, cleaners, woodcutters, landscapers, porters, and dining room
staff for the resort's charismatic owner, George Freeman Pollock. The
placement of their dwellings on the steep, uncleared slopes in the upper
hollow provided ready access to the Skyland Road. When the Depression
hit and Pollock's income dwindled, the Corbin Hollow laborers had
nowhere to turn.

Items discarded around the upper hollow dwellings reflect a   22
reliance upon purchased rather than cultivated foods. Far higher percentages of tin cans and glass food jars are found on Corbin Hollow
sites than on Nicholson and Weakley hollow sites, where we've found
higher percentages of Mason-style canning jars and agricultural items.
Not surprisingly, the vast majority of park publicity shots were taken
in this one hollow. According to *Hollow Folk*, the poverty there was the
result of social and economic isolation. Corbin Hollow (thinly dis-
guised in the study as "Colvin Hollow" to protect the inhabitants'
privacy) existed at the "lowest end of social development" with "no
general system of communication between the cabins" and "no road
to the outside world." Belying this bleak portrait, the Corbin Hollow
of today is still crisscrossed by the paths that once connected the
homes to the road leading up the ridge. Dating of the architectural
remains by associated artifacts demonstrates that settlement was
directly related to the accessibility of upper Corbin Hollow to the
Skyland Road: homes were built in the 1880s, when the resort was
established.

If the material record is so clear on the twentieth-century life-style [23] of hollow residents, where did the observations in *Hollow Folk* and in regional newspapers come from? And why did so many accept the descriptions as fact? From the mid-nineteenth century to the present, the region of the southern uplands—Appalachia—has been regarded as both all-American and un-American: the truest expression of an American folk culture and the most anathema to the American obsession with progress. Either way, the people of Appalachia have been consistently set apart from the rest of the country.

The creation of the idea of Appalachia is rooted in the nineteenth [24] century, when fiction writer Will Wallace Harney described the southern mountains in *A Strange Land and Peculiar People* (1869) and Berea College president William Goodell Frost weighed in with *Our Contemporary Ancestors in the Southern Mountains* (1899). Such romantic musings, part of the post-Civil War "local color" literary movement, graced the pages of new magazines such as *Harper's Monthly, Scribners,* and *Lippincott's,* publications aimed at northern middle-class audiences. Local color sketches took the form of travelogues, generally reporting on the foreign and unusual nature of backwoods southern life, inevitably emphasizing the otherness of the region. Literary scholar Henry Shapiro has written that magazines aimed to tell their audience "what it wished to hear: that it was the center of the universe and the true bearer of American culture." While stories of the rugged, pioneering adventures of the hardy mountaineers stirred the blood, readers felt a moral imperative to lift Appalachia from its state of "arrested development" and, not coincidentally, to develop its mineral, timber, and scenic resources.

By the 1930s, the notion of the peculiarity and degeneracy of [25] mountain folk had been codified, providing easy justification for the condemnation of land for Shenandoah National Park. Such was the context in which Sherman and Henry described the Blue Ridge inhabitants, influenced by what was already "known" about mountain life. As a sociologist obsessed by a belief in the evolutionary development of society, Sherman merely stacked the hollow communities in ascending order of civilization, with Corbin Hollow on the bottom of the heap, Nicholson Hollow ("a trifle bewildered by the sudden influx of new ideas") just above, Weakley Hollow ("continually running away from reality") slightly better, and two other nearby communities farther up the rungs of social development. Content to use data gathered by amateur sociologist Miriam Sizer, Sherman may not have conducted any field-work on his own. Suspiciously, Sizer was occasionally in the employ of Skyland owner George Freeman Pollock, a chief advocate for the new park. Thomas Henry was another staunch park supporter, who likely saw his partnership with Mandel Sherman as providing the seal of academic approval to the park movement. Folklife scholars Charles Perdue and

Nancy Martin-Perdue of the University of Virginia, who have conducted extensive genealogical and ethnographic research on displaced families and now work closely with a descendants' advocacy group, noted in 1979 that "the middle-class backgrounds of the researchers [of *Hollow Folk*] and the general tenor of the time precluded much of an attempt to consider the culture on its own terms."

Today, the image of a backward mountain past continues to be invoked. Restored by a local trail club, George Corbin's 1921 chestnut log home can be rented by hikers. According to the trail guide, "a night or two spent in the isolation of a restored mountain cabin—lighted by kerosene lantern, heated by a woodstove, lacking running water—provides a hint of the mountain lifestyle." In fact, woodstoves and kerosene lanterns were hardly unusual in rural America in the 1920s and 1930s. Furthermore, George Corbin lived within sight of five neighbors, and only three miles from a store and post office. Captured on tape in a 1977 interview, he fondly recalled, "I'd go down [to the store] once a week and take my eggs down, buy my sugar and coffee . . . buy the best coffee you ever seen, bring it home, and roast it in the stove." He engaged in day labor as far away as West Virginia, traveling by freight train; but also earned money from the potent products of his illegal still. He remembered proudly, "I made it and hauled it into Washington City [D.C.] right clear through Falls Church in a Model T car!" Still, those who opt for a hike up the winding and steep trail through Corbin Hollow learn from the trail guide only that it was "formerly the location of a very poverty-stricken and isolated community."

The archaeological examination of Nicholson, Corbin, and Weakley hollows demonstrates that the local cultures found in the Blue Ridge before the establishment of Shenandoah National Park were not the lifeless remnants of a hardy eighteenth-century pioneer society, as reported in the media and the sociological studies. Nor was life in the hollows an egalitarian utopia, replete with the kind of cooperative work, environmental stewardship, and wealth-sharing longed for by those who established communes just outside the park boundaries in the 1960s and 1970s.

Admitting the complexity of past life in the hollows and acknowledging the involvement of residents in the wider social and economic world is not to deny the existence of a community identity, one that was unique to the Blue Ridge. Instead, it is simply to return control of the past to the displaced, to affirm that hollow dwellers were not mere cultural flotsam stagnating in mountain hollows—to admit that inhabitants may have had a hand in their own destiny, clearly constrained, but not wholly controlled, by their mountainous environment, ethnic stock, or economic advantages or disadvantages. The archaeological, documentary, and oral historical record from the hollows highlights the relative diversity and complexity of the mountain past. Some "hollow folk" were

relatively well-to-do, some were undeniably poor, most owned land, but
a few were squatters; some planted orchards and corn, others raised live-
stock or ran businesses; some marketed traditional crafts locally, others
drove far away for employment; some meticulously swept their yards and
buried their trash, while others merely pitched their garbage down the
many convenient slopes. The mountain folk did not all deserve to be
tarred by the same brush, and neither do today's residents of that myth-
ical place known as Appalachia.

Questions for Reflection and Discussion

1. Have you ever seen houses or an entire neighborhood destroyed because
   of "progress," such as the building of a highway, a mall, a large office or res-
   idential complex? How did it make you feel?
2. Do you think city or state planners could do the same thing to the residents
   of Virginia's Blue Ridge Mountain as they did during the 1930s? Why?

Topics for Writing

1. Imagine that you are a resident of Blue Ridge and you learn that your
   house and your neighborhood are about to be destroyed in order for a
   park to be built. Write a letter to the city planners explaining why this
   should not be done. Be sure to use evidence from Horning's article itself
   to prove that Blue Ridge is a thriving, happy, productive community that
   should not be destroyed. Remember, you can certainly use exact words
   from the article, as long as you place them in quotation marks.
2. Return to the free write you completed before you read the article. Use the
   information there to write an essay in which you describe both the good
   and bad elements of your neighborhood. In order to make it easier to organize your essay, you may want to devote a paragraph to each good thing
   and a paragraph to each bad thing. Include descriptions, details, and
   explanations so that your readers can fully understand your meaning.

Additional Writing Topics about Class and Race in Our Society

1. The selections in this chapter provide evidence that people in our society
   are very much affected by what they look like, what they do for a living, how
   much money they have, the way they speak. Even four-year-old children are
   being judged to determine whether they will "fit in" at an exclusive private
   school. Write an essay in which you describe and explain how you judge
   people. Do you judge them by their appearance, income, race or ethnic

background, or manner of speaking? Or do you judge them based on other factors? If so, what are those factors? Then explain how you think people judge you. Do they judge you based on your appearance, income, race or ethnic background, or do they judge you based on other factors? If so, what are those factors? In your conclusion, decide if you judge people fairly or unfairly and decide if you are being judged fairly or unfairly.

2. Return to Chapter 4, and reread the article "When Money Is Everything, Except Hers." Then reread the first article in this chapter, "Shocking Visits to the Real World." After you have finished rereading these two articles, write an essay in which you decide who is actually better off, Wendy Williams or the very wealthy young adults. In your essay, be certain to explain the reason for your decision. You may certainly use your own experiences and observations of the rich and not-so-rich people you know to support your position.

Chapter
8

Working:
Pursuing Our Passions
or Paying the Bills?

According to an article in the *Utne Reader* magazine (January/February 1999), "Breaking the Job Lock," many Americans are working harder and faster than ever but are feeling less and less satisfaction, believing that they "accomplish little of lasting value" in their work. Many of us, it seems, are working because we *have* to, not because we want to.

Of course we have to work to pay the bills—unless we are like the privileged (and very spoiled) young adults described in the article in Chapter 7 entitled "Shocking Visits to the Real World." Do you remember the young woman whose job interfered with her traditional three-month family vacation in the south of France? The young man who got tired of working in Palm Beach and who described his co-workers as "rednecks"? Another young man who admitted he grew up "as a spoiled brat" and "didn't show up at the office when [he] was supposed to"?

But although most of us work because we have to, some of us are lucky enough to actually like the work we do; economists call this "good work," work that "truly expresses our values and fits our needs." How do we find such work? Through planning? Through luck? Or both? The selections in this chapter offer various perspectives about working for a living: from what not to do during a job interview to making it big in the high-tech industry—without a high school diploma. Hopefully, these readings will help you to think about the kind of work you have done in the past, the kind of work you do now, and the kind of work you want to do in the future.

Pre-reading Activity

Before you read the selections in this chapter, take about 15 minutes to respond to these free-writing topics. They will help you to think about your own working experiences and the working experiences of relatives and friends.

Think back to when you were a very young child: What did you want to be when you grew up? Have your career plans changed over the years? How? Why? Have you ever had to abandon the hope of having a certain career because you did not have the necessary educational background? What is most important to you as you make career or job plans: how much you earn, how much satisfaction you get from your work, or a combination of both? What have you learned about work from your parents or guardians?

You can answer the following questions by simply writing the numbers 1 through 10 and then writing the name of a person who fits into that category. You can use the names of family members, friends, co-workers, or yourself when answering these questions.

1. Who has a career (or job) that makes him or her happy?
2. Who has a career (or job) that makes him or her unhappy?
3. Who has a career (or job) that provides for a very comfortable living?
4. Who has a career (or job) that offers opportunity for advancement?
5. Who has a career (or job) that offers no opportunity for advancement?
6. Who has a career (or job) that requires him or her to supervise others?
7. Who has a career (or job) that requires him or her to take orders from others?
8. Who has a career (or job) that requires a college degree?
9. Who has a career (or job) that requires education beyond a college degree?
10. Who has a career (or job) that does not require a high school diploma?

NEXT TIME, EAT THE PIZZA AFTER THE INTERVIEW

Tom Kuntz

HOW TO AVOID GETTING HIRED

Anne Fisher

In the following two articles, the authors explain what *not* to do when applying for a job. Although these articles are meant to be funny—some of the job applicants described are really out to lunch—applying for a job is a serious, time-consuming, and difficult endeavor. It can take days, weeks, even months to land a good job, beginning with reading the want ads or going to an employment agency, preparing a résumé that will impress a potential employer, setting up interviews, choosing the right clothing to wear, making a good impression during the interview, performing well on employment tests, and getting letters of recommendation. And during this entire process, most people have other major responsibilities: going to school, caring for families, working at their current jobs. Finding a job can be a job in itself.

Vocabulary

From "Next Time, Eat the Pizza after the Interview":

Fortune 1000 companies (paragraph 3)   the top 1000 companies in the United States, based on profits

cum laude (14)   Latin for "with praise"—usually requires a grade point average of 3.5 or higher

From "How to Avoid Getting Hired":

chronicle (paragraph 1)   account; record

dispassionate (2)   without passion or emotion; objective

commiserate (3)   to sympathize with; the writer meant to write "commensurate", which means equal to

Source: "Next Time, Eat the Pizza After the Interview," by Tom Kuntz, *The New York Times*, Week in Review, January 24, 1999. Copyright 1999 by the New York Times Co. Reprinted by permission
Source: "How to Avoid Getting Hired," by Anne Fisher as appeared in *Fortune*, July 21, 1997. Copyright 1997 Time, Inc. Reprinted by permission.

Suggestions for Free Writing

Before you read the two selections, take about 15 minutes to free-write on the following topics:

Think about the job interviews you have had, both the successful and unsuccessful ones. Choose one interview that stands out in your mind and jot down as many facts about it as possible—what you wore, whether you arrived on time, who interviewed you, the questions you were asked, the tests you were required to take, the forms you were asked to fill out. Then explain what you think your greatest strengths are in a job interview situation, and finally, what you think your greatest weaknesses are.

Next Time, Eat the Pizza after the Interview

Clean your fingernails. Make sure no food is stuck between your teeth. Polish your shoes. And your résumé.   1

For years, self-help books have been preaching these basic rules for job interviews. Getting in the door is a good start, of course. It's your chance to separate yourself from that stack of applications, to impress the boss with all your personal charm. The goal isn't just getting in the door, though. It's leaving with a job.   2

But some sad sacks never get the word. A survey of personnel executives at 200 of the Fortune 1000 companies turned up a wide range of strange and self-defeating behavior by some applicants about a year ago. The results are a primer on what not to do on a job interview.   3

The survey was conducted for Commemorative Brands, a manufacturer of high school and college class rings, by the New York research firm Schulman, Ronca and Bucuvalas. Here is a sampling of comments from the interviewers: 4

- "The reason the candidate was taking so long to respond to a question became apparent when he began to snore."   5
- "During the entire interview, the applicant wore a baseball cap. . . . A few days later, another college graduate showed up for a management trainee position wearing overalls and sandals."   6
- "When I asked the candidate to give a good example of the organizational skills she was boasting about, she said she was proud of her ability to pack her suitcase 'real neat' for her vacations."   7
- "Wanted to know if employee perks included a swimming pool, paid lunches at the company cafeteria or a free computer to use at home."   8
- "Why did he go to college? His ill-conceived answer: 'To party and socialize.' "   9
- "He couldn't answer any of my questions because he had just had major dental work."   10
- "When I gave him my business card at the beginning of the interview, he immediately crumpled it and tossed it in the wastebasket."   11
- "I received a résumé and a note that said the recent high school graduate wanted to earn $25 an hour—'and not a nickel less.' "   12

- "He had arranged for a pizza to be delivered to my office during a lunch-hour interview. I asked him not to eat it until later." 13
- "Said she had just graduated cum laude, but had no idea what cum laude meant. However, she was proud of her grade point average. It was 2.1." 14
- "Insisted on telling me that he wasn't afraid of hard work. But insisted on adding that he was afraid of horses and didn't like jazz, modern art or seafood." 15
- "The candidate never looked directly at me once during the entire interview. Just stared at the floor." 16
- "An otherwise qualified candidate took herself out of the running when she opened her mouth. She had her tongue pierced." 17
- "She actually showed up for an interview during the summer wearing a bathing suit. Said she didn't think I'd mind." 18
- "He sat down opposite me, made himself comfortable and proceeded to put his foot up on my desk." 19
- "The interview had gone well, until he told me that he and his friends wore my company's clothing whenever they could. At which point, I had to tell him that we manufactured office products, not sportswear." 20
- "Applied for a customer service position although, as he confided, he really wasn't a people person." 21
- "When I mentioned that we had gone to the same college, he stood up and began to belt out the school football fight song." 22
- "Without asking if I minded, he casually lit a cigar and then tossed the match onto my carpet—and couldn't understand why I was upset." 23
- "On the phone I had asked the candidate to bring his résumé and a couple of references. He arrived with the résumé—and two people." 24

How to Avoid Getting Hired

So there you are, busily recasting your résumé—that crucial chronicle of just how much you have achieved and how indispensable you expect to be to the outfit that's thinking of adding you to the payroll—and you genuinely believe that everything on there makes perfect sense. 1

Think again. Better yet, ask somebody else (ideally, somebody smart who likes and admires you, but not overly much) to take a dispassionate look at the finished product. Then listen carefully while he or she points out just where you may have stepped off the pier into muddy water. Robert Half International, a worldwide executive-search firm based in Menlo Park, Cal., collects and publicizes bloopers like the ones listed below from real résumés—not to make anybody feel stupid but as a cautionary exercise. Here is a sampling of the kind of thing you don't want to send out. 2

"I demand a salary commiserate with my extensive experience." 3
"I have lurnt Word Perfect 6.0, computor and spreadsheat progroms." 4
"Received a plague for Salesperson of the Year." 5
"Reason for leaving last job: maturity leave." 6
"Wholly responsible for two (2) failed financial institutions." 7
"Failed bar exam with relatively high grades." 8

"It's best for employers that I not work with people." 9

"Let's meet, so you can 'ooh' and 'aah' over my experience." 10

"You will want me to be Head Honcho in no time." 11

"Am a perfectionist and rarely if if ever forget details." 12

"I was working for my mom until she decided to move." 13

"Marital status: single. Unmarried. Unengaged. Uninvolved. No commitments." 14

"I have an excellent track record, although I am not a horse." 15

"I am loyal to my employer at all costs. . . . Please feel free to respond to my résumé on my office voice mail." 16

"I have become completely paranoid, trusting completely no one and absolutely nothing." 17

"My goal is to be a meteorologist. But since I possess no training in meteorology, I suppose I should try stock brokerage." 18

"I procrastinate, especially when the task is unpleasant." 19

"As indicted, I have over five years of analyzing investments." 20

"Personal interests: donating blood. Fourteen gallons so far." 21

"Instrumental in ruining entire operation for a Midwest chain store." 22

"Note: Please don't misconstrue my 14 jobs as 'job-hopping.' I have never quit a job." 23

"Marital status: often. Children: various." 24

"Reason for leaving last job: They insisted that all employees get to work by 8:45 every morning. Could not work under those conditions." 25

"The company made me a scapegoat, just like my three previous employers." 26

"Finished eighth in my class of ten." 27

"References: None. I've left a path of destruction behind me." 28

Questions for Reflection and Discussion

1. A quick review of the "self-defeating behavior" described in the two selections shows that the mistakes made by applicants can actually be placed into a few categories. For example, some of the bloopers in the second article were caused by spelling or typing errors (commiserate/commensurate, lurnt/learned, plague/plaque, indicted/indicated). Reread both articles, and make a list of the categories into which the most commonly committed errors fall.

2. Job interviews are often nerve-wracking experiences, and when we are nervous, we tend to make more mistakes. What is the worst mistake you ever made during a job interview? Did it cost you the job? Did you ever apply for a job and the person interviewing you was not competent or qualified? Explain.

Topics for Writing

1. Imagine that you are responsible for hiring someone: a baby sitter for your children, a housekeeper to take care of your home, a tutor to help you with

your schoolwork, an assistant to work with you in your current job or to help you run your business, a caregiver for one of your parents or grandparents. Write an essay in which you explain what you would do to make sure you hired the person most qualified to do the job. Be certain to include a detailed description of the interview process, including the questions you would ask and the reasons for asking those particular questions.

2. Return to the free write you completed before you read the two articles. Use the information there to write an essay describing either the most successful job interview you have ever had or the most unsuccessful job interview you have ever had. Be sure to provide as much background information as possible, and also be sure to answer the important who, what, where, why, when, and how questions so that your reader can actually "see" your performance during the interview. In your conclusion, explain what you learned about yourself as a result of the interview experience.

Reading 8–2

A PATH OF ONE'S OWN: FIVE WHO TRANSFORMED THEIR DREAMS INTO CAREERS

Andy Steiner

The next selection describes five people who have managed to find the "good work" referred to in the opening paragraph of this chapter—work that truly expresses their values and fits their needs. This selection shows that it is not necessarily money or fame that makes people happy. In fact, the people described in the article are not going to be able to retire early on their earnings. And this selection also shows that there is no one type of work that provides satisfaction to everyone: The kind of work that makes us happy is as varied as everything else about us.

Vocabulary

domain (paragraph 1)   kingdom; place over which one has control

demeanor (3)   manner; attitude; bearing

banished (3)   forbidden to enter

bent (4)   attitude; position

pathologist (6)   a doctor who specializes in finding the cause of disease or death

Gray's Anatomy (6)   the "bible" of medical students and doctors; a standard text in the field of medicine

proprietress (16)   owner (feminine version of proprietor)

alternative news weeklies (19)   newspapers that cover offbeat but important stories or issues that the mainstream press does not cover

intriguing (21)   interesting

advocate (21)   supporter

prestigious (31)   highly regarded

outplacement services (36)   services to people who have been fired from their jobs

entrepreneurs (37)   people who start and manage their own businesses

401(k) (41)   a retirement account provided by the employer

existential (42)   philosophical

Source: "A Path of One's Own: Five Who Transformed Their Dreams into Careers," by Andy Steiner, as appeared in *Utne Reader*, January/February 1999. Reprinted by permission of Andy Steiner.

Suggestions for Free Writing

Before you read the next selection, take about 15 minutes to free-write on the following topic:

> If you could get paid for doing something that is very important to you, what would it be? If you could get paid for doing something you enjoy very much, what would it be? If you could get paid for doing something that would help others, what would it be? If you could get paid for doing something that would change things for the better, what would it be?

Sam Riley: He keeps the peace in his neighborhood

At Best Steak and Gyros House, Sam Riley Sr. is in charge. Most mornings he rolls in around 11, selects the best table—the one in the back by the window—and surveys his domain. From this command post, Riley can see the parking lot of Chicago Crossings, a small shopping center in the heart of one of Minneapolis' roughest areas. 1

The neighborhood may be poor, but since Riley's been on the job, it's gotten a lot more livable. The Minneapolis native started keeping an eye on things more than nine years ago, first as a self-appointed watchdog, then as an apartment building care-taker, and now as community liaison consultant to Project for Pride in Living (PPL), a local organization dedicated to improving life in inner-city neighborhoods. PPL manages or owns more than 400 low- to moderate-income housing units and numerous commercial developments, many of which are in the neighborhood Riley patrols. 2

He is known and respected for his confident manner, thoughtful demeanor, and large, powerful frame. What makes Riley so effective, though, is the fact that he knows the neighborhood and the people who live there. At Best Steak and Gyros, he greets nearly everyone who walks in the door with a deep bass "How ya doin'?" and a handshake or a watchful stare. When he spots a certain car pull into the parking lot, he calls out to uniformed security guards hired by PPL who are eating in the restaurant, "That's not Isaac, is it? He knows he's not supposed to be in here." He explains that the driver is a "banished individual. He's been doing bad things. I've told him that he's not to be on this property." The car drives away. 3

"Usually, when security companies come in, they have the guns strapped on, and they use forceful intimidation to get what they want from people," says Shari Pleis, PPL's division manager for property management. "Sam's bent on it is that these people are doing what they need to do to survive. While he doesn't agree with what they're doing, he's still very respectful. I've never heard Sam raise his voice. He just tells it like it is. And people listen. Thanks to Sam, this corner is much safer than it was two years ago." 4

Riley says his focus is on keeping drug dealers out of the neigh-   5
borhood and helping young people turn their lives around and realize
their dreams.

"When I was a kid, I wanted to be a pathologist," Riley recalls, his   6
eyes drifting toward the bustling parking lot. "I had a copy of *Gray's
Anatomy* and everything. I studied it every night. I was serious. Then in
junior high a teacher told me that I should pursue trade school instead
because my mother wouldn't be able to afford to send me to medical
school. That was it. I went into neutral."

After high school, Riley joined the army and then returned home   7
for a different kind of battle: making his community a better place to live.

"*Neutral* does not mean that you let go of the dream," he explains.
"You simply have to go to another level to let the dream survive in your
heart. I didn't go to medical school, but I've stood by the side of a man
who died in the street. Did I not become a pathologist? I've helped make
peace in my neighborhood. The work I do here is just as important."

Judy Wicks: Hearty conversation and spicy debate are on her café menu

Back in the 1950s, when Judy Wicks was growing up in suburban   9
Philadelphia, her favorite pastime was building clubhouses.

"I'd build a fort in the woods, and then each spring I'd tear down   10
the old fort and build a bigger one," Wicks recalls. "When my parents
asked me what I wanted for my birthday or for Christmas, I always asked
for more nails and tarpaper for my clubhouse. When it was done, I'd
plant flowers around it and invite the other kids over to visit."

The grown-up Wicks still runs a clubhouse: the White Dog Cafe,   11
which has evolved into a Philadelphia institution since it opened in 1983
in a converted brick rowhouse. While it *is* a business—with a mission
statement, a benefits plan, more than a hundred employees, and a $4
million annual gross—the White Dog retains a sense of fun.

That's fun with a purpose, of course. At the White Dog, customers   12
dine on pricey gourmet American cuisine, but at the same time they
hear from guest speakers who discuss topics dear to Wicks' progressive
heart. The "table talks" have titles like "Living with the New Welfare
Law" and "America: Who Stole the Dream?" and "Hatred in the Name
of God and Country."

"It's important to me to be able to express what I care about   13
through my work," she says.

Wicks knew for sure that she didn't want to work for someone else.   14
She did, for a while in the late '70s and early '80s, when she was a waiter
and later manager at La Terrasse, a nearby French restaurant. But after
a few years, she left to start a take-out muffin shop on the first floor of
the brownstone where she lived with her family. At first she baked in her
kitchen upstairs, and as the restaurant—located in a dense urban neigh-

borhood near the University of Pennsylvania—grew more popular, she expanded the menu. The restaurant itself also expanded bit by bit, first into her apartment and backyard, where entrees were sometimes cooked on a grill.

When the university threatened to demolish this block of brown-stones, Wicks managed to scrape together enough money to buy the building and expand into the apartment next door. Over the years she's added a fully equipped central kitchen, two levels of dining rooms, and a gift shop (appropriately named the Black Cat). 15

Through it all, Wicks has managed to provide a workplace where both the employees and the proprietress (as she refers to herself) can feel good about the food they serve and the message they spread to the community. 16

"Sometimes I think it's just like when I was a kid," she says. "I created my own environment and invited other people into it, and that's what I still do now." 17

Monte Paulsen: He's rewriting the rules of Washington coverage

Picture Washington correspondent Monte Paulsen wearing a bush-whacker hat, scaling a mountain, chopping down a tree. Then picture him out on assignment, hunting down a source, or seated at a keyboard, pounding out a story on deadline. 18

The two images are closer than you'd think. Paulsen, a one-man national bureau for a chain of alternative newsweeklies, says he applies the skills he learned during his rough-and-ready Alaska boyhood to his professional life. Well, maybe not the actual skills, but certainly the do-it-yourself attitude. 19

"In Alaska," Paulsen says, "if you need a house, you build one. You don't wait for something to happen." 20

In high school, Paulsen wanted to be a photographer, so he got a job developing film at the *Anchorage Daily News*. He was 15 and still in school, but also was working fulltime at the paper, learning the ropes from intriguing characters who taught him that a journalist's job is to expose corruption, to be an advocate for the underdog. 21

Paulsen soon took up writing, went to college, majored in philos-ophy and then journalism, and after graduation worked for the *Journal-Tribune* in Biddeford, Maine, for a year. He then moved to nearby Portland, where he and a few friends started an alternative paper, *Casco Bay Weekly*, on a shoestring. He was 24 years old. 22

Casco Bay Weekly broke several important stories right off the bat, and the paper grew quickly. But Paulsen, now editor and publisher, was moving away from the writing and reporting he loved. 23

Then, at an Association of Alternative Newsweeklies conference in Seattle, Paulsen got to talking with Ron Williams, then publisher of the Detroit alternative weekly *Metro Times*. Williams complained that his 24 paper needed better in-depth reporting. Paulsen griped that he didn't have any time to tackle tough investigative stories.

"We were sitting in a bar, and after half an hour of whining, we   25
looked up at each other and said, 'Oh,' " Paulsen recalls. "Not long after that, I left being a big-shot publisher and went back to being a writer. Ron hired me as his paper's first full-time investigative reporter."

After two years in Detroit covering stories like the disturbing poli-   26
tics of breast cancer came a stint heading the investigative team at *The State*, a Columbia, South Carolina, daily owned by the Knight Ridder newspaper chain. While he enjoyed the demanding pace of daily journalism, after four years Paulsen decided it was time to move on. He had grown tired of newspaper-chain bureaucracy, he says, and besides, he had an idea for a great new job.

He and Williams had been talking about starting an alternative   27
news bureau in Washington, D.C.—one that would focus not on mainstream politics and power brokers, but rather on the work of activists and nongovernmental agencies. They saw it as a chance to reinvent the whole idea of Washington coverage. Williams, who now heads Alternative Media, Inc., a chain that includes the alternative weeklies *Detroit Metro Times, Orlando Weekly*, and *San Antonio Current*, agreed to set Paulsen up with a D.C. office, a salary, and a regular byline.

An in-depth investigation of drug-war policies, an in-depth look at   28
the Christian Coalition's lobbying efforts, and a profile of Southern separatist Michael Hill are among Paulsen's recent efforts. He's also working on a book about hate crimes.

"Reporting is the art of not knowing," Paulsen says. "I have a dream   29
job, because I start out with only a working knowledge of a subject and learn so much more as I go along. I have an opportunity to use both my mind and my conscience."

Melissa Bradley: She's in business to spread the wealth

If Melissa Bradley didn't have such a good heart, she'd be dan-   30
gerous.

At 30, this one-woman achievement squad has already earned a   31
degree in finance from Georgetown University; landed a good job at Sallie Mae, a national student loan agency; founded two successful businesses; and been appointed to a prestigious fellowship with the U.S. Department of the Treasury. Lucky, you say? The truth is, she's been working on it a long time. And it hasn't been easy.

The child of a single mother, Bradley grew up in Orange, New   32
Jersey. Her mom worked two jobs. "She was a cleaning lady on the weekends, and an accounts-receivable clerk during the week," Bradley says. But even with two jobs, Bradley's mother didn't earn enough to keep her family above the poverty line.

"This stuck with me," Bradley says. "No matter how hard my mom 33
worked, it was still a struggle. I wanted to prove that it didn't always have
to be this way."

Bradley worked hard at school and got good grades. In the third 34
grade, she won a scholarship to a private academy, which she attended
through high school. She set her sights on Georgetown, even though
her guidance counselor told her she'd never be accepted. That was just
the beginning of proving doubters wrong.

After college, there was the job at Sallie Mae, which Bradley 35
describes as "the worst job I ever had, the biggest disappointment. A
woman in human resources told me that unless somebody dies or leaves
the company, you aren't going to be promoted."

When Bradley was given the choice to relocate or accept an exit 36
package, she took the money and left. She tried to get a bank loan to start
a consulting business but was turned down. So she borrowed $250 from
friends and family and set up Bradley Development, a consulting firm
that provided out-placement services to corporations and financial guidance to families with children in college. She was 23 when she started the
company. Three years later she sold it for more than $1 million.

She funneled the profits into her next venture, The Entrepreneurial 37
Development Institute (TEDI), a New York–based national nonprofit
agency that teaches low-income African American teens how to become
entrepreneurs. "I've always wanted to make money, and I'm not ashamed
to admit that," Bradley says. "But I want to bring other people like me
along for the ride."

She has now removed herself from the direct management of TEDI 38
so that she can concentrate on her next venture, a community bank that
will focus on loans and financial training for low-income customers. She
envisions a traditional bank with regular hours and services, plus "out-
reach branches" in public housing projects and poor neighborhoods.

With an eye to securing the backers and experience she needs, 39
Bradley accepted a 13-month U.S. Treasury fellowship. By April 1999,
her bank and finance organization. Black Star Community Development
Group, should be up and running.

"My mother always told me I could do whatever I wanted to do," 40
Bradley says, "and I believed her. So far she's been right."

Thomas Lynch: He finds poetry in death and life

It's not likely to make most people's list of dream jobs, but if you 41
ask Thomas Lynch, he'll tell you that being an undertaker has benefits
that go well beyond dental insurance or a 401(k).

"There's an existential component," he says. "In this profession, 42
you get to press your nose up against the larger questions, like 'Is that
all there is?' or a version of the question we all ask throughout our childhood: 'Are we there yet?' "

The son of a small-town undertaker in Birmingham, Michigan,   43
Lynch wasn't always certain that he wanted to follow in his father's foot-
steps. He and his eight siblings were all expected to help out at the
family funeral home, so he knew about the demanding hours, the
hands-on labor, and a certain notoriety in the community. "When I was
growing up, I was always called 'Digger' or some variant on that," he says.

After high school, Lynch worked at the state asylum and at a home   44
for alcoholic priests, then enrolled in college and started writing poems.
Lots of poems. "I've always written," he says. "Yeats once said sex and
death are the only things worth writing about, and at the time I thought
I had a leg up on the death thing, anyway."

Poetry, however, wasn't going to pay the bills, especially after Lynch   45
married and started a family. So in 1974 he bought a funeral home in
nearby Millford, Michigan, and for the past 25 years has seen his friends
and neighbors through countless deaths, both expected and unexpected. It's not always easy, but it is enlightening.

"There are times when a mother and father call you in the middle of   46
the night, and you have to make funeral arrangements for a daughter who
has been hit by a train," Lynch says. "I've learned to see life counterclock-
wise. When I discuss obituaries with people, I see what makes a difference
to them at the end of the day. In this way, I learn what's really important."

Experts often advise would-be authors to "write what you know."   47
Inspired by his work, Lynch did just that. His first published poem, titled "A
Death," focuses on the death of a woman Lynch knew at school. Since then
his poems and essays have appeared in *The New Yorker, London Review of
Books, The Paris Review, Harper's,* and other publications. Lynch's collection
of essays, titled *The Undertaking,* won the American Book Award for 1998.

Even though Lynch's writing career has taken off, he's not plan-   48
ning to give up his day job. There's something poetic, he says, about
arranging a suitable ending for a person's life on earth. And undertaking offers a chance to deal with many of the same questions about the
meaning of life that poets ponder.

"The older I get, the more convinced I am that either we have   49
invented God, or God has invented us," Lynch says. "Either way, it
doesn't matter. We need witnesses for our lives."

He pauses, and then adds, "Of course there are people selling Buicks   50
who are asking themselves those same questions. Doesn't everybody?"

Questions for Reflection and Discussion

1. Review the descriptions of the five people described in "A Path of One's
   Own," and estimate what kind of educational background, what kind of
   training, and what kind of experience each of the people needs in order
   to do his or her job successfully.

2. Are you attending college in order to be able to pursue a particular career, or are you attending for another reason? Explain.

Topics for Writing

1. Identify someone who is very satisfied with his or her work. Then interview him or her and use the information you gathered during the interview to create a "portrait" of that person that is very similar to the "portraits" created by Andy Steiner.
2. All of the people described in Steiner's article converted their dreams into careers. Return to the free write you completed before you read the selection, and use the information there to write a description of your "dream" job. Your essay should contain all of the following elements: a thorough description of the job itself, a full explanation of the reasons why this is your dream job, a full explanation of whether you are qualified to do this job, a full explanation of whether or not it will be possible for you ever to have this dream job, and a full explanation of the effect doing this job will have on you and others.

Reading 8–3

DREAM TEACHING

Edwin Romond

The next selection, "Dream Teaching," is a poem written by Edwin Romond, a high school English teacher from Pen Argyl, Pennsylvania. Realizing that most people understand that teaching high school English can be a difficult task, Romond imagines, or "dreams," what it would be like if everything went well in school: from the copy machine working properly to the students looking at him with eager eyes, waiting to be taught.

Vocabulary

serpentine (stanza 4)   winding; hard to follow or predict
cajoling (5)   encouraging
a revival crowd (5)   a crowd being inspired and excited by a preacher
exclamatory sentences (6)   sentences that end in exclamation marks

Suggestions for Free Writing

Before you read the next selection, take about 15 minutes to free-write on the following:

Choose a profession or job that you have some familiarity with (because you have done it or because you know someone who has done it), and then make a list of ten disadvantages about that profession or job. After you have completed the list, go back and write several words or phrases to further describe the disadvantage or to show how the disadvantage makes you feel.

I am first in line for coffee   1
and the copier is not broken yet.
This is how dreams begin in teaching high school.

First period the boy who usually carves skulls   2
into his desk raises his hand instead
to ask about *Macbeth* and, for the first time,
I see his eyes are blue as melting ice.

Source: "Dream Teaching," Edwin Romond, *English Journal,* (April, 1991). Reprinted by permission of Edwin Romond.

Then those girls in the back
stop passing notes and start taking them
and I want to marvel at tiny miracles
but still another hand goes up
and Butch the drag racer says he's found the
      meaning
in that Act III soliloquy. Then more hands join the
      air
that is now rich with wondering and they moan
at the bell that ends our class and I ask myself.
"How could I have thought of calling in sick
      today?"

I open my eyes for the next class and no one's late,   3
not even Ernie who owns his own time zone
and they've all done their homework
that they wave in the air
because everyone wants to go to the board
to underline nouns and each time I turn around
they're looking at me as if I know something they
      want
and steady as sunrise, they're doing it all right.

At lunch the serpentine food lady discovers smiling   4
and sneaks me an extra meatball. In the teachers
      room
we eat like family and for twenty-two minutes
not one of us bitches about anything.

Then the afternoon continues the happiness of   5
      hands
wiggling with answers and I feel such a spark
when spike-haired Cindy in the satanic tee shirt
picks the right pronoun and glows like a saint.
And me, I'm up and down the room now,
      cheering,
cajoling, heating them up like a revival crowd.

I'm living only in exclamatory sentences. They   6
      want it all
and I'm thinking, "What drug are we on here?"
Just as Crusher Granorski screams, "Predicate
      nominatives
are awesome!" the principal walks in
with my check and I almost say, "That's okay,
you can keep it." When the bell sounds
they stand, raise lighted matches

and chant, "Adverbs! Adverbs!"
I drive home petting my plan book.

At night I check the weather without wishing for a
    blizzard
then sleep in the sweet maze of dreams
where I see every student from years of school
    days:
boys and girls, sons and daughters who're almost
    mine,
thousands of them stretching like dominoes into
    the night
and I call the roll and they sing, "We're all here,
    Mr. Romond!"
When I pick up my chalk they open their books,
look up, and with eager eyes, ask me to teach them.

    7

Questions for Reflection and Discussion

1. Do you think Edwin Romond, the author of "Dream Teaching," is satisfied with his profession? Why?
2. Make a list of the three professions or jobs that you would find most satisfying and rewarding. Then make a list of the three professions or jobs that you would find least satisfying and rewarding. Compare your lists with those of your classmates. Are there any similarities that surprise you? Any differences that surprise you?

Topics for Writing

1. Write an essay in which you describe the worst job you have ever had, being sure to include adequate details and descriptions so that your readers can really understand why the job was so bad. Or write an essay in which you describe the best job you have ever had, being sure to include adequate details and descriptions so that your readers can understand why the job was so good. In your conclusion, explain what you learned as a result of having done that job.
2. Return to the free write you completed before you read "Dream Teaching." Use the information there to write your own poem (modeled on Romond's poem) in which you convert a job or profession that has many disadvantages into your "dream" job by imagining it as it could be in an ideal world. Insert the name of the job or profession in your poem, so it reads "Dream _____."

Reading 8–4

WHO NEEDS A DIPLOMA?
WHY THE HIGH-TECH INDUSTRY
WANTS DROPOUTS

Mark Wallace

The next selection, "Who Needs a Diploma?," describes the way the high-tech computer industry is providing job opportunities for high school dropouts, jobs that offer salaries that are higher than those being made by many professionals with college degrees. In fact, Dan Hammans, the young man described in this article, is making a lot more than the high school teacher who warned him that he "would never amount to anything."

Vocabulary

preoccupation (paragraph 2)   being intensely interested in something
forgoing (4)   giving up
garnered (12)   collected; earned
reminiscence (18)   reminder; remembering the past
intuitively (19)   naturally; by instinct, without having to be taught

Suggestions for Free Writing

Before you read the following article, take about 15 minutes to free-write on the following topics:

What kind of worker are you? Do you like to work with your hands? With your head? Do you like to interact with people, or do you prefer to work alone? Do you like to be busy and rushed, or do you need peace and quiet so you can do your work carefully?
Where do you perform better: in school or at work? Why? Which do you prefer: school or work? Why? Where you do feel more confident and comfortable: school or work? Why? Are you attending college because you need a college degree to pursue the career of your choice, or are you attending college for other reasons? What are those reasons?

Source: "Who Needs a Diploma? Why the High-Tech Industry Wants Dropouts," by Mark Wallace, as it appeared in *The New York Times Magazine,* March 5, 2000. Reprinted by permission of Mark Wallace.

226

A couple of years ago, just before Dan Hammans dropped out of high school, his guidance counselor told him that he would never earn more than $15,000 a year, that he would never hold a job for more than six months at a time and that, to put it plainly, he would never amount to anything. "He pretty much told me I was a loser," Dan says. He is sitting in his 1999 Mitsubishi Eclipse, which is fire-engine red, cost $23,000 and boasts 210 horsepower off the factory floor—though with Dan's modifications, that's up to 260. Dan is on his way home from a job at which he earns roughly $2,600 every two weeks, or about $25,000 more each year than a certain Mr. Sternberg of Gilbert High School in Iowa would have thought possible.

"What the heck?" Dan mutters at a passing car. "That's a real interesting body kit. It's got Ferrari side skirts or something." When traffic is light (and the Eclipse running well), the drive to Richardson, where Dan lives, just outside of Dallas, takes about 15 minutes door to door, though on bad days it can take more than an hour. Commuting is one of the small annoyances Dan has learned to put up with in his new life as a computer networking engineer, though it is clearly not as frustrating as walking a mile through subzero Iowa winters to grade school. Such experiences, Dan says, help explain his preoccupation with fast cars. There is that, of course, and then there is the fact that he is 19. "I'm also fascinated by traffic patterns," he says after being cut off by another driver. "It reminds me of fluid dynamics."

Mr. Sternberg can perhaps be forgiven his pessimism: in the United States, 25-year-old male high school dropouts make less than $25,000 a year, on average. Their compatriots with high-school diplomas make only about $31,000, the same starting salary as college graduates with engineering degrees.

The Department of Education does not compile data for 19-year-old high school dropouts with a natural working knowledge of computer systems who teach themselves fluid dynamics in order to design airflow parts for their new cars. But perhaps they should: more and more American teenagers are forgoing college educations or even dropping out of high schools to "drop in" to jobs created by the technological revolution. "I've talked to some people who go to college," says Anthony Yarbrough, 19, a network engineer who graduated from high school last year. "They say, 'O.K., we read this book all day; we get to do a little of this.' From what they're telling me, I'm learning a lot more just working than I would've in the college system."

Bonnie Halper, whose high-tech placement firm, Sendresume.com, occasionally finds jobs for such young people, says: "When I look at some of the résumés that I get from people right out of college, I think, Why are they teaching you these useless technologies?" Dan and Anthony, by contrast, learned their skills not in classrooms but in pursuit of the passions that grip so many teenagers these days: computer games, digital music, video editing, computer animation and film. They are hobbyists whose hobby just happens to be part of the fastest-growing industry on the planet, and they are learning to take advantage of it.

Though Dan wouldn't like to admit it, we are lost. It is early after- 6 noon, and a brief stretch of President George Bush Turnpike (estimated completion date: 2004) stands weirdly overhead to the left, connecting one patch of flat Texas sky to another. Orange detour cones have left us well north of the customer we are to see, but Verio, the company for which Dan works, gives him 31 cents a mile to take the Eclipse on site visits, and we've skipped lunch to arrive on time.

At the site, a long, low concrete commercial block that houses a 7 telecoms company, we are led through an open-plan cubicle warren so vast that the paths between cubes have been given street names. Just off Crowley Avenue, between Colleyville Road and Clyde Boulevard, sits the "electrical room," where Dan is to test three network lines. To do this, he has brought a small device known as a router, with which he will "ping" a similar device back at the office, some 15 miles away.

Routers are the traffic cops of the Internet, guiding countless bits 8 of information between computers, e-mail servers and Web sites around the globe. An intimate knowledge of routers comes in handy at Verio, one of the largest Web-site hosting companies in the world, but this is a knowledge Dan has only imperfectly at present. Most of his morning was spent back at Verio trying to get the two routers to talk to each other— though at one point there was a break to check out a new screen saver, based on "The Matrix" ("awesome," in Dan's estimation).

At the site visit, the problem is solved with a call to Dan's boss, but 9 the morning has not been in vain. This is what passes for training in an industry that moves too quickly for textbooks and knows precious few rules. "When I got this job," Dan says, "they'd ask me, 'Do you know how to do this?' And I'd say, 'No, but I will by the time I get it done.' "

That Dan came to Verio with gaps in his skill set is fine with his boss. 10 "I learned stuff on the job from scratch, which is the way I feel people should learn their jobs," Ric Moseley says. "I'm not sure Dan's quite as mature as he needs to be—a lot of that maturity I think is learned in college—but four years anywhere is going to do something to you, being out on your own for the first time, meeting new people, having to deal with different situations by yourself. Which is what he's doing now."

The network test takes only a few minutes, and Dan is back in the 11 office by 4 o'clock. "I'm going to be glad when this day's over," Dan says. "I guess I'm always just paranoid about doing things wrong."

I first met Dan in Manhattan, where he was competing in a pro- 12 fessional computer gamers' tournament. A past champion, Dan estimates he has garnered almost $100,000 in cash, prizes and endorsements since he began competing in 1995. Computer games have also been Dan's ticket to the job market. He learned his networking skills at "LAN parties" in the mid-90's, wiring friends' computers into Local Area Networks for all-night sessions of video games like Quake. (Ric Moseley, who is 28, learned his trade the same way.)

And even in the Internet age, it's who you know. Dan landed his first job in Dallas, testing computer games, through contacts made at Quake tournaments. In March 1999, he moved out of his parents' house and joined the skilled labor force. Most of us take much longer to reach that point. For Dan, it came when he was barely old enough to vote. 13

Teenagers, of course, have been dropping out for as long as schools have been in session. While most probably still become manual laborers or minimum-wage toilers, our fast, new information-age economy allows some dropouts to move along productive paths rather than simply run from age-old conflicts. Like Dan, some even seem to be doing both. "It really was hard having a pager in high school," says Michael Menefee, a 21-year-old product developer who dropped out of college after just a few months. "The principal would say, 'I'll just hold this for you, and if you get a page, I'll come get you.' Well, that's not the point. The point is, I'm making more than my teachers." 14

Still, as Dan's mother, Alice Hammans, says, dropping out is no guarantee of a good job: "You don't get something for nothing. Daniel hasn't just begun in the work world without first acquiring a lot of knowledge." His schooling in computers, in fact, began around the age of 3, when his father got a Commodore 64, one of the first home-computer systems. By 7, Dan was programming in Basic. In high school—just as the World Wide Web was exploding into America's consciousness—Dan got a part-time job at a local Internet service provider. Dan describes his childhood as happy, sort of, until he got into school. "Dan had a really hard time in grade school," his mother says, "so he just chose an alternate path. Luckily, because of everything that he has internally, he was able to make it." 15

Other "drop-ins" echo Dan's frustration. "I was always one of those people who sat there and argued with my teachers about why I should be in school all the time," says Matt Levine, who, at 18, has decided that starting an Internet-based media company is more important than college. "I looked at the opportunity and the opportunity cost, and sort of went where my heart desired, at least for the moment." 16

Furthermore, says Peter Pathos, founder and chief executive of Theplanet.com, a Dallas start-up specializing in "advanced" Web hosting, "Right now, I think there's much more opportunity diving into the phenomenon than going to college." Pathos employs both Anthony Yarbrough and Michael Menefee, as well as other "drop-in" young adults. "There's almost a gap between the ones you catch right out of 17 high school and the ones who've been used up and burned out by the time they're 21 or 22 by the high-tech jobs," he says of his employees. "The younger ones are some of the most talented people."

It's a busy Friday night, and Dan is having dinner at Campisi's   18
Egyptian with his girlfriend, Wendy, an 18-year-old pre-med student at the University of Texas, and his roommate, Mike, a 23-year-old college dropout who works in computer game design, something Dan hopes one day to pursue. The place is aclatter with waiters and barmen and locals cheering the Dallas Stars, but none of this seems to reach Dan, who is lost in a video game on the tiny screen of his cellular phone. "Take this away from me," he tells Mike, after we have put off ordering a second time. The episode sparks a reminiscence of early video games and the Commodore 64's Dan and Mike both owned as children. "We had one we actually used for a stepping stool," Mike says, "because it was so solid." Dan describes with pride loading games onto the Commodore system at the age of 4, which involved typing commands his father had printed on the disk. Though he couldn't yet read, he was able to copy letters well enough to get the computer to play the game.

"Even back then," Mike says, "even when we didn't know anything   19
about computers, I always thought it was silly that it didn't just load the game, that you had to type something." It is a small point, but a telling one. When the Commodore 64 came along, those of us old enough to read followed the instructions. But Dan and Mike are unburdened by such received wisdom. They are first-generation citizens of the information age, not immigrants to it, and are intuitively familiar with its language and its ways. We who remember the dawn of the personal computer may feel that the future has at long last arrived, but Dan and Mike were born into that future. It is nothing more exciting than their present day.

Though Dan is currently wrapping up his G.E.D., his education is   20
not over yet. With Verio's help, he plans to go after a Cisco Certified Internetwork Expert certificate, the information-age equivalent of an M.B.A. According to Cisco, the starting salary for the 2,000 or so C.C.I.E.'s awarded thus far in the United States is roughly $75,000. Even without a Cisco certification, it's impossible to tell how far Dan could go in the high-tech job market, where brain sweat and elbow grease are still the best predictors of long-term earning potential.

Dan's stormy relationship with school may have cost him little in   21
terms of salary and the kind of statistics tracked by the Department of Ed., but even at 19, he recognizes that stepping through the door to the adult world of work has left other doors to swing shut behind him. "The day I realized I would never go to college, I was really bummed out," he says. "I wanted to play hockey. In high school, I was, like, twice as good

at hockey as I am now at Quake, and as much as I love Quake, I loved hockey twice as much.

"That's really the only regret that I have. I watched people that I played with go on to play for Iowa State, and they won the national championship last year and they were awesome." 22

Questions for Reflection and Discussion

1. Are you or your friends as comfortable with computer technology as Dan Hammans is? Do you have friends, relatives, or acquaintances who are making large salaries because of their expertise in this field?
2. Although Hamman says his only regret over not going to college is that he won't be able to play hockey for a college team, do you think that he will later regret not going to college for other reasons? Explain. If you could get a job earning $75,000 a year right now, would you drop out of college? If so, what would you miss about college? What wouldn't you miss?

Topics for Writing

1. Although Dan Hamman seems to be doing okay without college, there are certainly advantages that he is missing. Based on your college experience thus far, and on the experiences of family, friends, and acquaintances who have attended college, write an essay in which you explain the advantages of attending college before entering the work world. In order to make it easier for you to organize you essay, you could devote each of your paragraphs to one of the advantages of attending college.
2. Return to the free write you completed before you read "Who Needs a Diploma?" and use the information there to write an essay in which you explain which you prefer: the world of work or the world of school. If there are things about both worlds that you like, then you should explain what you like about each of these worlds. Be certain to give descriptions, details, and examples so that your readers can understand why you feel the way you do about school and work.

Reading 8–5

WHO AM I TODAY?

Claudia Shear

The next selection is very different than the other readings in this chapter: It's not really an essay or an article; rather, it is a *monologue* (a speech) that the author, Claudia Shear, performed in a one-woman play several years ago. It is meant to be funny and ironic, showing how difficult it is to earn a living. In her case, because she is an actress, she cannot hold a full-time, permanent job because she must always be available for auditions. So she must rely on temporary jobs in order to survive. However, many of us are forced to hold low-paying, temporary jobs because we do not have the necessary skills, because we must juggle work with school, child care, or other responsibilities, or because employers are not willing to provide their employees with the security and benefits that come with full-time positions.

Vocabulary

centenary (paragraph 3)   one hundred
roux (4)   French for sauce or stock; a liquid cooking base
insubordinate (6)   rude; disobedient
careen (8)   move fast without control
engorged (13)   stuffed

Suggestions for Free Writing

Before you read the monologue, take about 15 minutes to free-write on the following topic:

No matter how much we enjoy our work, most of us do it primarily to earn money to live. Think back as far as you can remember and make a list of *every* job you have ever had in which you earned a salary—from your very first job helping around the house, selling lemonade, delivering newspapers, to the job you hold now. Next to each job on the list, jot down a phrase or sentence explaining what you learned from that job in terms of skills or in terms of discovering something about yourself (your talents, your likes and dislikes, your work ethic).

Source: "Who Am I Today?" by Claudia Shear, *The New York Times*, September 29, 1993. Copyright 1993 by the New York Times Co. Reprinted by permission.

At last counting, I've had 64 jobs. Now, I'm not 236 years old, so obviously some of them were of unusually short duration. The briefest was at a restaurant called Bar Lui—got hired, went in, drank an iced coffee, made a few phone calls, after about 10 minutes the manager interrupted me: "Um, we have very specific policies regarding personal calls."

Out the door, on to a subway, a train, a plane, a bus, or walk to an address, a corner, a park, a bar. Life can spin on a dime—you can stop for a doughnut and end up living in another country.

Who am I today? Who do you need? Today, I'm a bartender at a Chinese restaurant. I'm a proofreader at an investment bank. I'm the take-out book at a "gourmet" kitchen, opening onto a yard strewn with dog feces. I'm the translator for an Italian pop music band. I'm a brunch chef on Fire Island. I'm Mrs. Rip Van Winkle in the Centenary Parade of the Brooklyn Bridge. I'm the fake secretary for a guy pulling a con involving pens.

I carry up cases of beer, stacks of documents, flats of eggs, trays of lipsticks. I set up the computer, the desk, the roux, the stock. Then I begin to read the documents, chop the onions, wash the walls, wash the dishes, wash the pots, pour the drinks, answer the phone, answer the phone, answer the phone: "Good afternoon, Finley Kumble; Good morning, Shakespeare Festival; Buonasera, Il Toscano; Hi, we have five very pretty girls, two brunettes, a red head and two very busty blondes; Medical Center Patient Information, what room please?"

And they tell me, chill on the conversation, don't stand over there, be nice to the customers, put your book away, no personal calls, don't sit down, here's a club in case they come to rob the restaurant late at night when I'm not here, watch your mouth, no eating, don't detach yourself from the console without permission, don't forget to always give your name, remember to never give your name.

And then they tell me, Uh, there's been complaints about your attitude. You were heard whistling in the elevator. Singing in the dining room. You laugh too loudly. You were insubordinate. You have to do what we tell you without arguing. You spend too much time on the phone. Maybe you should drink less coffee so you won't have to go to the bathroom so much. It doesn't matter if you're good, the floor runs better when it's all men. You were warned about reading at the desk. No standing around, you have to look busy. The girls wear leotards because that is what our customers like.

And my personal favorite: I don't have to give you a reason, it's my restaurant.

Today, I'm a room service waitress for a midtown hotel. Only woman, only non-Hispanic. Arrive at 5 A.M., put on a stupid uniform, then ride in huge elevators with a cart piled with giant trays. Elevator stops. A couple of guys, smiling encouragement, help me heave the tray onto my shoulder and I stagger down the corridor, chanting the room number, "214, 214." Stop at the door, tray weighs a ton, and my arms shaking, let go for a minute to ring the bell. "Bing-bong . . . room service" (oh please oh please). Sssssh (sound of shower) "Out in a minute." *Finally*, door opens and I careen into the room at a pitched run "Goodmorningroomservicehere'syourbreakfast" *Boom!* tray is down. Go to the kitchen and get the next one.

How much for the day—$100? I'll do it. Job for a catering company 9
in a huge warehouse preparing lunch for a convention at Madison Square Garden—hairnets, huge plastic aprons, up to my elbows in processed turkey in vats of brine. Great spheres of turkey meat encased in a rind of fat and gelatin that wedges painfully under your fingernails as you lean over and lift them out. The brine stunk and left the floors and tables slick with grease. I showered that night for an hour and a half.

How much is the tax on $13? Do you serve from the left or the 10
right? Do you type, do Word for Windows, take dictation, do french service, arm service, tray service, own a tuxedo, have a beeper, drive a car, live in Manhattan? Will you work Sundays, midnights, every weekend, no weekends, just lunches, only dinners, on call, when we need you?

$1.05, from the left, yes, yes, yes, yes, yes, yes, no, no, no, no, yes, 11
yes, yes, yes, yes, yes, yes, yes.

You see you always have to say yes to get a job. Never have a per- 12
sonality, a life, a light, an opinion.

And smile when you say yes. Oh, no, yes isn't good enough. I don't 13
just have to say "yes" to some jerk in a cheap suit engorged with the majestic power to hire and fire at some steak house on Second Avenue, I have to *smile* at him and if I don't, it means that I have a bad attitude.

Great, that moment when you get a job. *Great*, that moment of the 14
first paycheck. All too soon, there's that clench in your stomach as the dreaded punch-in, sign-in, be on the floor time approaches. And as you walk to the first table, pick up the first document, push the button to take the first call, you think, "I'll never get through this." And then you finally finish your shift and it's time for the late night ride in the taxi, counting your cash by the street lights. And sitting down. Ohh, sitting down after hours on your feet is as pure as drinking water, as satisfying as biting into an apple.

And you're too fired up to go to sleep, you sit at the kitchen table. 15
It's really late, it's really quiet, you're tired. Don't wanna go to bed, though. Going to bed means this was the day. This Feb. 12, this Aug. 3, this Nov. 20 is over and you're tired and you made some money but it didn't happen, nothing happened. You got through it and a whole day of your life is over. And all it is—is time to go to bed.

Questions for Reflection and Discussion

1. Although Claudia Shear's monologue is meant to be funny and flip, she is also trying to make the point that her employers often treated her as if she were not human. However, it is often important for us to see the employer's point of view. Find examples in her monologue that show that she may not have been doing what she was supposed to be doing at her place of employment.

2. In paragraph 14, Claudia Shear describes the terrible feeling she has when she first begins a difficult or boring job, saying, "I'll never get through this." Make a list of some of the tasks or jobs you have had to perform that have made you feel the same way. Compare your list with those of your classmates. Are there any similarities?

Topics for Writing

1. In "Who Am I Today?" Claudia Shear presents a *monologue* (a speech) in which she shows the difficulty, the boredom, and the frustration she felt while trying to earn a living. Create your own monologue in which you show the difficulty, boredom, and frustration of one or more jobs you have had. Try to imitate Shear's style of repetition, intentional fragments, use of dialogue, and action-packed descriptions of the tasks she performed.

   In her conclusion, Shear expresses her frustration and lack of a sense of accomplishment by saying, "You got through it and a whole day of your life is over. And all it is—is time to go to bed." In your conclusion, try to sum up the way the job or jobs made you feel by writing a sentence or two similar to Shear's.

2. Return to the free write you completed before you read the monologue, and use the information there to write your work history. Begin with the first job you can remember and end with your most recent (or current) job. However, you should not simply write an essay that lists and explains each job in the order in which you had them. Instead, this work history should provide your readers (and you) with an explanation of the impact that each and every job you have performed has had on you: How did performing the job make you feel? What skills did you learn from performing the job? What experience did you gain from performing that job? What did you learn about yourself and/or others from performing that job? What career decisions did you make from performing the job? In your conclusion, reflect on the way all of the jobs you have had thus far have helped you to plan your career goals and plans for the future.

Reading 8–6

WARNING: THIS IS A RIGHTS-FREE WORKPLACE

Barbara Ehrenreich

The next selection, an article entitled "Warning: This Is a Rights-Free Workplace," explains the way workers in the United States "have lost ground in recent years" in their ability to work in an environment where their rights and values are respected—from a limit on the number of times a worker can go to the bathroom to mandatory drug testing. As Barbara Ehrenreich says in her conclusion: "We can hardly call ourselves the world's pre-eminent [leading] democracy if large numbers of citizens spend half of their waking hours in what amounts, in plain terms, to a dictatorship."

This article is similar to the type of reading that would be assigned in a college-level economics or sociology class.

Vocabulary

autonomy (paragraph 1)   individuality

palpable (1)   something that can be felt

probing (2)   examining

foray (4)   trip

seditious (4)   rebellion against the government

harangues (4)   long-winded, one-sided speeches

comprehensive (6)   total; complete

innocuous (7)   innocent

ubiquitous (8)   seeming to be present everywhere

enhanced (11)   made better

concerted (14)   well planned

A.F.L.-C.I.O. (14)   American Federation of Labor, Congress of Industrial Organization; organizations to help workers gain and retain their rights

sustained (15)   continued with regularity

pre-eminent (16)   leading; best

Suggestions for Free Writing

Before you read this article, take about 15 minutes to free-write on the following topics:

Think about the jobs you have had, and make a list of the restrictions and limitations that were placed on you in those jobs—for example, were you told what to wear? When you could use the bathroom? When you could take a break? To whom you could speak? Where you could be? Whether you could use the phone? If you had to work overtime? Then, review the list and decide which restrictions and limitations seem fair and which ones seem unfair. Next, write the reason why you think they were fair or unfair. Did you ever do anything to try to change the restrictions that you thought were unfair? Did you ever do anything to try to improve your working conditions? If not, why? If yes, what was the result of your efforts?

If the laws of economics were enforced as strictly as the laws of physics, America would be a workers' paradise. The supply of most kinds of labor is low, relative to the demand, so each worker should be treated as a cherished asset, right? But there have been only grudging gains in wages over the last few years, and in the realm of dignity and autonomy, a palpable decline. 1

In the latest phase of America's one-sided class war, employers have taken to monitoring employees' workplace behavior right down to a single computer keystroke or bathroom break, even probing into their personal concerns and leisure activities. Sure, there's a job out there for anyone who can get to an interview sober and standing upright. The price, though, may be one's basic civil rights and—what boils down to the same thing—self-respect. 2

Not that the Bill of Rights ever extended to the American workplace. In 1996, I was surprised to read about a grocery store worker in Dallas who was fired for wearing a Green Bay Packers T-shirt to work on the day before a Cowboys-Packers game. All right, this was insensitive of him, but it certainly couldn't have influenced his ability to keep the shelves stocked with Doritos. A few phone calls though, revealed that his firing was entirely legal. Employees have the right to express their religious preferences at work, by wearing a cross or a Star of David, for example. But most other forms of "self-expression" are not protected, and strangely enough, Green Bay Packer fandom has not yet been recognized as a legitimate religion. 3

Freedom of assembly is another right that never found its way into the workplace. On a recent journalistic foray into a series of low-wage jobs, I was surprised to discover that management often regarded the most innocent conversation between employees as potentially seditious. A poster in the break room at one restaurant where I worked as a waitress prohibited "gossip," and a manager would hastily disperse any gath- 4 ering of two or more employees. At the same time, management every-where enjoys the right to assemble employees for lengthy anti-union harangues.

Then there is the more elemental and biological right—and surely   5
it should be one—to respond to nature's calls. Federal regulations forbid employers to "impose unreasonable restrictions on employee use of the facilities." But according to Marc Linder and Ingrid Nygaard, co-authors of "Void Where Prohibited: Rest Breaks and the Right to Urinate on Company Time," this regulation is only halfheartedly enforced. Professionals and, of course, waitresses can usually dart away and relieve themselves as they please. Not so for many cashiers and assembly-line workers, some of whom, Linder says, have taken to wearing adult diapers to work.

In the area of privacy rights, workers have actually lost ground in   6
recent years. Here, too, the base line is not impressive—no comprehen-sive right to personal privacy on the job has ever been established. I learned this on my first day as a waitress, when my fellow workers warned me that my purse could be searched by management at any time. I wasn't carrying stolen salt shakers or anything else of a compromising nature, but there's something about the prospect of a purse search that makes a woman feel a few buttons short of fully dressed. After work, I called around and found that this, too, is generally legal, at least if the boss has reasonable cause and has given prior notification of the company's search policies.

Purse searches, though, are relatively innocuous compared with   7
the sophisticated chemical and electronic forms of snooping adopted by many companies in the 90's. The American Management Association reports that in 1999 a record two-thirds of major American companies monitored their employees electronically: video-taping them; reviewing their e-mail and voice-mail messages; and, most recently, according to Lewis Maltby, president of the Princeton-based National Workrights Institute, monitoring any Web sites they may visit on their lunch breaks. Nor can you count on keeping anything hidden in your genes; a growing number of employers now use genetic testing to screen out job applicants who carry genes for expensive ailments like Huntington's disease.

But the most ubiquitous invasion of privacy is drug testing,   8
usually of urine, more rarely of hair or blood. With 81 percent of large companies now requiring some form of drug testing—up from 21 percent in 1987—job applicants take it for granted that they'll have to provide a urine sample as well as a résumé. This is not restricted to "for cause" testing—of people who, say, nod or space out on the job. Nor is it restricted to employees in "safety-sensitive occupations," like airline pilots and school-bus drivers. Workers who stack boxes of Cheerios in my local supermarkets get tested, as do the editorial

employees of this magazine, although there is no evidence that a weekend joint has any more effect on Monday-morning performance than a Saturday-night beer.

According to a recent report from the American Civil Liberties 9 Civil libertarians see drug testing as a violation of our Fourth Amendment protection from "unreasonable search," while most job-holders and applicants find it simply embarrassing. In some testing protocols, the employee has to strip to her underwear and urinate into a cup in the presence of an aide or technician, who will also want to know what prescription drugs she takes, since these can influence the test results.

According to a recent report from the American Civil Liberties 10 Union, drug testing has not been proven to achieve its advertised effects, like reducing absenteeism and improving productivity. But it does reveal who's on anti-depressants or suffering with an ailment that's expensive to treat, and it is undeniably effective at weeding out those potential "troublemakers" who are too independent-minded to strip and empty their bladders on command.

Maybe the prevailing trade-off between jobs and freedom would 11 make sense, in the narrowest cost-benefit terms, if it contributed to a more vibrant economy. But this is hardly the case. In fact, a 1998 study of 63 computer-equipment and data-processing firms found that companies that performed both pre-employment and random drug testing actually "reduced rather than enhanced productivity"—by an eye-popping 29 percent, presumably because of its dampening effect on morale.

Why, then, do so many employers insist on treating their workers 12 as a kind of fifth column within the firm? Certainly the government has played a role with its misguided antidrug crusade, as has the sheer availability of new technologies of snooping. But workplace repression signals a deeper shift away from the postwar social contract in which a job meant a straightforward exchange of work for wages.

Economists trace the change to the 1970's, when, faced with falling 13 profits and rising foreign competition, America's capitalists launched an offensive to squeeze more out of their workers. Supervision tightened, management expanded and union-busting became a growth industry. And once in motion, the dynamic of distrust is hard to stop. Workers who are routinely treated like criminals and slackers may well bear close watching.

The mystery is why American workers, the political descendants of 14 proud revolutionaries, have so meekly surrendered their rights. Sure, individual workers find ways to cheat on their drug tests, outwit the electronic surveillance and sneak in a bit of "gossip" here and there. But these petty acts of defiance seldom add up to concerted resistance, in part because of the weakness of American unions. The A.F.L.-C.I.O. is currently conducting a nationwide drive to ensure the right to organize, and the downtrodden workers of the world can only wish the union well. But what about all the other rights missing in so many American workplaces? It's not easy to organize your fellow workers if you can't communicate freely with them on the job and don't dare carry union literature in your pocketbook.

In a tight labor market, workers have another option, of course. 15 They can walk. The alarming levels of turnover in low-wage jobs attest to the popularity of this tactic, and if unemployment remains low, employers may eventually decide to cut their workers some slack. Already, companies in particularly labor-starved industries like ski resorts and software are dropping drug testing rather than lose or repel employees. But in the short run, the mobility of workers, combined with the weakness of unions, means that there is little or no sustained on-site challenge to overbearing authority.

What we need is nothing less than a new civil rights movement— 16 this time, for American workers. Who will provide the leadership remains to be seen, but clearly the stakes go way beyond "labor issues," as these are conventionally defined. We can hardly call ourselves the world's pre-eminent democracy if large numbers of citizens spend half of their waking hours in what amounts, in plain terms, to a dictatorship.

Questions for Reflection and Discussion

1. Review the article and make a list of employer practices that Barbara Ehrenreich believes are unfair to workers. Then review the list and decide if you agree that they are unfair. Have you been subject to such practices in your jobs?
2. In paragraph 13, the author notes that "America's capitalists launched an offensive to squeeze more out of their workers. Supervision tightened, management expanded, and union-busting became a growth industry." Have you ever been the victim of one or more of these practices? Or, if you have functioned as a supervisor or manager in a job, have you ever had to "squeeze" more out of the workers? How did you do this?

Topics for Writing

1. Based on the information in the article, combined with your own work experiences, write an essay in which you agree or disagree with Barbara Ehrenreich when she claims that workers in the United States are being deprived of their dignity and freedom in the workplace. Be certain to take specific information from the article, quote that information (remember to use quotation marks), and then explain why you agree or disagree, based on your own work experiences, your knowledge of the topic, and your observations and knowledge of other workers whom you know.

2. Return to the free write you completed before you read the article. Use the information there to write an essay in which you describe the restrictions that have been placed on you in the jobs you have had. As you describe each restriction, analyze whether you think the restriction was a reasonable one, or if you would have been able to perform your job more effectively without that restriction. In your conclusion, based on your own experiences, explain what kind of restrictions you would impose on employees.

Additional Writing Topics about Working

1. The selections in this chapter offer an overview of the world of work, from how to behave during an interview to the way workers' rights are being eroded in the United States. These selections can provide you with an opportunity to better understand the conditions and circumstances that will have an impact on your own working career and goals. Reread each selection (including the poem "Dream Teaching" and write a one- or two-paragraph summary about *each* one, explaining what you learned about the world of work.

   In order to practice identifying and incorporating quotations from your reading into your essays (a skill that is essential in college-level writing assignments), be certain to include at least one quotation from each selection in your essay. Remember to place the words you are quoting in quotation marks. Select a quotation that reflects the point or points that were most helpful, interesting, or useful to you as you strive to understand the conditions and circumstances that will have an impact on your own working career and goals.

2. Return to the free write you completed at the beginning of this chapter, and review the names you wrote in response to the ten questions. Use these names to help you choose two people to interview (classmates, parents, teachers, friends, co-workers). One of your subjects should be someone who is satisfied with his or her employment situation, and the other should be one who is not satisfied.

   After you have completed the interviews, write an essay in which you compare the two people's experiences and feelings about their employment situation. In your conclusion, try to identify those factors that lead to satisfaction and those factors that lead to dissatisfaction, based on the information you obtained in both interviews.

Chapter
9

Relationships:
The People in Our Lives

The chapters in this book have covered many topics that are important to our happiness, success, and well-being: childhood, parenting, adolescence, education, work, class and race, and careers. But perhaps there is nothing so important in our lives as our relationships with others. Unless we have people with whom we can share our experiences, our joys, our sorrows; with whom we can spend time; in whom we can confide and place our trust—then everything that we do, even our greatest successes and achievements, may, somehow, seem hollow and empty.

And it is not just our intimate relationships that affect our well-being and our ability to function in a world that can sometimes be difficult and challenging. The way we interact with people over the course of a typical day can also affect us: An argument with a salesclerk can ruin an otherwise fine day; being of help to a stranger or being helped by a stranger can make us feel happy to be alive.

The selections in this chapter cover a wide range of relationships. By reading and writing about these selections, perhaps you will be able to better understand the significance not only of the relationships you have with family members and close friends but also the way that the relationships you have with people at school, at work, and in your community help to clarify your values and priorities.

Pre-reading Activity

Before you read the selections in this chapter, take about 15 minutes to respond to these free-writing topics. They will help you to think about the relationships you have had that have helped to form and sustain you in your childhood and adolescence, the relationships you are having now, and the relationships that you hope to have for the rest of your life.

You will be making four separate lists, consisting of words, phrases, or complete sentences.

1. Make a list of the qualities you value in your relationships with your family members.
2. Make a list of the qualities you value in your relationships with your friends.
3. Make a list of the qualities that you value (or will value) in your relationship with your spouse.
4. Make a list of the qualities that you value (or will value) in your relationship with your children.

Review these four lists, and identify those qualities that reappear in each list. Then describe why you think these qualities are so important, and decide if you could have a successful relationship without these qualities.

Reading 9–1

INSTANT INTIMACY

Roxana Robinson

In the essay entitled "Instant Intimacy," Roxana Robinson describes an encounter she had with a stranger on a subway car at Grand Central Station in New York. Everyone knows that subway cars and platforms can be very dangerous places, but in this selection, Robinson explains that the opposite was true—that the experience enabled her to see that an encounter with a stranger can also provide us with an opportunity to help another human being, and to learn something about ourselves and humanity in the process.

Vocabulary

reverberant surfaces (paragraph 1)   surfaces that cause sounds to vibrate again and again

cacophonous (1)   horrible, jarring sounds and noises

Michelangelo's last and little-known commission (2)   Michelangelo is most famous for his painting on the ceiling of the Sistine Chapel in Rome

anonymity (2)   not being known or recognized by anyone

lethal (4)   deadly

plangent (10)   with a deep sound

demonic (15)   demons are evil spirits, devil-like

tumult (15)   confusion; disorder

galvanizing us (15)   pulling us together to act

Suggestions for Free Writing

Before you read the selection, take about 15 minutes to free-write on the following topic:

Think about a time when you had an encounter with a stranger or strangers. Recall as much as you can about the incident or event, not only about the details of the encounter itself but also the emotions the encounter aroused in you. Describe what, if anything, you learned about yourself and others as a result of the encounter.

Source: "Subway," by Roxana Robinson, originally published in *The New York Times Magazine,* April 4, 1999, as "Instant Intimacy." Reprinted by permission of the author.

Generally, the rule in the subway is silence. This is not, of course, 1
to say that you are in a silent world. You are in a metal car weighing
several tons, riding on rimless metal wheels, driven by crackling electrical charges and surrounded by hard, reverberant surfaces. The noise,
especially on corners, when all the moving metal parts of the train seem
to rub horridly together, is high, piercing and cacophonous enough to
drive you mad. So that simply standing alone in the subway car, without
anyone else in it, you are under a kind of attack.

But your own silence is the rule. When the car is full, there may be 2
60 or 70 complete strangers crammed into it, any one of whom may be
poised on the brink of madness. Your neutral request that he move over
may be all that's needed to send him down into a black pit of manic
rage. And not only will he hurtle downward, he'll try to pull you with
him. So silence and no eye contact. Eyes are often raised upward in stu-
dious attention, as though Michelangelo's last and little-known commission had been discovered on the curved white ceiling of the No. 6 train.
Or focused discreetly on the floor. This is safer than the ceiling, because
looking downward partly conceals your face and throat: no one can cast
his mad eyes across your features, measuring your cheeks for slashes,
your neck for fingers. Silence and anonymity are the rule that most
people obey.

Which is why it is so startling when someone breaks it, plunging a 3
carful of strangers into unsettling intimacy.

Last week I was standing in the middle of a fullish car that 4
stopped at Grand Central. As the crowd outside pushed its way in, a
man among it fell. I saw him go down, just as he was stepping into the
car: I saw his head slide downward. He was falling down onto the
tracks, through that narrow opening between car and platform. As he
went down, he gave a wordless shout—a loud, low, dull cry. Everyone
turned, electrified. Everyone saw him going, sliding away from the
world. He was grabbed by the people closest to him: suddenly we were
together in this. Suddenly we were all survivors, connected, and one of
us was in peril. There was the man's head, slipping downward in the
crowd, and in all of our minds was the unspeakable notion of being on
the tracks, in that lethal black underworld between platform and train.
Urgency flashed through us: the man was grabbed by his arms and his
elbows and his shoulders and pulled magically back up. He was saved;
he stood. He was terrified, but upright. He moved inside the car to
stand directly in front of me.

He was a white man in his 40's, gray-haired, grizzled and stout, 5
wearing black plastic-rimmed glasses, a white T-shirt and a brown leather
jacket. He looked like a deliveryman, perhaps, someone used to taking
orders, not giving them. He took hold of the pole and stared at me. His
face was 10 inches from mine. He began talking. His voice was still loud
and urgent, but oddly low, dull, without variation.

"I fell down, I fell down," he roared. "I fell down between the   6
train." He was looking into my eyes.

"I know," I said, "but you're all right now."   7

At once he frowned. His eyes were black with fear, his pupils huge.   8
"I didn't hurt myself, did I? I'm all right, aren't I? My leg isn't broken or
nothing, is it?"

"No," I said steadily. "You're all right."   9

"I'm all right, aren't I?" he repeated, loud and plangent. He was   10
desperate.

"You're all right," I said. I looked deeply and directly into his eyes,   11
as you never do in the subway with strangers. "You're all right now."

"They pushed me," he roared mournfully. "I fell down."   12

"They pulled you up again," I answered. "You're all right now. Your   13
leg isn't hurt. You're all right."

His fear was contagious. I felt as though I were soothing a fright-   14
ened horse, as though my own certainty was all that would save us both
from rocketing helplessly down into terror. But the man had chosen to
stand in front of me. This was my task, just as it had been the task of
those at the door to grab his arms, his elbows, his shoulders and pull him
powerfully to safety as he slid screaming down.

Now it was my task to look into his eyes and tell him that, though   15
all his fears were real, though we were surrounded by demonic tumult
and silent strangers, though we were hurtling dangerously through the
darkness, though we were continually at risk of losing our places and
falling out of the world, still, just at this moment, because of luck and of
that sudden reflex of humanity that strikes a crowd like a flash of light-
ning, galvanizing and electrifying us and revealing us as our true selves,
we were all right. We were fine.

Questions for Reflection and Discussion

1. If you had been on that subway car, would you have behaved in the same
   way as the author did when the frightened man made eye contact with her
   and began to talk to her? Why? Explain.
2. Why do you think people are so fearful to have any contact or interaction
   with strangers? Do you think this fear is justified? Do you think the world
   is a better place or a worse place because of this fear?

Topics for Writing

1. In paragraphs 1 and 2, Roxana Robinson describes the way that strangers
   behave on the subway in order to protect themselves from those who "may
   be poised on the brink of madness." Reread these paragraphs carefully, and

then create your own essay in which you describe the way you behave in certain situations or circumstances to protect yourself from danger, either real or imagined. For example, you can describe how you behave when you are walking or driving alone at night, when you are doing a dangerous job or task, or when you are performing a dangerous or challenging sport.

Or, if you have actually survived a dangerous situation, write an essay describing that incident or event in full and complete detail, being sure to answer the who, what, where, why, when, and how questions. Tell if you were helped by others, either strangers or people whom you already knew. In your conclusion, explain how the experience changed you, for better or worse.

2. Return to the free write you completed before you read "Instant Intimacy." Use the information there to write an essay in which you compare and contrast an experience you had with a stranger or strangers with the experience Robinson had with the man on the subway car. Begin by describing your experience in full, being certain to answer the important who, what, where, why, when, and how questions. Decide which elements of the experiences were the same (compare) and which were different (contrast). Then devote a paragraph to describing and explaining each of these similarities and differences.

   Use this writing assignment as an opportunity to choose and incorporate quotations directly from the selection into your essay. This is an important writing skill for college-level assignments because it enables your reader to see that you have comprehended the reading assignment and are able to select those phrases and sentences that are important to your topic and that back up your point of view or opinion.

   One of the most important elements to compare or contrast in your essay is the result of the experience. Robinson explains in her final paragraph that the experience helped her and the other people on the subway car to realize that "we were all right. We were fine." In your final paragraph, explain what the experience with a stranger or strangers helped you to realize.

Reading 9–2

BUD

Jennie Phillips

The next selection is not about the relationship between two or more people; it is about the relationship of people in the village of Adamant, Vermont, to a dog named Bud that decided to "adopt" them. As the author explains, Bud didn't need other dogs; "people were Bud's pack."

Vocabulary

politesse (paragraph 4)   formal politeness
vulnerable (5)   open to being hurt
imperious (12)   proud, haughty
homeopathic veterinarian (15)   an animal doctor who uses natural medicines and treatments
shrouded (18)   wrapped

Suggestions for Free Writing

Before you read the next selection, take about 15 minutes to free-write on the following topic:

> Some of us are "animal people," and some of us are not. Describe your feelings, your relationships, and your experiences with animals. Are you one of those people who believe that animals are more wonderful than people? Or do you not like to be around animals?
>
> Describe your relationship with the pets you have had. Which was your favorite? Why? What did you learn from having a relationship with this pet? What can we learn about ourselves based on the way we treat our pets and other animals? If you have not had pets in your life, describe your relationship with animals in general—how you feel about them, what your experiences with them were and are (there is quite a difference between seeing animals in a zoo and working with animals on a farm, for example), what they mean to you (for example, are you a vegetarian because you do not believe in eating animals), what you know about them, how you feel about protecting animals from poachers and other people who want to make profits from their skins or husks, what your favorite animals were when you were young, what your favorite animals are now.

Source: "Bud," by Jennie Phillips, as it appeared in *Yankee*, December, 1999. Reprinted by permission of the author.

Bud was a Vermont dog, a purebred malamute. He lived in and 1
about Adamant, a village bounded by mountains and set in a curving
bowl of fields, woods, marshes, and ponds. Bud was brought to Adamant
by Louis Porter, a ten-year-old boy, during the summer of 1986, but in
September of that year, when Lou returned to school, Bud started taking
trips to the village on his own. At first he would come home in the late
afternoons. Soon he wasn't coming home at night at all. Louis's mother,
Ruthie, spent hours driving around looking for Bud.

If Bud had shown any inclination toward hunting, his wanderings 2
would not have been tolerated. Vermonters are passionately protective
of their deer, and even a dog chasing a butterfly is thought to be showing
early signs of the instinct to run deer. But Bud didn't give a whit about
deer, or even other dogs. People were Bud's pack.

Bud liked to visit people. He would stand on the threshold of your 3
home, look you in the eye, and wait. He would not enter until you
greeted him and invited him in. In the next stage, Bud would come to
visit and stay for several days. The last barrier of reserve was removed
when Bud was invited into that most private human sanctum, the
bedroom. At this stage, special bowls and food were seen around the
house in anticipation of Bud's next visit.

According to Forrest Davis, a local retired philosophy professor, 4
author, and volunteer firefighter. "It wasn't that he was so all-fired easy
to know. There was a certain politesse; he observed the more formal
courtesies, like any other Vermonter. He waited for the proper
moment."

Bud's first friends were Lois and Elbridge Toby, who lived in a 5
house on a knoll overlooking the general store. Elbridge had been
wounded in World War II. Bud always seemed attracted to those who
were hurt, sad, or somehow vulnerable. Lois recalls, "Bud came nosing
around. I'd never seen him before. Elbridge patted him. Bud wagged his
tail. That was it. They were friends."

In Elbridge's last years, as he became more ill, he and Bud would 6
lie together on the lawn for hours. When Elbridge died, Lois says she
"sat Bud down and told him." Although Elbridge had died in the hospital, Bud seemed to understand. "He immediately walked through
every room in the house, howling," Lois says.

When Arlene, the village postmistress, lost her brother to an early 7
death, Bud was there. "I was devastated, but I didn't want to share my
grief with anyone in the village. Every day, after I sorted the mail, it was
my custom to walk home. Throughout that spring, Bud would meet me
at the store when I was finishing. Then he would walk up the hill with
me. I would sit in the window and cry, just sobbing. Buddy would sit
there beside me and listen to my crying. Sometimes I would put my arm
around him. It was so helpful."

Alison Underhill is a staunch defender of wildlife and a skeptic about dogs. She used to call Ruthie to complain whenever she saw Bud roaming loose. But Bud won her over. "Bud belonged to himself. He was all of ours, but we were also his. He was aloof and independent, not needy like many dogs. He seemed to let people know, 'You may pat me if you like,' yet he had a way of showing real affection and caring. He let you know that he visited you because he wanted to be with you. He chose you. I always felt honored when he came to visit."   8

Dogs were not allowed in the community store back then, but gradually the rules were relaxed for Bud until, at some point, he was expected and welcome. On cold days, he spent hours in front of the woodstove, a handy place for him to meet new owners and generally work his social traplines.   9

Tim Cook, whose sister Polly manages the general store, moved into a cabin in the woods on the quarry road a half mile from the village. Tim was 85 percent deaf and blind from a progressive neurological condition. By living in a cabin without water or electricity, Tim was fending off the realization that he couldn't live independently much longer. Bud must have noticed Tim's struggle because he became a self-made seeing-eye dog, walking back and forth with Tim, guiding him away from traffic and obstacles.   10

The amazing thing was that Bud could maintain such a tight schedule of duties, obligations, and social calls. Over the years, Bud knit the village together with his zigzag trail. One resident said, "We all had this dog in common. We called around on the phone to see what he was doing." In the end, nobody really owned Bud. He became a public institution.   11

Dr. Eleanora Sense, at 100-plus years old, was one of the deans of the Adamant Music School, which draws piano students and masters from around the world every summer. She is described by those who remember her as imperious and magisterial, with a daunting ability to control and dominate those around her. The story goes that Eleanora would bring a string when she walked down to the general store. If Bud happened to be at the store, Eleanora would loop her string through Bud's collar and lead him to her cabin. Bud would spend a few days and nights under her tutelage. It is also said that she and her willing prisoner enjoyed tea and Lorna Doones together. On one Fourth of July, Eleanora led Bud in the village parade with a crown of flowers on his head.   12

It was on a wintry walk with Marion Parauka and Lois Toby up by the county road that Bud first showed signs of kidney disease. "Buddy took his first spell over by Mary Radigan's house. He fell down in the road for no apparent reason," Lois remembers. The local veterinarian prescribed a special diet and, pretty soon, village houses and the general store were stocked with cans of the right food. The store bulletin board carried alerts on Bud's condition. Word spread that people should stop feeding him   13 cookies and ice cream: Bud needed protein. People took cooked meat, often moose meat, to the store for Bud when he stopped by.

Later, Bud's declining health necessitated that he be administered   14
medication every day. A sign-up sheet was posted in the store with instructions on when and how to give Bud his medication. Bud began to spend more time in front of the general store's woodstove as he became less able to work his territory. He shifted his locations less frequently, and he lengthened his visits.

When Ruthie noticed that Bud was failing to the point that he   15
could no longer maintain his customary lifestyle, she took him to a homeopathic veterinarian and left him there for several days of treatment. "We were just trying to help Bud feel more comfortable, but when we brought him home, he was so sick he couldn't even walk. We knew we were going to have to put him to sleep. We decided we would give Bud a few final days so everyone could come and say good-bye." Word spread quickly. Someone posted a notice: "Buddy is dying."

Ruthie recalls that over the next few days there was a steady stream   16
of Bud's people. "There were so many people I didn't even recognize, much less know. But Bud knew everyone."

Some chose not to visit Bud's deathbed. As one person put it, "I didn't want to embarrass Bud. He had had such dignity in his life."

On February 24, 1996, Ruthie's journal reads, "Buddy can't even   17
stand. His face is all swollen and he can't stop shivering." On February 28 she wrote, "Today is the day. My heart is aching. I found a little girl sitting and sobbing by Bud's side. I had never seen her before." That afternoon, the veterinarian was called, and Bud died in Louis's kitchen surrounded by a small circle of family and friends.

They brought Bud's body down into the village at nightfall on   18
March 3. An icy wind blew fresh snow in swirling eddies. His body was shrouded in a blanket and laid across the back seat of an old red sedan. As the car slowly wound its way along the steep, twisting dirt road, a crowd of Bud's friends, lining both sides of the road, was caught and held by its headlights. Next to a frozen pond and beaver dam was an open grave bordered by mounds of loose dirt. The body was lifted out of the car, gently lowered into the grave, and then covered with a brilliant red scarf. The villagers silently took turns shoveling dirt into the grave. Someone murmured, "We're sure going to miss him."

An Adamant Music School postcard with Bud's picture on it is still   19
sold in the general store today. And a granite gravestone, paid for by donations collected in the store, still marks Bud's grave by the upper Adamant Pond dam.

An old dog named Eric now enjoys Bud's spot in front of the woodstove. Some say that Eric is trying to take Bud's place. But everyone agrees that no dog can really ever do that.

Questions for Reflection and Discussion

1. According to the author, Bud was able to sense people's needs, and he was able to satisfy them. Do you believe that animals can sense the needs, desires, and emotions of human beings? Explain.
2. Some people believe that you can tell a lot about a person based on the way he or she reacts to animals. Do you agree? Explain.

Topics for Writing

1. Reread the article about Bud, and write an essay in which you explain the many and various needs he satisfied, both for individual citizens of the town of Adamant and for the citizens of the town in general. In the first selection in this chapter, Roxana Robinson explained how the stranger's falling helped to unite the people on the subway. In your conclusion, explain how Bud united the people of Adamant, and explain whether a dog such as Bud could have the same effect on the people in your neighborhood or town.
2. Return to the free write you completed before you read the article about Bud. Use the information there to write an essay in which you explain your relationship to your pet(s) or other animals, covering as many aspects as possible: What are your experience(s) with pets or animals? What have you learned about them? How do they make you feel? What have you learned about yourself as a result of your relationship with animals? What have you learned about other people as a result of watching these people interact with pets or animals? Do you think pets and/or animals are superior to human beings? In what ways? In your conclusion, explain whether, as a result of your feelings and experiences with pets or animals, you would have been one of the people in Bud's "pack."

Reading 9–3

WHO SAYS YOU CAN'T HURRY LOVE?

Monte Williams

The first selection in this chapter dealt with the relationships that form—quite unexpectedly—among strangers, and the second selection dealt with the relationships that form between animals and humans. This next selection, "Who Says You Can't Hurry Love?" deals with the kind of relationship that is perhaps most important to us: the choice of a companion or spouse. But this article contains a "wrinkle" on the usual dating/mating pattern: Most of the people described in the article are trying to meet other people who are also Jewish in order to "discourage intermarriage and preserve Jewish heritage," and they are trying to do it in eight minutes or less!

Vocabulary

affable (paragraph 1)   friendly; outgoing
secular (6)   nonreligious
assimilating (6)   blending into
interminable (7)   never ending
initiate (15)   start
amorous (17)   from the Latin *amour*, meaning "love"
reciprocal (26)   mutual
logorrhea (28)   excessive talking; the inability to stop talking to let others speak

Suggestions for Free Writing

Before you read the next selection, take about 15 minutes to free-write on the following topic:

Imagine that you have only eight minutes to meet and interview the person whom you are going to marry or with whom you are going to spend the rest of your life. Make a list of the ten most important questions you would ask him or her, and then number them in the order of importance, with one being the most important and ten being the least important.

Source: "Who Says You Can't Hurry Love?" by Monte Williams, *The New York Times*, March 5, 2000. Copyright 2000 by the New York Times Co. Reprinted by permission.

The host and hostess, an affable husband-and-wife team, stood   1
erect and at the ready, she with a hotel desk bell in hand. "On your
mark, get set, date," shouted Alan Weiss, and his wife, Nikki, rang the
silver bell.

Twenty men and 20 women shook hands across morsel-size cafe   2
tables in the private back room of a Glatt kosher restaurant on the
Upper West Side [of Manhattan] and rapidly conversed. "What do you
do for a living?" "Where are you from?" "What's the most exciting thing
you've ever done?" "What do you do in your spare time?"

The questions came faster than a hungry greyhound. There was,   3
after all, only eight minutes to chat before the men were told to rotate,
round-robin style, to other tables, where women eagerly (or apprehen-
sively) awaited them. In the end, each person would have seven "dates,"
each eight minutes long.

Seven dates? Eight minutes? What is this?   4

It's called SpeedDating, and it's the latest wrinkle in the Jewish   5
singles scene. Its inventors at Aish HaTorah, an international Jewish educational resource center, said they came up with the idea more than a
year ago during a brainstorming session on how to discourage intermarriage and preserve Jewish heritage.

"We're trying to reach secular Jews, who are in danger of assimi-   6
lating and disappearing and not keeping their heritage alive," said Rabbi
Yaacov Deyo, the educational director of Aish HaTorah in Los Angeles.

Of course, its founders are also trying to promote SpeedDating as   7
an alternative to seemingly interminable blind dates, in which men and
women with no chemistry struggle to make small talk. In SpeedDating,
participants fill in a yes or no answer on a rectangular card after each
date indicating whether they would like to see the person again. If a
match is made—if a man and woman both decide they want to see each
other—coordinators provide them with each other's phone number
within 48 hours.

The rapid-fire matchmaking was begun in Los Angeles, then   8
spread to 15 cities and 5 countries, including Australia and South Africa.
After two months in New York, there is a waiting list for a chance to
locate love in the asphalt canyon, for a fee of $20. Mr. Weiss said that 18
or 19 matches came out of the SpeedDating session he held at Levana,
a kosher French Mediterranean restaurant on the Upper West Side. "It's
a novel idea, and I got the impression people liked it," he said.

The program's participants, on the other hand, gave it mixed   9
reviews.

"I had two matches," said Rob, a handsome Manhattan doctor with   10
a Pepsodent smile. He went out with both women. "Let's just say I'd like
to meet someone on a more conventional basis. It's not for me."

But Gary Lowitt, a vice president at a national real estate company,   11
is wedded to the notion of SpeedDating, since he's still seeing a woman

he met at one of the events. "You have to be open minded," said Mr. Lowitt. "I'm not into bars or clubs or that whole scene. It's interesting, different and fun."

Last week, at a SpeedDating gathering at Levana, the participants were in their 20's and early 30's. But there are also events for people in their late 30's and 40's.   12

Lissa, a graduate student in black pants and a green sweater, had eight-minute dates just like the others, but three minutes would have been sufficient. "The women were very good looking, and the men were balding," she said. "I was wondering where are all the good-looking Jewish male genes. Even in the bathroom I had more fun talking to the women than the men."   13

At the beginning of the night, the participants, all wearing name tags, filled out an evaluation card with their names, phone numbers and e-mail addresses. This being SpeedDating, they were also asked to sum up each of their seven dates with yes or no answers to two questions: "Would I like to date this person?" and, "Was this person polite and respectful?"   14

After matches were made, the organizers asked men to place the first call. This is no hard and fast rule, but research suggests that women prefer men to initiate things, said Michelle Chandler, an Aish spokeswoman.   15

Rabbi Yitz Greenman, executive director of Aish New York, added, "The Talmud says that it is the way of man to pursue a woman."   16

At these dating affairs, clients are not allowed to exchange phone numbers themselves or give any indication that they have amorous intentions toward any particular date. What draws SpeedDating participants? Clients say they are tired of the bar and party scene and the awkwardness of asking for someone's number or being pressured into giving someone theirs.   17

On average, coordinators say the program has a 50 percent success rate: Half of its clients make at least one match.   18

It is quite different from the work of traditional Jewish matchmakers, known as Shadchens, who generally set up Orthodox Jews. "Much more thought goes into traditional matchmaking," Rabbi Deyo confessed. "But SpeedDating, because it's not just one person, certainly increases the odds."   19

Besides matchmaking, some Jewish singles, mostly Orthodox, meet at Sabbath meals at the home of a rabbi, Mr. Weiss said. Other unmarried Jews are finding their mates at Shabbaton, a Sabbath dinner for as many as 150 people, most of them single. Shabbatons are sponsored by synagogues or other Jewish institutions, and are sometimes held at a hotel or during weekend getaways.   20

Lissa, a 28-year-old with blue-green eyes, curly brown hair and catwalk cheekbones, was interested in only one man she met during a   21

SpeedDating session. She sensed he was spiritual. She is a Reform Jew from Manhattan and goes out only with Jewish men because there is, she says, "a spiritual and cultural bond." Some of her Christian friends don't understand. "I have to reverse things for them," she said. "I ask, 'Well, would you go to synagogue with me? And they say 'No.' "

Unlike most people at the gathering, Lissa, who spoke only on the condition that her full name not be used, came equipped with a few written questions. "I only had eight minutes, after all," she said. "I didn't want any dead airtime." Among her questions: "What are you passionate about—family, music, sports? And do you believe in magic?" Not the David Copperfield variety. But knowing instantly that you have met your soul mate. 22

In Los Angeles, SpeedDating has resulted in one marriage and an engagement. "In New York, in one case, we had a guy who wanted to date all seven women he was paired with and all seven wanted to date him," said Rabbi Greenman. "At first, people think this is kitsch, you know, cute. But we're fighting assimilation head on." 23

Rabbi Greenman said Aish is also studying the possibility of starting a separate SpeedDating organization for other groups. "We just don't know if other groups care about marrying within their own group," he said. "Do you think Irish only want to date Irish or Italians only Italians?" 24

Not everyone at SpeedDating events are devoted to the idea of marrying a Jew. Consider Ren, who spoke only on the condition that his full name not be used. He said it doesn't matter to him if his future wife is Jewish or not. He was born to a Portuguese Roman Catholic father and a Jewish mother. "My family is not interested in being Jewish," he said. "My grandmother, who was a Jew and a Communist in Vienna in the 30's, didn't sit well with the Nazis. So she wanted her children to assimilate." 25

Did Ren, a tall, dark literary agent in Manhattan, meet his match? He chose two women, but the interest was not reciprocal. 26

Still, he thought eight minutes was enough time for participants to decide on whether to pursue a conventional date. "It's all in the body language," he said. "And in the rhythms of your conversational style. It's not good if there are long silences or you're interrupting each other." 27

It's also not good if your date has logorrhea. Jennifer, a willowy, dark-haired 27-year-old, complained that one of her companions talked the full eight minutes about himself. "He didn't ask me anything," she said. Although Jennifer's parents do not care if she marries outside the religion, her grandmother is uncompromising in her position that she marry a Jew. "If I didn't, she would disown me," Jennifer said. 28

Alas, Jennifer didn't select anybody at Levana. But like several others who have tried SpeedDating, she said she would give it another shot. "I had a great time," she said. "Even though I was taller than 90 percent of those guys." 29

Questions for Reflection and Discussion

1. In the article, Lissa, the graduate student, complained that the men she met "were balding." And Jennifer, the willowy, dark-haired 27-year old, complained that she "was taller than 90 percent of those guys." How important is a person's appearance to you in terms of whom you date or whom you would marry or have married? Explain why you feel this way about appearances. What is more important to you than a person's appearance? Less important?

2. Many of the people who participated in the SpeedDating event were doing so because it was important for them to meet someone of the same religion. How important is it or was it to you to meet and marry someone of your religious, cultural, ethnic, or racial background? Would you marry someone who is very different from you in these categories? Why?

Topics for Writing

1. Choosing a mate or a partner is one of the most difficult, and important, things we do, and we often do this by going out on dates. Write an essay in which you describe a date that turned out to be a happy, satisfying experience, or a date that resulted in a sad, embarrassing, or disastrous experience. Be sure to answer the important who, what, where, when, why, and how questions. In your conclusion, give your reader advice on how to choose a date, a mate, or a partner, based on your own experiences.

2. Return to the free write you completed before you read the article. In that free write, you composed ten questions that you would ask a potential mate or spouse and you numbered them in order of importance. Write an essay in which *you* answer the questions you composed (devoting at least one paragraph to each question) fully, accurately, and honestly. In your conclusion, decide if you would be a good "pick" based on the answers you provided to the questions.

Reading 9–4

TO MY DEAR AND LOVING HUSBAND

Anne Bradstreet

In these days of speed dating, of meeting people via the Internet, or even being too busy to meet anyone because of our work and school schedules, we tend to forget the romantic nature and pleasure of meeting someone, falling madly in love, and living happily ever after. Maybe we need to go way back in time to be reminded of the days when "true love" was accepted and celebrated. The poem, "To My Dear and Loving Husband" may be just such a reminder. Written more than 300 years ago by Anne Bradstreet, it describes a wife's love for her husband as more valuable than "whole mines of gold."

Vocabulary

recompense (line 8)   return; payment
manifold (10)   many times over
persever (11)   persevere, last

Suggestions for Free Writing

Before you read the poem, take about 15 minutes to free-write on the following topic:

Think of two or three couples you know and decide if you would consider them "romantic" or "practical," based on their behavior toward each other. First, define what you think "romantic" means—for example, does it mean sending flowers on Valentine's Day or does it mean something deeper? Then describe what you think "practical" means—for example, does it mean saving money for a rainy day or using money to buy snow tires rather than for an exciting vacation or going out to a fancy restaurant? Next, describe each couple briefly to decide if they are romantic or practical based on your definitions. Finally, decide if *you* are romantic or practical based on your definitions. Has being one or the other ever caused problems in your relationships? Has being one or the other contributed to the success of your relationships?

If ever two were one, then surely we.   1
If ever man were loved by wife, then thee;   2
If ever wife was happy in a man,   3
Compare with me ye women if you can.   4
I prize thy love more than whole mines of gold,   5
Or all the riches that the East doth hold.   6
My love is such that rivers cannot quench,   7
Nor ought but love from thee give recompense.   8
Thy love is such I can no way repay;   9
The heavens reward thee manifold, I pray.   10
Then while we live, in love let's so persever,   11
That when we live no more we may live ever.   12

Questions for Reflection and Discussion

1. Some people would find Anne Bradstreet's poem inspiring, thinking that all relationships should be so perfect and all couples should be so devoted to each other. Others would find it absolutely unrealistic, thinking that such devotion and adoration are impossible and impractical. Which position do you take, or are you somewhere in the middle? Explain.
2. What do you think Bradstreet means when she writes in the final line of the poem: "That when we live no more we may live ever"?

Topics for Writing

1. Interview a couple who has a good (and if possible, long) relationship to find out their secret to success and happiness in their relationship. (You will probably get more interesting and informative information if you interview each member of the couple separately.) Then write an essay in which you describe the couple's methods, practices, and philosophy for having a successful, happy, and long-lasting relationship. (Be sure to include the way they deal with their problems—this is the true secret to success in any relationship.) In your conclusion, explain what you learned about a successful relationship as a result of conducting the interviews and writing the essay.
2. Return to the free write you completed before you read Anne Bradstreet's poem. Use the information there to write a poem in which you describe the advantages of being practical in a relationship, or in which you describe the advantages of being romantic in a relationship. Notice that Anne Bradstreet's poem is written in paired rhyming lines; that is, the first two lines rhyme, the second two lines rhyme, and so forth. Try to follow the same pattern in your poem. It's not an easy thing to do, but the results can be worth the effort, and it's a good way to practice developing your vocabulary by having to choose just the right word that fits and rhymes.

Reading 9–5

CITY MAP

Daniel Stolar

In the next selection, "City Map," Daniel Stolar explains the long and complicated relationship he had with Lillie Bausley, the African-American woman who cared for him from the time he was an infant and who cleaned and cooked for his family in their home in St. Louis, Missouri.

Stolar acknowledges the awkwardness of being a privileged white person writing about a woman of color who is employed by his family when he says that he is embarrassed by his inability to know what to call her. "I have played with giving her titles," he says, "maid, housekeeper, nanny, even good friend of the family, or adopted aunt, surrogate mother."

Vocabulary

proliferation (paragraph 1) large number of; growth of
dank (2) damp
neuronal connections (3) connection between the nervous system and the brain
alderman (3) a political position with some power and authority
ward (3) political district
fledgling (3) young; just starting out
regentrification (3) the changing of a neighborhood by the arrival of wealthier residents
cliché (4) an expression that is used so much that it loses its meaning
keloid (5) a scar or a tumor; in this case, a scar (see paragraph 20)
mimic (6) imitate
conjugated verbs (6) changed the ending of the verb to agree with the subject
switch (7) a tree branch
indulged (7) spoiled; pampered
invincible (8) unbeatable; indestructible
precarious (8) fragile; hanging on the edge
aloof (8) standoffish; distant
prognosis (9) probable or anticipated outcome of a disease
proximity (10) closeness
gall (10) nerve; audacity
reconcile (13) bring together; make sense of
traipsing (14) walking

Source: "City Map," by Daniel Stolar, originally published in *Doubletake Magazine,* Spring 1997, reprinted as "The Color of Love" in *Utne Reader.* Reprinted by permission of the author.

incessantly (14)   to repeat over and over

enlightened advocates (15)   those who understand a situation, although it is not their own

frailty (15)   weakness

innuendo (16)   something that is suggested but never said clearly or out in the open

calloused conservatism (16)   to grow hard and careful because of experience

condescension (16)   humoring or looking down on someone

continuum (16) a line or path of growth and change

implication (16)   the real meaning although it is not stated outright

coerced (19)   forced

irreducible (20)   cannot be reduced any further; clear and apparent

permeated (23)   affected every aspect of life

religious fatalism (31)   accepting what happens without question

manifestations (32)   expressions; examples

reverie (32)   dreaming or imagining

metaphysical journey (32)   a journey that symbolizes or represents something important

deride (34)   criticize severely; dismiss

Suggestions for Free Writing

Before you read the next selection, take about 15 minutes to free-write on the following topic:

> Think about a relationship or encounter you have had or have on a regular basis with someone of a different race, economic class, ethnic background, or professional status. Do the differences between the two of you have an impact on your relationship? If yes, explain and describe the impact. If no, explain whether you have had to overcome the differences or if neither of you noticed the differences in the first place. Next, consider and describe whether the relationship or encounter you described is an ordinary, accepted one in the environment in which it occurs, or it is out of the ordinary and exceptional.

I turn left out of Kingsbury Place, through the turn-of-the century stone gates, and head north on Union. Soon I cross Delmar, and the change in scenery indicates the line in St. Louis's social geography that I have just crossed. There is a flatness to the streetscape, a two-dimensionality to the buildings that front Union north of Delmar, an absence of lawns, a proliferation of liquor stores and drive-thrus. There are groups of black men hovering on corners, front stoops. Several miles farther north, I turn right on Natural Bridge, then left on Shreve and right on San Francisco. From the time I was born until I turned sixteen I rode this route with my mother and sister to take Lillie home. Since I have been able to drive, I have taken her home myself.

1

Often, I go inside and sit downstairs in the two-family flat where 2
Lillie lives, visiting with Janice, her daughter, and Gemila, her baby
granddaughter. The entry hall slants to the far corner where a yellow
box of mouse poison spills out its gray pellets. There is a proud, dusty
display of glassware in the armoir. The kitchen beyond is a dank and
close place. It is wallpapered halfway around where Lillie's son, James,
left it unfinished fifteen years ago. The wallpaper ends in a vertical line,
the end of one day's work, to be taken up the next. The exposed wall is
gray cement with a jagged crack running diagonally like a scar across it.
In twenty-seven years, I have never seen the upstairs of Lillie's house.

I know this drive as well as I know anything. If we could somehow 3
tease apart the neuronal connections that let us know what we know, the
map of this drive would be found in thick relief on my brain, a part of
me. In fact, the whole neighborhood around Kingsbury Place and the
house where I grew up (and where my father still lives) has a history that
is tangled inseparably with my own personal history: my father was
alderman of the twenty-fifth ward for four years; my mother succeeded
him and held the post for eight years after that. For twelve years the
battles of the old twenty-fifth ward were my dinnertime introduction to
the adult world. It was a ward of both the best and worst urban St. Louis
could offer; a unique pocket of majestic 1904 World's Fair–era private
streets, dismal boarded-up slums and tenements, a chunk of the second-
largest urban park in the country, a street of fledgling cafés and bou-
tiques. A ward of subtle and not-so-subtle boundary lines between white
and black, safe and dangerous, developing and forgotten. And it was a
ward that experienced unparalleled growth during my parents' time in
office—regentrification, rehabilitation, redevelopment—for which both
my parents, and particularly my mother, received a handsome amount of
credit and local celebrity. Into this ward, into our home, Lillie came three
times a week from her home in the heart of black north St. Louis, a part
of the city that otherwise I probably never would have known existed.

I was raised, in large part, by Lillie Bausley. I have played at giving 4
her titles—maid, housekeeper, nanny, even good-friend-of-the-family, or
adopted aunt, surrogate mother in my inability to explain her role in my
life and my embarrassment about it. But these are not titles which clarify.
In their very inadequacy, they point to the underlying cliché. It is a
cliché colored perhaps with racist underpinnings and assumptions:
Jewish white boy and girl raised in a tiny pocket of inner-city private
streets surrounded by black slums, raised by professional parents with a
black maid coming Monday, Tuesday, and Friday, and whenever my
parents were on vacation. She was hired a week before I was born and
works for my family to this day. And, cliché as it may be, there can be
little doubt that there are only a handful of people on this earth with
whom I have spent more time than I've spent with Lillie Bausley.

For the first twelve years of my life, Lillie's son, James, was also a fixture in our house. And even more, in my young imagination. He was like no one else I knew. Seven years older than I, he treated me inconsistently. Sometimes he would brush by without a word, his eyes fixed in the distance. But sometimes he would grab my hand in his and pull me to him to whisper in my ear. To me, he was eight feet tall, black as night, rippled with muscles. I remember the thick raised keloid on his neck—mean and dangerous, dizzying. At the age of sixteen, he'd had a tryout with the baseball Cardinals: he was a catcher with a rifle arm, a year or two away, they told him. It was the same year he taught me to pitch.

When James was aloof, I felt painfully little and awkward, and, something more, I felt painfully white, as if this were a part of my awkwardness. He was all power and confidence striding into our kitchen, twirling a toothpick in his mouth, and I literally paled in comparison. But more often, he would call me "partner" as he pulled me to him, and our kitchen became charged with his presence. I couldn't help but try to mimic his speech when we were together: "no" became "naw," "isn't" became "ain't"; I dropped words and conjugated verbs incorrectly.

Lillie will always tell the story of the time she went out back and tore a switch off the hedge "to get after" James and me. She tells the story as if this singular incident happened regularly, once a week, her putting us boys back in line, and to this day, she'll threaten to do it again if I give her a hard time. But the truth was she indulged us. When my parents were away on vacation, I stayed up to all hours watching movies on television while Lillie dosed on the couch. If James was out of school, he would stay with us, too. I stayed awake for the movie while they slept, their heads lolling slack-jawed on the other's shoulder. Together, James and I could get away with murder.

James was her only son of four children, and though he took the invincible part of a star high school athlete, his life had been a precarious one. He had juvenile-onset diabetes, and on a couple of occasions had been near death in a diabetic coma. When he picked Lillie up at our house, he guided her gently to the car, two fingers and his thumb on her elbow, and Lillie, who needed no help walking, let herself be guided. When I think of their relationship, this is the image I see: it was the way they were with each other. None of this thought was conscious at the time, of course, but I could feel what they brought into my house: in a place as familiar as my own kitchen, they brought not only warmth, but the excitement—danger, even—of another world, a poor and black world, which I had heard about on the news, which I heard in James's slang, and which I thought I saw in his hard, aloof walk. Sitting with them around the kitchen table, watching the afternoon soaps on TV, it was a world to which I was allowed the illusion of belonging.

The years 1978 and 1979 brought great, unwanted change to both my family and Lillie's. In the spring of 1978, when I was ten years old, my mother was diagnosed with breast cancer. Though she would live the remaining nine and a half years of her life mostly free of symptoms, she (and we) would never be free of the prognosis that accompanied her cancer, already present in four lymph nodes at the time of her mastectomy. We lived many of those years wondering if each one would be her last.

A little more than a year later, in the summer of 1979, Mr. Jule Gordon, a middle-aged Jewish man, a fixture at the handball courts in Forest Park for over twenty years, was shot dead there as he stopped for a drink between games. It was a brutal, headline-making murder, occurring within the boundaries of my mother's ward. It was a murder that terrified and outraged all of us, not simply because of its proximity, but also because of its sheer gall: the black man who shot Mr. Gordon walked up to less than ten feet away from him in broad daylight with dozens of people watching and shot him twice. There was another black man waiting behind the wheel of a car, and together the two men sped off. With plenty of witnesses to describe the make, model, and license number of the car, the police needed only a couple of days to make the arrests. One of the men arrested was James Bausley; he drove the car. It is likely that he drove north on Union, past the gates to Kingsbury Place, across Delmar, and back into north St. Louis—the same route I have taken myself so many times with Lillie.

The details of the following weeks and months, of James's trial and conviction, are no longer clear to me nearly two decades later. There was no question that James was driving the car, and no question that the other man had pulled the trigger. Apparently robbery was his intent, though the eight dollars in Mr. Gordon's pocket and the hundred dollars in his car were untouched. What lay in doubt was James's intent. He testified that he did not know why his friend wanted to stop at the handball courts, that he did not know his friend was carrying a gun. James said that he drove away because he was scared. He said that a black teenage man in north St. Louis does not go to the police after being involved in a murder. A black teenage man does not seek out the police for anything, James said.

Eighteen years old, James was tried as an adult, and convicted of second-degree murder. He was sentenced to ten years. With a call to the lieutenant governor of Missouri, a fellow Democrat, and a member of our temple, my mother was able to ensure that James was imprisoned in a minimum security prison, instead of the maximum security penitentiary in Jefferson City. It was a small victory, but one we were proud of at the time—something, finally, that we could do.

More than anything, I remember the conversations I had with my mother during that time. (How I must have tormented her.) I knew

James. He had hung around my house for as long as I could remember. He had taught me how to pitch—as a ten-year-old and for three or four years to come, it was my most prized ability. And, of course, I knew Lillie. I could not reconcile what I knew and what had happened. And so my twelve-year-old mind stopped on this question: what, really, had James done? What did he think as he drove to the park that day, as he slowed the car and his friend got out? As his friend rushed back in and they sped away?

Over and over I asked my mother these questions. (I would not dare ask Lillie.) Did my mother believe James? Did she think he knew what his friend had planned? At the dinner table, traipsing into my parents' bedroom in the middle of the night, I asked her. For a time, my mother sidestepped my questions—somehow it was the vital issue to her. Probably, more hardened to the city, she did not want to tell me what she really thought. We would never know the truth, I said incessantly, we would never know what James knew. Finally my mom settled on an answer: someday, she told me, we would know. If James was able to put his life together after prison in a good and moral way, if he was able to stay out of trouble, that would be our answer.

The black vote was one that my parents as liberal Democrats depended on. The dynamics of urban black poverty, the tension of black and white relations, these were part and parcel of my parents' daily work. And there is no question in my mind that they felt themselves to be enlightened (as I confess to feel now)—advocates of the poor and discriminated. I still believe—will always believe—that it was a cause to which they were truly dedicated. But it was a cause decidedly more likely to be met with frustration than success. A complex cause confounded endlessly by personal interest and human frailty, not to mention centuries of social, economic, and political inequality. I imagine now that more often than not, my parents came home from City Hall convinced of the futility of their work, and that, even as they ate the dinner prepared by a black maid, they searched for ways to steel themselves against this futility.

I wonder at the role of innuendo at our supposedly liberal dinner table. Between them, my parents spent twelve years on the board of aldermen, and a lifetime in the city, and I came to understand that this time in the trenches gave them license to make pronouncements that they would never have tolerated in their suburban peers. It was a sort of calloused conservatism born of the wounds of a raw and frustrated liberalism, still tender at its center. An "I've-been-there" conservatism, "I know how it is." Our dinner-table conversations were often heady and heated. How well I remember their gentle condescension: "It's good that you feel that way while you're young." And, etched permanently in my memory as a further point on this same continuum, were the subtle suggestions that Lillie's lenience and indulgence—the same indulgence she always showed me when my parents were away—were somehow responsible for James's downfall. What exactly was said? I am not sure. My parents would not dare suggest it openly—perhaps not even to themselves. "He should have been working," I may have heard at some point. "Major league baseball—that was a pipe dream. I don't know why she encouraged it." I could not swear to either of these quoted sentences, only to the felt truth of their implication. Something, somewhere had gone deathly wrong. And quietly, in the spaces between words, blame inevitable settled in around us on 59 Kingsbury Place.

"Come on, white boy, you ain't got a bad arm," James would say. 17 "Focus on my glove." Like a Zen master, James would tell me to focus only on the details of the thing: his glove hovering over the bare spot of earth that served as our plate, the hard, cracked grip of the ball, its dry seams under my fingers. "Forget everything else," he would tell me, until, at last, I could do it. There was only his glove, the ball, and my body moving smoothly through the wind up he taught me: the step back, the kick, my weight flying forward, propelling my arm like a whip, my back bending into the pitch, a moment of glorious silence and frozen time when only the ball moved, and then the satisfying pop of the baseball hitting leather. Pitch after pitch, only this pop of ball in leather punctuated the hot stillness of those St. Louis summer days. Over and over, I brought my focus back to his glove, my target, like a mantra until everything else fell away and experience became purely sensory, purely experiential. Maybe in those moments of athletic Zen, we were able to play ball on some common field.

Ten years old, I had a flawless windup. 18

But what lay behind our pitching sessions in the parkway outside 19 my house? Had Lillie asked him to play catch with me? Forced him to play with this geeky white kid seven years younger than he was? I imagine now that this was the case, and I imagine furthermore that she did it partly out of pity for the skinny kid who spent his afternoons watching television and whose father's fatherly gifts were obvious earlier and later in life but not at this vulnerable age. (To this day my dad loves to tease me when I am watching baseball on television by asking me who's winning the Super Bowl.) It is, indeed, a short leap to cynicism: was James's teaching me to pitch nothing more than an extension of the servant-employer relationship his mother had with my parents? Was this childhood idol of mine, this mentor, merely working for me?

I think now that this is the question that I was really asking my 20 mother. The reality of what happened—of murder, of prison—shed new light on the afternoons sitting around my kitchen, the late nights watching television, the pitching sessions in the parkway. Suddenly, the utter inequality of our two worlds and the relationship between them was as clear, as boldly black and white, as the newspaper headline and underlying photograph of James in his handcuffs. Here was truth irreducible, the subtext lain bare. (How well I can see that photograph to this day: his head lowered in shame, the thick scar on his neck as mean and expressive as his face was blank.) Now the enlightened talk of my liberal politician parents seemed nothing more than talk, hollow and false. The line between us and them was as solid and fixed as Delmar Boulevard.

I hardly dared to ask myself the questions that logically followed from those I asked my mother. If James had done it, if he had gone to the park that day with the intention of helping his friend kill Jule Gordon, what then? How was it possible? I imagined James gripping my hand, holding Lillie by the elbow. How could he be led to such brutality? What had happened on the streets of north St. Louis? Or, maybe, in the house at 59 Kingsbury Place? If, somehow, I could only believe that James had gone there innocently, unknowingly, then maybe I could reconcile it all. It could happen to anybody, this mistake, this lack of judgment. I saw my own pale hands on the steering wheel of James's Cutlass. I felt the presence next to me of that other black man whose face I knew from the newspaper. I think now that this is what I so desperately wanted to believe. That James and I were not so different, That I, too, could have followed the path that took James to that place on that day. 21

Each day for years after James went to prison, I brought home a dollars worth of change. I set it on my mantel, and Lillie collected it every two weeks. In prison, she told me, you needed change for everything. At the time, I allowed myself to think that I was really helping out. Now, I realize, of course, that Lillie could have gotten change anywhere, that she took it for me. Every other week she left bills on my mantel and took my dimes, nickels, and quarters to James in prison. It was my only connection to him. (I thought of the English class assignment of following the life of a penny, and I imagined my nickels, dimes, and quarters, leaving my house on Kingsbury Place, taking the familiar drive into north St. Louis, then another longer drive and finally passing beyond the prison walls to James. I imagined them in James's hands, being traded for soda, food, cigarettes.) In exchange for my silver, Lillie brought me statistics from James's games in the prison baseball league. She scribbled the numbers on the back of an envelope—otherwise, she said, she would never remember "all that nonsense." James was tearing up the league, hitting homers and doubles, throwing out ten consecutive base-stealers at one point. Lillie always said that he asked after me, but he never returned the notes I sent with her, and eventually I stopped writing. 22

Lillie continued to come Monday, Tuesday, Friday, just as I continued to make my way through school, summer camps, Little League. Every other weekend Lillie visited her son in prison. And the new given of my life was that my mother was dying of cancer. It permeated our house. My mother continued to work—finishing law school during her second aldermanic term, leaving politics for a law practice, and then, for 23 the last two years of her life, returning to public office as the appointed director of Forest Park. But the cancer and, more important, the doomsday prognosis were ever-present in the countless chemotherapy and radiation treatments, the three major surgeries, the wigs and scarves and hats. I wouldn't dare leave dishes in the sink—not because my mom worked hard and deserved better, but because my mom had *cancer*.

On the most basic level, Lillie kept our household running 24 smoothly as it suddenly became a thing of utmost importance. But there was more. My mother took on an almost untouchable presence in our family—cancer having greatly upped the ante of disturbing her. If my sister and I needed last minute help with a term paper, or got in trouble at school or just came home grumpy, my mother would always be our last resort, the final defense. But short of crisis, we would no longer bother her. We went instead to my father or to each other. Or to Lillie, who was there three times a week sitting in the kitchen—her thick elbow on the table, her chin in hand—ready to talk when we came home from school. She cooked our dinners and helped with math; she knew our friends by name; she told us that our mother was a strong woman, that she would keep fighting.

The question of James stayed lodged in my mind. Eventually, I 25 stopped asking my mother. By now I knew her exasperated response; only his life after prison could really prove his innocence to us. (I realize now how much she probably wanted to believe this herself.) And as time passed, and the murder and conviction receded further into the past, the questions burned less fiercely. New routine developed, took precedence. Even as I depended more on Lillie daily, the questions about her son, and all that they stood for, faded.

But in the end, there would be no long moral life after prison for 26 James to prove his innocence. Five years after he was convicted, a year shy of his probable release, he was stabbed to death in prison. Apparently another inmate tried to steal a small color television from him, there was a fight, and James was stabbed. I knew that television; I sat next to Lillie on the couch in our den as she picked it out of a catalogue. We had given it to her for Christmas. She, in turn, gave it to James.

I did not go to James's funeral. I cannot remember why. Recently, 27 I asked my father and my sister, and they are likewise at a loss to explain why I was not there. My father vaguely recalls taking the trip with my mother into north St. Louis to the funeral home during the wake. They went to see Lillie, he says, and she was not there when they went. In black communities, he explains still, it is customary to have a very long period of formal mourning, and nobody stays the entire time. I was sixteen years old, and it was during a time shortly after my mother's cancer had reappeared in some new part of her body, a time when things looked particularly bad. But I know that this is a best a partial explanation for why I was not at this man's funeral.

At my mother's funeral, four years later, Lillie stood in the row behind me in United Hebrew Temple on Skinker Boulevard, the western boundary of Forest Park. The rabbi motioned over our heads to the doors of the temple and invoked the image of that shining park beyond—at the time of her death, my mother was still the director of Forest Park. Its restoration would be my mother's legacy, the rabbi said. Lillie squeezed my hand while the rabbi spoke. At the time of his death, James was serving a prison sentence for a murder committed in that park. Lillie's palm was warm and moist. Tears streamed down her face. She would tell me later that she was crying for the both of us, as I was not yet able. 28

Lillie Bausley still works for my family. She is seventy-six years old and she comes only Mondays and Fridays now. She cooks dinner, washes the clothes, and goes on a weekly grocery-shopping trip. A professional maid service comes once a week to do what my father and stepmother call "the real cleaning." I still look for clues as to what exactly Lillie's role has been in my life. Yes, I love her. Yes, I have depended on and confided in her. But have I ever really known her? Have we ever met on equal ground? She flew to Boston with my family for my college graduation. On her own, she came to see me at medical school, clutching my mother's old flight bag as she came off the plane that terrified her. And when I visit St. Louis now as a young adult, she gets roughly the same amount of face-time as my three grandparents, more than my aunts, uncles, and cousins, less than my father, sister, and girlfriend. 29

We still sit around the kitchen talking. If my dad and stepmother happen to be out of town, Lillie still stays at our house (she says she likes the peace and quiet), and I pretend to feel indulged as we sit up late watching movies. I cannot help but cringe as she calls me "my only boy, now." 30

Silent tears still fall down her face if we talk about James. She is peaceful as she talks, resolved. She has gone to the same church every Sunday for as long as I can remember (and with her, twice a year, all of my newly outgrown clothes), and she has a religious fatalism that I can only envy. "It was his time," she says. "And when God calls, there's nothing we can do. Everybody's got their time to go. Just like when God called your mother. Maybe if he'd have gotten out of that prison he'd be running the streets on crack. You know how them streets are where I live. All that matters is I know in my heart that he was a good boy. I never did howl and carry on at his funeral like all the rest." 31

My parents were responsible for the bike paths in Forest Park. The original loop, 6.2 miles around the perimeter, was my father's idea during his aldermanic term; the later addition, slicing through the center of the park, my mother's. I ride or run or walk these paths with great pride. They are invariable crowded, and in St. Louis, they represent one of the most culturally and racially mixed assemblages of our population. Moving along these real-life manifestations of my parent's 32 vision, I fall easily in reverie, the progress of my physical body symbolic of the metaphysical journey these paths afford me. The newer path invokes my mother in its every turn and twist. The original path, my father's, passes by the handball courts where James helped kill a man. They are paths that permit remembering and contemplation, but they seem to defy arrival. Surely there is symbolism in this unending series of loops and circles lain down for me by my parents.

No matter how I try to approach the subject now, I could never 33 have arrived at the handball courts that afternoon. It never, ever could have been me in the car with the black man who became a murderer that day. This is the real answer to the questions that lodged permanently in my twelve-year-old mind. The reality of living twenty-four hours a day in a black man's skin in north St. Louis is unimaginable to me. How could it be otherwise? Even as I pictured my own hands on James's steering wheel, I could not hear the conversation in the car. I could not feel the expression on his face or see the look on his friend's. The simple truth is that I can never know what was on James's mind that day as he drove to and from Forest Park.

But at my mother's funeral I hold Lillie's hand. She cries my tears. 34 A cynic would deride this moment, this relationship. It is false, he would say, a servant-employer relationship, rich-boy-poor-woman relationship, what can you share? This logic is convincing, but wrong. At some point we do come together, It may not be a complete union, but what union between people is? The lines dividing us are deep and complex. I may not go upstairs in Lillie's house, but I do come inside and sit awhile.

Questions for Reflection and Discussion

1. In the last line of paragraph 2, Stolar says, "In 27 years, I have never seen the upstairs of Lillie's house." And then in the very last sentence he says, "I may not go upstairs in Lillie's house, but I do go inside and sit awhile." What is the significance of going upstairs in Lillie's house? Explain the balance he creates between the two sentences by placing one early in the essay and placing the other at the end of the essay.

2. Do you think Lillie's son, James, liked Daniel Stolar? Or do you think Stolar was correct when he wondered in paragraph 19, "Had Lillie coerced James to play with me?" and when he asked at the end of the same paragraph, "Was this childhood idol of mine merely working for me?" If you were James, how would you have felt about growing up with Stolar and having your mother work for his parents?

Topics for Writing

1. Write an essay in which you explain how you choose your friends: Are they all very similar to you in terms of race, class, professional and economic

status, and gender, or are your friends from various backgrounds and walks of life? Be sure to give details and examples so that you *show* your readers what kind of friends you choose rather than just *tell*. By showing, you are giving your readers the evidence to understand and accept what you write.

2. Stolar tries to explain in the last paragraph of his essay that although some people would find his relationship with Lillie "false," because of the differences between them (she is black and he is white; she is poor and he is rich; she works for his family and thus he is her employer), he believes that "at some point, we do come together." Return to the free write you completed before you read Stolar's essay. Based on the information there, the information in the essay, and your own experiences and observations in the environment in which you live, work, and/or attend school, do you think it possible for such people to come together as friends?

Additional Writing Topics about Relationships

1. You have just read five selections about relationships. Hopefully they have helped you to think about your relationships and enabled you to better define your values and needs in terms of your relationships with others. Reflect on the readings and the essays you have written in response to them, and use this information to write an essay in which you describe the most important relationship you have ever had (or still have) in your life. It could be a relationship with a spouse, a lover, a friend, a teacher, a family member, even a pet. Remember to describe the relationship in full and accurate detail, being sure to answer the important who, what, where, when, why, and how questions. Also be sure to explain why the relationship is the most important one in your life. In your conclusion, explain what benefits you and the other party have received as a result of this relationship.

2. Review the selections in this chapter, along with the many selections in other chapters, on relationships. See, for example, "Theme for English B" in Chapter 1 (between student and teacher), "Angry Fathers" in Chapter 2 (between father and son), "The Call" in Chapter 3 (between an imprisoned mother and her son), "When Money Is Everything, Except Hers" in Chapter 4 (between a poor girl and the other students in her school), "Driving Lessons" in Chapter 5 (between a child and his parents), "The Mother Tongue" in Chapter 6 (between mother and daughter), "First They Changed My Name" in Chapter 7 (between a girl and her teachers), and "Who Am I Today?" in Chapter 8 (between worker and employers).

Use the information in these articles, in addition to your own experiences and observations, and the information you recorded in the free write that you completed at the beginning of this chapter, to write an essay in which you discuss the importance of having various relationships in our lives. Be certain to incorporate at least one quote from each essay in order to gain practice in this important skill, one that will be required of you in college writing assignments. Use of quotes will also enable your reader to understand the importance to you of each type of relationship described.

Chapter

10

Growing Older and Wiser

You probably have not given too much thought to growing old because, if you are like most college students, you are probably in your late teens or early twenties, very far from your "golden years." However, you are also probably watching your parents or guardians make plans for retirement, and most of you have grandparents who are growing older.

Although old age is a time when one's health or mental capacities sometimes fail, it is also a time when older people are able to enjoy their families, particularly their grandchildren, and share with them the wisdom and knowledge they have gained over the course of their long lives.

The selections in this chapter deal with the aging process. They show that aging does not always have to be a time of pain and loss; it can also be a time to make new discoveries, to learn new skills or hobbies, and to meet new friends or mates. And most important, these selections show that growing old provides us with the time we need to reflect on the past and to pass along important information to the younger people in our lives.

Pre-reading Activity

Before you read the selections in this chapter, take about 15 minutes to free-write on the following topics:

Think about the people in your life whom you consider "older." How old are they? What age does someone have to be for you to consider him or her "old"? What kind of relationship do you have with these "older" people: Do you learn from them? Enjoy their companionship? Or are they a burden to you because they are ill or unable to care for themselves? What qualities do they possess that you admire? What qualities do they possess that are not so admirable? Do you feel there is a "generation gap" between you and these people, or do you feel that the difference in age actually makes the relationship better? Do other family members respect these older people and appreciate their wisdom? Or are these older people not able to care for themselves and thus are a burden on their families? Do you feel that these people are discriminated against by society because of their age? Or are they given respect and admiration in our society? Give examples. What are their greatest fears? What are their greatest pleasures?

Reading 10–1

THE KARATE KIDS AND ME

Marlene Demarco

In the next selection, "The Karate Kids and Me," Marlene Demarco describes the way that beginning karate lessons at the age of 51 helped her to discover that "age isn't as limiting as I'd thought." While she is proud of the fact that she earned her white belt, the real value of her experience was the opportunity to be accepted as an equal by the 10- to 12-year old boys in her karate class.

Vocabulary

plight (paragraph 1)   problem; difficulty
persevered (8)   stuck with it

Suggestions for Free Writing

Before you read the article, take about 15 minutes to free-write on the following topic:

What is the most extraordinary thing you ever accomplished? What circumstances led you to do this extraordinary thing? What circumstances made it extraordinary? Did this accomplishment require physical strength and stamina, mental ability, or perseverance? Were other people impressed with your accomplishment, or was it something only you knew about? What did you learn about yourself as a result of this accomplishment? If you could repeat it, what would you do the same? What would you do differently?

My plight is the direct result of the mild winter of '97. If we'd had   1
the usual blizzard followed by subzero temperatures that turn snow, salt
and cinders into high-tech igloo-building material, I would have been
huddled inside my home office. Last February was so mild I was broom-
scrubbing the garage when Chris walked in to gab. The six families in
our town-house complex rarely phone each other, but anyone standing
in front of his or her house is fair game for conversation.

Chris mentioned that her 10-year-old was taking karate, and I casu-   2
ally remarked it was something I wanted to try—someday. She promised
a set of registration forms, then delivered them and prodded: "Did you

Source: "The Karate Kids and Me," by Marlene Demarco, from *Newsweek*, November 24, 1997. Copyright 1997 Newsweek, Inc. All rights reserved. Reprinted by permission.

call yet?" In the name of town-house peace, I phoned the karate club and talked to a young woman.

"I'm interested in taking karate, but I'm 51, overweight and completely out of shape. I know your current session started several weeks ago, so when does the next session begin? Next fall?"   3

"Oh, I'm sure you will fit in perfectly. Our oldest beginner was 72. I'll have *Sensei* call you." Sensei? From watching Saturday-morning cartoons, I knew Sensei was a teaching rodent. It was difficult to envision a human with that title.   4

On the phone, Sensei was calm and encouraging. He assured me I could catch up with the rest of the beginners and that karate was for me. In person, he was a sensitive-looking fellow seated in an office crammed with trophies and press clippings. This couldn't be all that bad. Anyway, I could always quit if I didn't like it. That proved to be a naive thought.   5

Age is meaningless among beginning students, so I found myself in a class of 10- and 12-year-olds, who looked at me with gaping mouths. My first class began with a bow and a warm-up. I made it through the jumping jacks, stretching twists and push-ups with the help of supreme determination and a body that was surprised enough to do what I asked of it. This was the first time I had tried these moves since PE class decades ago.   6

After that first hour, I got into my car knowing that getting out might not be possible. In a few hours, the pain had increased until breathing hurt and crawling was the only way of getting around the house. By the time I could consistently stand erect again, I had to go to the next class. Anything that caused this much pain had to be good exercise.   7

As the weeks passed and I learned to tolerate the pain that never quite goes away, I became fascinated by my classmates. The girls always stopped talking whenever I was around, and I was amazed at how easy it is to be transported back to fourth-grade feelings of not being part of "the group." The boys were very different. After a few sessions, they accepted me as an equal and asked me to practice with them before class. I became one of the guys. I couldn't disappoint my pals, so I persevered.   8

Gradually, all the chauffeur-mothers, who were considerably younger than I, realized I was a peer of their children. After they individually told me how they would really, really like to take the class but just couldn't, I started feeling like a defender of the baby boomers, and I had to continue. When I met the mother of my 16-year-old tutor, a talented young man charged with the responsibility of catching me up to the class, she told me she would have taken the class if she were my age. She is four years younger; that spurred me on again.   9

Then Sensei got into my head. This slightly built, quiet person turned into a taskmaster in class. He talked of self-defense, the need to develop strength and what we must know to test for our white belts. As   10 we prepared for the test, the pressure became intense, but the competition was against oneself.

Students of karate naturally respect those of higher rank because 11 the superiority of skill is so obvious. The "colored" belts encouraged us "no" belts as our test day approached, but the anxiety Sensei's own brother exhibited before testing for a purple belt wasn't comforting. We knew Sensei would be a brutal judge. This was crazy. Why was I giving such power to this stranger?

Five days before the ordeal, I sat in church thinking that I was stupid 12 for beating myself up over something that was supposed to be fun. Then the priest started his homily. As I sat there persuading myself not to go through with the test, I heard the priest say, "Never give up . . . strive for new accomplishments." It is impossible to quit with God on your back.

Sleepless before the test, I started eating compulsively in the middle 13 of the night. On D-Day, I washed my *gi* (white heavy cotton pants and top) and had it professionally pressed. It was a hot, humid summer evening, and two of my pals and I agreed to warm up in the hallway until we were permitted to enter the gym. Then my exquisite luck held. I ripped my pants when I tried a split. The tearing sound got the boys' attention; they assured me the top of my uniform concealed the damage.

I wish I could say my fears vanished and I performed brilliantly, but 14 I can't. I tried to concentrate as I watched the others. Then it was my turn. I could feel myself getting weaker as I went through the series of blocks and punches and kicks. Sensei called for a *maegeri*, a front kick, and my mind went blank. As I looked into the mirror, I saw the reflection of the boys' stunned faces, and I kept thinking that this kick must be more complex than I knew it was. After a couple of false starts, I did it. But there was no thrill of victory.

After we completed the test, one of the boys put his arm around 15 me. "I know why you messed up on the kicks. You were thinking about the rip in your pants, 'cause you know that kick." He patted me on the shoulder and left. It is amazing how encouraging a kind word from a 10-year-old can be.

I had learned much more than karate in those four months. 16 There's great pleasure in realizing that the time of tests is not over. And that, just maybe, age isn't as limiting as I'd thought because I did earn my white belt and I'm working toward the yellow.

Questions for Reflection and Discussion

1. In paragraph 8, Demarco notes that although the boys in her karate class accepted her, the girls did not. In fact, the girls "always stopped talking" whenever she was around, leading Demarco to remember what

it was like to not be part of the group. Why do you think the young boys in the class reacted so differently than the young girls?

2. Demarco mentions that she is 51 years old. Do you think 51 is old? Consider what "old" means to you: Does it depend on a person's age, or does it depend on the person's attitude, condition, and behavior?

Topics for Writing

1. Think of an accomplishment achieved by someone whom, you know who is older, and write an essay describing the accomplishment, including the same type of information that Demarco includes in her essay. Be sure to give all the important background information, about both the person and the accomplishment, and be sure to answer the important who, what, where, why, when, and how questions. In your conclusion, explain the significance of this accomplishment to the person, and then explain what *you* learned about the person, and about aging, as a result of the accomplishment. (If possible, give a copy of your essay to the person you wrote about and ask him or her to respond to it.)

2. Return to the free write you completed before you read the article, and use the information there to write an essay very similar to Demarco's in which you describe and explain an accomplishment that you are very proud of. As you model your essay after Demarco's, be sure to give all the important background information explaining why you undertook the challenge that led to your accomplishment. Answer the important who, what, where, why, when, and how questions. In your conclusion, explain what you learned or gained as a result of the accomplishment, just as Demarco does when she says, "I had learned much more than karate in those four months. There's great pleasure in realizing that the time of tests is not over. And that, just maybe, age isn't as limiting as I'd thought."

I AM ASKING YOU TO COME BACK HOME

Jo Carson

The next selection is a poem entitled "I Am Asking You to Come Back Home," written by Jo Carson, in which a mother asks her grown son or daughter (it isn't clear which) to come home "before you lose your chance of seein' me alive." "I'd rather you come back now and got my stories," she says to her adult child. "I've got whole lives of stories that belong to you."

Vocabulary

No vocabulary

Suggestions for Free Writing

Before you read the poem, take about 15 minutes to free-write on the following topic:

All families have stories, and they are almost always told by older members of the family. Often, they are about what life was like in the "olden days," and they describe hardship, sacrifices, hard work, and change. Just as often, however, they are funny stories describing unusual relatives, friends, or behavior.

Think of the stories you have been told by your parents, grandparents, guardians, or other older relatives that you want to pass on to your own children. Write down as much as you can remember of these stories, recalling as many details as possible. Then explain why each story is significant to you and why it will be (or is) significant to your children.

I am asking you to come back home   1
before you lose your chance of seein' me alive.
You already missed your daddy.
You missed your Uncle Howard.
You missed Luciel. I kept them and I buried them.
You showed up for the funerals.
Funerals are the easy part.

You even missed that dog you left.
I dug him a hole and put him in it.

2

It was a Sunday morning but dead animals
don't wait no better than dead people.

3

My mama used to say she could feel herself
runnin' short of the breath of life. So can I.
And I am blessed tired of buryin' things I love.
Somebody else can do that job to me.
You'll be back here then, you come for funerals.

4

I'd rather you come back now and got my stories.
I've got whole lives of stories that belong to you.
I could fill you up with stories,
stories I ain't told nobody yet,
stories with your name, your blood in them.
Ain't nobody gonna hear them if you don't
and you ain't gonna hear them unless you get back home.

5

When I am dead, it will not matter
how hard you press your ear to the ground.

6

Questions for Reflection and Discussion

1. Do you think it is important for family stories to be shared and passed on? Explain.
2. Do you think the son or daughter who is being addressed in the poem *will* come back home to hear the stories? Explain.

Topics for Writing

1. Think of an older person in your life who has had an important impact on your upbringing—who has taught you, guided you, helped you, loved you. Write a poem to this person explaining what he or she has done for you, what he or she has taught you, and the effect he or she has had on you. Be certain to give specific details in your poem, just as Jo Carson gives specific details about how her child missed seeing daddy, Uncle Howard, even the dog, and about how she buried the dog on a Sunday morning. Avoid making large, empty statements about how wonderful the person is; that kind of writing belongs in greeting cards. Be specific and precise so that your reader can see and know the person you are describing in your poem.

2. Return to the free write you completed before you read the poem, and use the information there to write an essay in which you recall your favorite story passed on to you from an older relative. Write the essay in such a way that you can save it and pass it along to your children and grandchildren, so they will be able to know at least one family story that is important to you. In your conclusion, explain why you chose to describe this particular family story, what it means to you, and what it taught you about your family.

THE OLD IN ONE ANOTHER'S ARMS

Davida Rosenblum

Although there are several selections in this book about older people, most of them simply describe the older person's wonderful qualities (as in Henry Louis Gates's description of his mother in Chapter 3) or the older person's needs or problems (as in Daniel Stolar's description of Lillie's loneliness after the death of her son in Chapter 9). What hasn't been covered yet is the need that older people have for companionship and love.

The next selection, entitled "The Old in One Another's Arms," written by Davida Rosenblum, does just that. It is an essay filled with romance and passion, but it is also filled with the wisdom and grace that the old acquire as a result of their life experiences—both joyful and painful.

Vocabulary

iconoclastic (paragraph 1)   one who is untraditional, different, finds new ways to do things
charismatic (1)   an appealing, attractive personality
euphemism (2)   a nice way of saying something (lavatory instead of toilet, for example)
deified (2)   made into a god
entrancing (4)   pleasing, romantic
suffused (6)   filled
obliterated (7)   no longer existing; destroyed
dewlaps (7)   loose folds of skin
invariably (7)   without fail, always
preamble (11)   an introduction
manifest (15)   showing itself
stigmata (16)   signs
accretion (16)   accumulation
beguiling (17)   attractive, enticing
viable (17)   capable
immobilized (20)   frozen, unable to move
aghast (20)   shocked
intolerable (21)   unable to bear
excruciating (23)   extremely painful
increments (23)   amounts, sections
elliptical (27)   avoiding facts and descriptions
conduits (27)   carriers
paradoxically (29)   a contradiction causing confusion

Source: "The Old in One Another's Arms," by Davida Rosenblum, *The New York Times Magazine* June 29, 1997. Copyright 1997 Davida Rosenblum. Reprinted by permission of Sterling Lord Literistic, Inc.

Suggestions for Free Writing

Before you read the next essay, take about 15 minutes to free-write on the following topic:

> Describe the way you think a relationship can suffer with the passage of time. Think of the oldest couple you know in a strong relationship: How is age affecting their lives together? Is it making their relationship better or worse? Stronger or weaker? Is age bringing them wisdom and comfort, or is age depriving them of health and happiness? If one of these people died, do you think the other one would ever enter another relationship? Why? How would you feel if one of the people entered another relationship after the death of his or her partner? Would you be happy or upset?

Ralph, my brilliant, adored, iconoclastic, charismatic film-maker husband of 47 years, died suddenly in the fall of 1995. A little more than two months later I learned that the wife of my very first lover, whom I hadn't seen in almost half a century, had passed away at the same time. I was stunned by the double coincidence: Marc and I married our respective mates within a month of each other, and we had become widowed two weeks apart. 1

Marc was not only my first lover; he was also my first love. For nearly two years we'd "dated," a word that in those days could mean anything from a weekly movie to "sleeping together," another euphemism of the late 40's. Besides a commonality of interests, we shared a hearty appetite for sex, though we were novices at the time. Ultimately, Marc chose to marry Kitty, his English sweetheart, whom he'd met during World War II, but his image remained with me over the entire course of a difficult but richly textured marriage. Though in his last years Ralph had mellowed into almost the mate I'd always wanted, he was not Marc, or at least not the Marc deified by memory into the model of a lover no mere mortal could match. 2

Overwhelmed by conflicting emotions, I spent the next several hours agonizing over the news. Finally I sent him a brief condolence note: "My deepest sympathy on your recent loss. Having just suffered a similar loss myself, I know what you must be feeling." It ended with a three-word sign-off, the exact configuration of which eluded me for the better part of an hour. I chose, finally, "With remembered affection." 3

Marc's reply arrived three days later. I opened it with a pounding heart. Inside were thanks for having written, and an invitation to call if I shared his view that meeting again might be "therapeutic at worst, entrancing at best." And call I did, after a long afternoon of staring at the phone, wondering what I would say. 4

After some awkward conversation punctuated with long silences— how does one gracefully span 50 years?—Marc suggested meeting for dinner. 5

"Why don't you come here?" I proposed. We made a date for the 6
following night. Never were 30 hours so suffused with a combination of
dread and eagerness.

At precisely 6:30 the doorbell rang. I took a deep breath and 7
opened the door. There, bearing a bottle of wine, a bouquet of tulips
and an expression as tragic as the one I'd been seeing in the mirror
since the death of my husband, was an almost unrecognizable Marc. He
looked older than the 72 years I figured him to be. His jaw line was
nearly obliterated by the dewlaps that age invariably brings, and there
was a swath of bare scalp where wiry reddish hair had once grown. My
young lover was nowhere to be seen. We stood staring at each other for
some time; I suppose he was looking at me with the same thought.

We spent the next four hours weeping over our losses and 8
describing our lives during the intervening years, all the while picking
with little interest at the lavish spread I had prepared.

As we said goodbye, Marc put an arm around my shoulder and 9
gave me what started as the barest of hugs, only to become a full body
hug that lasted for an astonishing several minutes. As it ended, he kissed
me lightly. There was a faint suggestion of tongue. Hesitantly, I met his
with the tip of my own.

"Oh, God!" I thought despairingly, "here we go again." 10

Marc phoned two days later. "I owe you a dinner," he said, without 11
preamble. "What are you doing this afternoon?"

We decided on a movie. I suppose we weren't sure we had anything 12
more to say to each other. We both arrived at the theater a full half-hour
early. As we talked, I gradually became aware that his depression was
gone. He was cheerful, lively and amusing.

"What on earth happened between Monday and now?" I asked, 13
unable to hide my astonishment. "You're so different!"

"It was the hug," he said. 14

We took our seats just as the lights dimmed. Within minutes, a 15
creeping anxiety overtook me and blotted out whatever was taking place
on the screen. During our conversation, everything about Marc that I
had once found irresistible was again manifest. I knew that some land-
mark events would soon be taking place, chief among them bed. And I
had a problem with that.

I, too, had changed. My body now bore all the stigmata of 50 years 16
of aging, stretch marks from two pregnancies and a hysterectomy scar
the least of them. With sinking heart, I did a quick inventory of every
defect, sure that they would be an immediate turn-off for anyone who
hadn't experienced their accretion gradually over the years.

When I finished contemplating my own shortcomings, I tried to 17
visualize Marc's. The prospect of dealing with a body that might be in
comparable shape, even if I had known it intimately half a century
before, was less than beguiling. Besides, it occurred to me that he might

no longer be sexually viable—my impression was that most men in their 70's weren't. And even though at our age it probably wouldn't matter one way or another, the process of discovery was unimaginable.

As we walked toward Sixth Avenue looking for a place to eat, Marc mentioned that he'd become a bird watcher since his retirement, and asked if I'd like to accompany him to his favorite wildlife preserve that Saturday. By now I was crazed. Here was Marc laying himself out for me like a picnic lunch, and all I could think of was the dreaded moment when we would find ourselves in bed. Between bouts of panic and the need to keep up my end of the conversation, I considered the possibilities. On the one hand, he might run screaming from the room. On the other hand, *I* might run screaming from the room. And even if we could tolerate the sight of each other, we might not be moved to do anything more than—literally—sleep together. In light of our youthful passion, I found this scenario the most depressing of all. 18

As we neared the corner, I turned to face him. My next words came as a complete surprise. "You'll be staying over tonight," I said in a conversational tone. "Shall I pick up some bagels for breakfast?" 19

I stood there immobilized, aghast at my audacity. Marc looked at me thoughtfully for a long moment. "Bagels would be nice," he said. 20

Dinner was tense, at least for me—just one more intolerable delay on the way to the moment of truth. One block from my apartment, we stopped to pick up the bagels. I nearly groaned aloud when Marc expressed a preference for poppy seed. I have always hated poppy seeds. By unhappy coincidence, they'd been Ralph's favorite too. 21

I managed to kill five minutes by completely rearranging the closet as I hung up our coats. I killed another five moving the bagels with exaggerated care into poppy-seed-proof plastic bags. It was now seven minutes after 9. There was nothing to do but make a pot of coffee and talk some more; bedtime at 9:07 was for impatient lovers, and I was certainly not that. 22

Time passed in excruciating increments. I kept looking at my watch, hoping both that the hands wouldn't move and that they would move faster. Marc seemed unnaturally calm. After several centuries, midnight arrived. The next move would have to be mine, it appeared, as Marc seemed perfectly content to sit and chat all night. I stood up. 23

"Well," I said, in a voice more suitable to an execution than a seduction, "I guess it's time." 24

One of my flowered flannels was hanging on the back of the bathroom door. For a moment I considered getting under the covers in the altogether rather than putting it on; but that, I felt, would be giving myself an unnecessary handicap. Better to wear the flannel with its pink peonies and red cabbage roses and take my chances. I am by character 25 more flannel than silk, and on flannel would my future rest. Shivering, I slid the nightgown over my head and got into bed.

"O.K.," I called weakly, and placed my fate in the hands of the gods.   26

There will not be here a description, elliptical or otherwise, of   27
what ensued. I am the wrong generation for that. Suffice it to say that yes, he could, and our lovemaking was as delicious, intoxicating and graceful—yes, graceful, as it had ever been in our youth. There was not one moment of awkwardness; however altered, our bodies were merely the conduits of our mutual need and our joy in having rediscovered each other.

It has been more than a year since that momentous night. We con-   28
tinue to mourn our lost companions, but grief is now part of the back-drop of our new life rather than a wrenching interruption of it. Each day, however we choose to spend it, is a miracle; we are endlessly sur-prised by this unexpected gift and the pleasure we take in each other's company. It is all the proof we need that there is indeed life after death.

I gaze at Marc blissfully over our morning bagels—still poppy seed,   29
I regret to say—hold onto his hand during our afternoon walks and at night lie spoon-fashion against his large, comfortable body. He is old and so am I, but that knowledge, too, is part of the backdrop. Sometimes I think wistfully of the years I will never have with my husband—and, paradoxically, those I missed spending with Marc. But mostly I am content. The young Marc is gone forever, the dream is gone as well. But I no longer need either. The circle has been closed, and with gratitude, love and mutual delight, we are in it together.

Questions for Reflection and Discussion

1. In paragraph 27, Davida Rosenblum says that she will not give her readers a description of the love making that occurred between her and Marc. Do you think this was a wise decision? Explain.
2. How would you feel if one of your parents or grandparents died and the other began an intimate relationship with a former boyfriend or girlfriend within one month? Explain.

Topics for Writing

1. Write an essay in which you explain why you agree with Rosenblum's deci-sion to sleep with Marc, or write an essay in which you explain why you dis-agree with her decision to sleep with Marc. If you do not want to take such a firm position on the topic, you can explain why you feel uncertain about whether you agree entirely or disagree entirely. (Some people, for example, may be put off by the fact that they slept together so soon after

the death of their spouses; others may be put off for religious or moral reasons; and yet others may think Davida and Marc are simply too old to be engaging in a sexual relationship.)

2. Return to the free write you completed before you read the essay, and use the information there to write an essay describing the kind of relationship you want to have when you grow old. You can use as your inspiration the experiences of the couple you described in your free write. Be sure to include in your essay all of the aspects of a relationship that are important to you. (If you chose to answer writing question 1 in Chapter 9 relating to Anne Bradstreet's poem, you may want to go back to that essay for information and inspiration as well.)

Reading 10–4

A TATTOO IN TIME

Marian Haglund Juhl

The next selection, "A Tattoo in Time" by Marian Haglund Juhl, deals with a topic that all of us, but particularly older people, are concerned with: Who will make the decision to "pull the plug" if we become too ill or incapacitated to make the decision for ourselves? In this essay, Juhl considers getting a tattoo to ensure that her wishes will be followed.

Vocabulary

resuscitate (paragraph 1)   bring back to life; use life-saving measures on a very ill person

incapacitated (2)   unable to care for onself; unable to function independently

idiosyncrasies (2)   peculiar habits

oblivious (4)   completely unaware of what is going on

flippant (6)   a lighthearted remark not meant to be taken seriously

elicit (10)   draw out, find out

mortality (18)   the fact that we are all going to die

irrevocable (21)   not changeable; not reversible

Suggestions for Free Writing

Before you read the following article, take about 15 minutes to free-write on the following topic.

Death is an unpleasant subject, something we would prefer not to talk or even think about. Yet, it is certainly something that we must all confront: not only our own death but the deaths of those we love very much. Think about the kind of death you want to have and answer the following questions in as much detail as possible: Do you want to be kept alive as long as possible, or do you want to make sure the medical establishment does not take any extraordinary measures to keep you alive? Do you want something in between? And after you die, what do you want to happen to your body? Do you want to be buried or cremated or frozen? Do you want to donate your organs so they can be used by someone who needs them and can benefit from them? What kind of ceremony do you want after your death? Do you want a religious service, or do you want your friends to go to a bar and drink a toast for you instead?

Source: "A Tattoo in Time," by Marian Haglund Juhl, from *Newsweek*, October 13, 1997.
Copyright 1997 Newsweek, Inc. All rights reserved. Reprinted by permission.

Seventy-one may seem an odd age at which to get your first tattoo, 1
especially for a woman. Just about the only reason I haven't gone ahead
and had it done is that I haven't quite figured out the wording. It will
read something like this: DO NOT RESUSCITATE. And I'll have it written
right across my chest.

I've always enjoyed good health, despite a mastectomy 15 years 2
ago. But I do have a genuine fear of becoming incapacitated by a serious
accident or illness. For me, the fear has not so much to do with dying
but with remaining alive and dependent on others for my care. I've
always been fiercely independent—my hair has never been touched by a
hairdresser, for instance. My family knows that when I die, I want to be
cremated. No one could ever apply my makeup the way I do, and I'm
not about to be dolled up by some undertaker. My husband attributes
my idiosyncrasies to a stubborn Swedish heritage.

Maybe I am a bit peculiar. And I do admit to a touch of crotcheti- 3
ness. But as far as DO NOT RESUSCITATE goes, I'm deadly serious.

The legal and medical communities have several systems in 4
place that recognize my right to refuse extreme measures to keep me
alive, should it come to that. Still, I remain skeptical. What if I am
treated by a doctor who believes it is a physician's responsibility to
apply all the heroic efforts available, despite the patient's wishes?
What if my paperwork gets lost? What if my paperwork is exactly
where it is supposed to be, but no one stumbles across it until after
I've been resuscitated, and my oblivious body is kept alive by life
support?

I don't want my children to have to make the decision to "pull the 5
plug" on Mom. I've lived a wonderful life. I'd prefer, when the time
comes, to have a wonderful death, as well.

So what to do? It occurred to me that a tattoo right across my chest 6
would be impossible to lose or ignore. (As an artist, I truly believe a
visual display is worth a thousand words.) The idea, which at first was
simply a flippant remark I tossed out to amuse my painting group, has
merit. Think about it: the first thing they do to you in most emergency
situations is rip your shirt open to attach monitors and other gizmos of
the trade. Who could miss my message?

Determined I may be, but even I cringe at the thought of all those 7
letters being pricked a dot at a time into my bony chest. Something
shorter might work; the obvious abbreviation is DNR.

But that one could lead to other problems. Suppose something 8
happens to me while we're visiting our daughter in Michigan, a state
where DNR stands for the Department of Natural Resources. Might I be
mistaken for property of the state, just another road kill that ended up
in a hospital's emergency room?

No, a shortened tattoo alone would leave too much to chance. 9
As the notion continues to swirl in my mind, I envision a network

much like Medic Alert. A tattoo, backed by the Do Not Resuscitate Society, should convince even the most reluctant rescue worker that I'm serious about this.

Seeing the letters, emergency-room personnel would know to contact the society at 1-800-HEYU-DNR. That call would confirm my membership and even elicit my degree of commitment:

Level 5: I really don't mean this, but I want to impress my friends with how urbane I am. Please do absolutely everything you can to revive me.

Level 4: If I probably won't die, but can be expected to live a compromised, dependent, yet relatively pain-free life, please do what you can to keep me around a while longer.

Level 3: If it looks like I'm going to be dead by this time tomorrow, and those next 24 hours will be extremely painful, go ahead and let me die peacefully right now.

Level 2: I mean it. If I'm going to be a vegetable, or what I define as a burden to my family, let's get this over with as soon as possible.

Level 1: Not only do I mean everything I said in Level 2, but while we're at it please help yourself to any of my usable organs so that others may enjoy a rich, full life.

"Yes, Ma'am, Mrs. Juhl is a DNR subscriber, Level 1. She asks that you please make every attempt to summon her family so they can say their goodbyes before you allow her to die with dignity."

Some people will no doubt be offended by this idea, and to them I say: Go soak your head. I don't care what you think. This is *my* life I'm talking about, and I'll decide how I want to live it.

It all boils down to mortality. If you have ever been diagnosed with a life-threatening disease, you know the issue of mortality looms large. If you're lucky, as I was, the outcome will be positive and you'll return to good health. But then, before you know it, you're 70. Suddenly, once again, you come face to face with mortality.

While I may feel decades younger, the fact is I'm in my "golden years." Although I certainly have no interest in seeing my life end any time soon, I need to be realistic. So this is far from a death wish. If anything, it's a *life* wish.

I've always been an idea person, and my family generally offers only a pat on the head ("good dog") when I try to work up some enthusiastic support for my latest brainstorm. I'm taken seriously much less often than I should be—and that's too bad, because I've had some darn good ideas. My friends, though, think I might be on to something with this one.

Yes, you say, but history is full of people who get tattoos and live to regret them. Wouldn't something like this be irrevocable? What if you change your mind? Easy enough. Society membership would include a coupon for a free, second tattoo. It would be the universal symbol for

"Do Not"—a bright red circle with a slash mark across it. Have it applied right over the top of the old tattoo, and you're back among the living.

Living as well as I can is what I intend to do until it's time for me 22 to go for my reward.

Questions for Reflection and Discussion

1. What would you do if one of your parents, grandparents, or other older family member decided to get a tattoo instructing medical personnel not to resuscitate him or her? And even if the person didn't do something so drastic as getting a tattoo to prove the seriousness of his or her wish, would you still honor his or her wishes? Explain.
2. Reread paragraph 20, and use the information there to decide if you think Juhl's children will honor her wish to not be resuscitated.

Topics for Writing

1. Think about the death of someone who you knew very well. Write an essay explaining whether this person died with dignity and whether his or her wishes were followed. In your conclusion, explain what you learned about the dying process as a result of watching this person die.
2. Return to the free write you completed before you read the essay, and use the information there to write a set of complete instructions to your survivors, in the form of a letter. Explain precisely what you want to happen to you from the moment you get too sick to take care of yourself all the way through to the disposal of your body, your possessions, and any money you may have. In your conclusion, decide on the wording of a tattoo that you would have needled into your chest to make sure your wishes are followed and explain to your survivors that if they don't believe what you say in the letter, they should take a look at your chest.

PAST IMPERFECT:
A KANSAS WOMAN
PENS HER MEMOIR AND FINDS,
AT LAST, REDEMPTION

Clare Ansberry

Because "Past Imperfect" is the final selection of this chapter, and of this book, it is fitting that it is about the subject of writing. In this article, originally published in *The Wall Street Journal*, we are told how Jessie Lee Brown, who when she was 80 years old (she is now almost 100 years old), began one morning to "pour her life onto a pad of paper." The result? A 208-page memoir entitled *The Life of Jessie Lee Brown from Birth Up to 80 Years*. Through her writing, Brown was able to let her children and grandchildren (to whom she dedicated the book) know the story of her life, but far more important, through her writing Brown's own life was enriched. Friends and relatives marveled at the many difficulties she endured, and strangers wrote to her to share their thoughts and experiences. And Brown, it seems, discovered the most important reason of all for writing: "It did me a lot of good to get things out in the open."

This article is similar to the type of reading that would be assigned in a college-level psychology course, sociology course, anthropology course, or history of the family course.

Vocabulary

watersheds (paragraph 3)   important events
redemptive (9)   freeing, inspiring
enigma (11)   mystery
encephalitis (15)   a very serious disease causing swelling of the brain
pinochle (18)   a card game
domineering (18)   bossy; taking control
reproach (36)   scolding
mustered (50)   pulled together, gathered

Source: Republished with permission of The Wall Street Journal Co., from "A Kansas Woman Pens Her Memoir and Finds, At Last, Redemption," by Clare Ansberry, as it appeared in *The Wall Street Journal*, March 7, 1997. Permission conveyed through Copyright Clearance Center, Inc.

Suggestions for Free Writing

Before you read the next article, take about 15 minutes to free-write on the following topic:

> If you were to write a seven-chapter book about your life, what would the titles of each of the seven chapters be? After you have decided on the chapter titles, write a paragraph or two for each chapter title in which you outline the topics and information you would include in that chapter. Remember, a life story does not have to be told chronologically (in time order); it can be told by topics or themes. In fact, you may want to use some of the chapter topics and themes in this book as a model: childhood, adolescence, parents, education, relationships, careers, class and race in society, and growing older.

Manhattan, Kansas—At the age of 80, Jessie Lee Brown Foveaux 1
accompanied a few of her lady friends to Harvest of Age, a program for senior citizens in this town on the Big Blue River in northeastern Kansas.

The teacher, Charley Kempthorne, who was also a farmer and a 2
wallpaper hanger, asked them to write stories about growing up. Reluctant, but too polite to refuse, she produced innocent tales of her grandmother and a distant Aunt Clara who chewed tobacco and could spit in a cat's eye.

Then one morning she went into the kitchen of her white two- 3
bedroom house on Thurston Street, where she raised eight children and two grandchildren. She sat down at the table and, aided by scrapbooks, letters and photographs, began pouring her life onto a pad of paper. Week after week, she came to class with a handful of pages, written in longhand. She was one of the few who did write, the others preferring to chat. She duly noted the watersheds—births, deaths, one marriage, three wars, one flood—as well as the things that just struck her fancy, like the first time she saw Lawrence Welk.

Having described the world around her, she revealed for the first 4
time the world within. She explained why she never spoke of her late husband and why she left the room when his name was mentioned; why he was absent from family photos lining her shelves, and why there was no hint of him on her doily-topped tables.

Her children and grandchildren had always seen her as kind and 5
loving. But she also wanted them to know she had her share of bitterness, hate and pride, hoping they might forgive her and learn from her mistakes.

About 30 copies of "The Life of Jessie Lee Brown from Birth Up To 6
80 Years" were printed at the local college. She gave them to family members, with a note asking if they were troubled or embarrassed by her writings: she initially asked them not to show it to anyone else.

That was nearly 20 years ago. 7

Over the years, with her blessing, her 208-page book made its way 8
across streets, fences and state lines, to the nightstands of friends, distant

cousins and strangers. More than 200 people requested copies before she stopped counting a few years ago. The local Riley County Historical Museum has one, as does the First Baptist Church. Four of the pastors there have read it, as have their wives.

She recently wrote a note to Mr. Kempthorne, thanking him for his support. Wandering through the years, pausing to examine forgotten passages and acknowledge shortcomings, proved redemptive.   9

"Thank you so much for not giving up on me," she wrote. "I am not a writer, but my poor efforts have made a great difference in my life."   10

And in the lives of her family. Her children, now grandparents themselves, are still her son and daughters, their identities wrapped in their parents'. Their father was an enigma, feared and loved. Now, they see and understand things they never did before. "As children you don't ask questions, but as you grow older you want to know," says Sadie Rutledge, the eldest of her three living children.   11

Jessie had, so it seems upon reflection, a magical childhood, fishing by moonlight, pushing cats named Dolly and Polly in a buggy. Around her lived characters like old man Dinsmore with his white hair and beard, who, for a dime, would crawl inside a coffin and pose as dead.   12

The oldest of three, she was proud, thin as a sunflower and spoiled with attention from her Irish-American parents and dozens of aunts, uncles and cousins. To her, happy homes were a birthright, and largely the handiwork of women content to be loving mothers and devoted wives. Out back of a family farm, she would sit under a big shade tree and dream. "I was going to have the most wonderful life and live in a big house. I'd have a fine carriage and horses and a large family. We would have parties and happy times," she wrote.   13

When World War I started, she worked at the laundry at nearby Fort Riley. There, she met a handsome doctor named Howard Nichols with deep brown eyes. He called her Dixie. They wanted to marry before he was sent overseas, but her mother convinced them to wait until he returned.   14

Jessie wrote him letters; a friend made a wedding dress of white satin. Near the end of the war, his letters stopped coming. A year later, he died in an Army hospital. The same year, her mother died, and Jessie, stricken with encephalitis, was left broken. "I folded my dress, with all my beautiful dreams gone. I put it away. Mama gone, Howard gone—not much to look forward to. But life goes on," she wrote.   15

Months later, a neighborhood boy named Bill Foveaux returned from the war to find that his mother and two older sisters had died of tuberculosis, leaving his father with four younger children. She knew of him. His family lived a block away, and their fathers had worked together over the years. Bill called on Jessie several times and finally convinced her to meet his family. The house was a mess, and the chil-   16 dren seemed lost. She felt sorry for them and for him. He was pleasant, nice-looking and lonely.

For months, be begged her to marry him. "At last I began to think, 'Why not?' Bill won't be Howard, but he is kind and does need a home after all those years in a terrible war," she wrote. On the way to the local judge, she told Bill she had changed her mind, but was assured that every bride-to-be got cold feet. They exchanged vows on Dec. 6, 1919, and then ate lunch in a cafe in nearby Junction City. 17

In the first five years, she bore three boys and a girl. She and Bill played pinochle with neighbors and his war buddies. Bill could be domineering, telling her whom she could visit, but he worked hard on his construction jobs and taught the children to obey her. Then, one night in 1925, he went to the American Legion for a meeting. His friends brought him home sick, blaming the food. It happened again a few weeks later, which she thought odd. When she mentioned it to her best friend, she was told that the guys sometimes went drinking after the meetings. 18

Jessie knew nothing of alcoholism, and to her knowledge had never, until then, seen anyone drunk. She confronted Bill, and he promised not to do it again. The day their fifth child was born, he stayed out all night toasting another son. He apologized and for a few months came home every night, but more sprees chased by more apologies followed. With each, she lost a little more respect for him. 19

Meanwhile, she was overwhelmed trying to care for her children and asked her doctor how to stop having them so fast. He said he didn't know and said she was simply the type who was supposed to have a lot of children. Her sixth child arrived 14 months later, her oldest not yet seven years old. Her husband blamed her for having so many children. He began staying away from work and spending paychecks before he got home. Some weeks, they had no money. 20

"It was changing me from a happy-go-lucky character into someone not nice to know," she wrote. "Each time I had to tell someone I couldn't pay a bill, I died a little. I was so ashamed, even of my name. I thought everyone was talking about me. . . . All I asked was food and clothing." 21

She canceled life-insurance policies to buy food and got a job at the grocery store across the street. The owner, Elmer Holbert, let her bring the babies to sleep in the back room. She earned extra money peddling cosmetics, spices and extracts, carrying a suitcase of samples and pushing the youngest in the carriage. The older ones followed on foot. 22

She didn't want anyone to know Bill drank, for she felt both embarrassed and somehow responsible. But it was hardly a secret. He spent many nights in jail after getting into fights. When he came home, he insisted that she and the children get out of bed and sing with him on the front porch, or make breakfast for him and his friends. 23

"I wasn't a wife. I was a darned slave with no pay," she wrote. "I 24
became so full of hate for that husband of mine, only God above kept
me from killing him."

When her children first read those passages, they were struck by 25
their mother's contempt and despair. They were saddened too, realizing
her loneliness. "We never picked up that she was that unhappy. She kept
her feelings to herself," says Sadie, 69 years old. Part of it was the era.
Grown-ups didn't talk in front of the children; women were stoic and
loyal. When Jessie was troubled, she would sit and tat, a delicate crochet-
like craft she learned from her grandmother.

She kept silent, too, so as not to ruin their affection for their father. 26
He drank, but so did many others. When he did, Jessie sent the younger
ones outside to play or over to a neighbor; the older ones stayed to
protect her, because sometimes Bill would threaten her with a broken
bottle. And when he was sober, he would tell wonderful stories and make
huge vats of oyster stew. They loved him as they did their mother.

He was in jail for getting into fights when the two last children, 27
Marion and Dee Dee, were born. While giving birth to Dee Dee, Jessie
almost died—and prayed she would. Overwhelmed with caring for
another child and afraid of having more, she refused for weeks to leave
her bed. A friend scolded her: "Where is the old gal we used to know?"
She died long ago, Jessie responded.

Ultimately she was sustained by her eight children and their needi- 28
ness. It wasn't just food and clothes. They counted on her to keep the
family together, to make Christmases and birthdays happen, to send them
to church. She found she wasn't alone. Other wives, mostly those of war veterans, were likewise trying to make life normal for their children and
would help each other out, quietly passing clothes from family to family. At
the time, alcoholics weren't considered sick, just old drunks and jailbirds.

Dee Dee Torgerson remembers kids teasing her when her father 29
didn't come to school programs, even when she was Mary in the Christmas
pageant. "I'd say, 'He's coming.' Finally, I learned to just shut up," she says.

Jessie often felt that she had failed her children. Mothers were
responsible for providing a happy, carefree home and childhood. But 30
life seemed relentless, not carefree.

"I had so little time to spend doing things with them. There was so
much to do for them, work, work all the time. Oh, I was here in the house 31
and watched over them, settled fights and put bandages on cut fingers,
but there was no time to play games. Just stories at bedtime—and then I
was so happy to get them all safely into bed and then asleep," she wrote.

Finally, Jessie said a prayer. She promised that if she could find 32
work to support her children, she would try to stop hating her husband.
Not long after, she again got a job at the Fort Riley laundry, this time for
the men fighting in World War II. But she remained bitter.

"I wish I could tell you that I changed real fast, but I didn't. That 33
old hate had eaten in like a canker sore and wouldn't let loose," she
wrote. "This man had ruined my life, and I was going to get even."

She threatened divorce; he told her if she did, it would be her last 34
day on Earth. She was less terrified of his threats than of actually going
through with it. It was the early 1940s, and divorce was a shameful spectacle. "I didn't want to be the first one," she says. It was against her religion, her upbringing.

When she finally decided to seek a divorce, she told her children 35
it was time. Bill could no longer keep a job. The older children were
working, and she could manage the two youngest ones with her job.
They never questioned her, having been raised not to talk back, but also
because they weren't sure she would do it. She had managed to live with
their father's drinking for so long.

She took a day off work and went to the local judge, expecting 36
reproach. He told her, "We have been wondering here how much longer
it would be before you woke up." For the filing fee, she needed $65,
which she didn't have, so two of her children chipped in. The sheriff
came home to make sure Bill left the house. That night she slept
soundly. "I made up my mind to live my life so that I need not be
ashamed to look at myself in the mirror," she wrote.

Bill was supposed to pay $50 in monthly alimony, but didn't, though 37
he would visit and treat the two youngest children to movies or slip them
$5. He bought Marion a bicycle. "Mom probably could have used that
money to buy a lot of milk," says Dee Dee. "But she just said, 'That's nice.'
She never put him down. She let us have our relationship with him."

Jessie knew she had to manage on her own. She had a large 38
garden, and her older children pitched in. She still has a slip of paper
from a local bank saying she was a person of "stability, honor and
integrity." She wrote poems, confiding her loneliness when her 24-year-
old daughter died of tuberculosis and finding in verse a voice for her
humor, often muted in the noise of getting through the day.

She got a job at a hospital as a nurse's aide and gained a new appre- 39
ciation of life and its frailty. She couldn't continue hating all alcoholics:
Though she refused to believe it at first, her oldest son, who has since died,
had a drinking problem. But she had yet to forgive Bill. When she was in
the hospital once having an operation, he sent flowers. She refused to
allow them in the room. "Childish? Yes. Foolish? Yes and just plain mean-
ness (I think now)," she wrote. "I am sorry about that, but much too late."

In 1951, Bill died of cancer. She took her two youngest children to 40
see him one last time. She arranged the funeral and paid for it. The
Veterans of Foreign Wars post gave him a military salute, and he was
buried next to his father. "As far as I was concerned, it may as well have
been a complete stranger that service was for. I had no feelings beyond
wanting him to have as nice a funeral as we could give him," she wrote.

It struck her children that their mother never said she loved their   41
father, not even in the beginning. Dee Dee remembers questioning in
disbelief after reading the memoir, "You would marry him and not love
him?" But they saw that Jessie had seemed to surrender to marriage
rather than embrace it. There were other telling passages. Jessie wrote
of her grandmother dying soon after her grandfather. "The doctor said
she just didn't want to live without Grandpa. It must be wonderful for a
husband and wife to care that much . . . to be so in love." When asked
recently her happiest memory with her husband, Jessie stops and looks
away. "Gosh, I don't know. I can't think of any that would really cause me
to swoon. I guess that's the reason I felt guilty. I did marry someone I
didn't care that much about."

Jessie never wanted anyone to walk away from the book hating   42
him or pitying her. She had been full of pride and self-pity, she says,
and he of unrealized expectations. "After World War I was over, he
returned home with great dreams of what he wanted from life.
Without much education, he couldn't hope for a high-salary job.
When difficulties came along, instead of facing them, he reached for
a prop. . . . We started out with good intentions. We got lost along the
way."

She dedicated the book to her grandchildren. She wanted to leave   43
them something aside from scrapbooks and some Fred Waring albums.
She knows they won't agree with everything she wrote. Young girls, she
says, should pass cooking classes before they marry; she questions the
wisdom of planting a flag on the moon where no one can see it. Still, she
hopes they might find her writings useful.

They have learned many things, the family lore about remote ties   44
to President McKinley and contacts with the Jesse James clan. The family
members were touched by her pride, as she acknowledged and praised
them as the Vietnam veteran, the carpenter's apprentice, the champion
bowler. They have come to see her as more relevant as they grow older,
their struggles—alcoholism, divorce, illness—having been her own.
When her oldest granddaughter, Linda Rutledge, was going through a
painful divorce last summer, she took a plane from Georgia to Kansas to
spend a week with Jessie. "I thought if anyone can help, Grandma can.
She puts life into perspective," she says.

Jessie's message to her grandchildren has been as simple and   45
complex as faith and forgiveness. "I had to talk to our Lord a lot and
admit I had been so wrong to hate people. . . . It wasn't easy to look deep
inside and take my share of the blame for the mess I was making of my
life," she wrote. "As soon as I felt I was forgiven, it was much easier. . . .
I am sure your grandfather suffered much more than I did." Says Danny
Torgerson, Dee Dee's 39-year-old son, "The fact that she can still come
out of it loving people blows me away."

The grandchildren, many of them scattered around the country, keep in touch with letters and make trips when they can. Diane Waddell, who lives two hours away, bakes Jessie a birthday cake every year and asks her advice in raising her own teenagers. She now keeps notes of her own life. 46

Jessie is 97 now. One lady called her Grandma Snowball, her head wreathed by soft white curls. She gets around her house using a cane, or reaching table to chair to table. Her son, Marion, checks on her daily. She buried her fifth child last summer. 47

When younger, she always wondered why old people wanted to live on. It seemed so dull. She imagined herself getting a rocking chair, a canary and books. She did get a canary named Bing, which died, followed by another named Jimmy Dean. After he died, she bought ceramic animals. 48

Old age, she found, is not bad. She has new carpet, a new washing machine and a microwave. She reads detective stories and the Manhattan Mercury, clipping articles for her scrapbook. She visits the U and I club (U for Uplifting and I for Interesting) and takes classes at Sunday school. Her two daughters are her best friends and she theirs. Until a few years ago, she would pack tomatoes and peppers from her garden into her suitcase, board a bus and visit them for a month or more. 49

Her writings haven't made her wealthy, but they have enriched her life. "It did me a lot of good to get things out in the open," she says. People who read her memoir admired her courage. Most found something in common with at least a sliver of her past. She may have lived their busy routine or worn the same silent face. One woman wrote to say she had eight children, and her husband was an alcoholic who blamed her for everything. They moved nine times in one year. She wished she had mustered the same courage to get a divorce: "I just felt like you were doing my story, too. . . . Hope you have a nice Christmas." 50

At Jessie's last birthday, nearly 150 people came to an open house in the basement of the VFW. Many were children or grandchildren of friends, most of whom had in some way appeared in her writings—the neighbor who gave her a red teapot with little gold birds, the woman who decorated cakes so beautifully. 51

She has completed two more books since her first memoir, the latest, "Granny's Ramblings of This and That Two," in 1993. They are scattered snapshots of vacations, a history of Thurston Street where she has lived for 73 years. She included a letter from Bill to his sister during World War I, showing him homesick and longing for a piece of his aunt's cake. Now, there is an old picture of them together, on her shelf; she put it there after writing her memoir. "He was a fine-looking young man," she says. 52

Questions for Reflection and Discussion

1. Sometimes, the conclusion or the last line of an article or book contains a very important message. The message may not be stated; rather, it is *implied* (hinted at). What important message is implied by the last two lines of the article: "Now, there is an old picture of them [Jessie and Bill] together, on her shelf; she put it there after writing her memoir. 'He was a fine-looking young man,' she says."
2. In what ways did Jessie Brown's memoir benefit the people who read it? Explain.

Topics for Writing

1. Write an essay in which you identify, describe, and explain the many values and uses of writing, using as evidence and example Jessie Brown's story, but also using as many of the other readings in this book as possible. Explain how the writer and/or reader benefited from having written or read the various essays and excerpts.

    For example, most of the readings in Chapter 1 show people using writing to examine or solve problems: Mark Levensky's letter to his English teachers telling them to stop giving spelling tests; Langston Hughes's poem to his English teacher explaining how the differences in their race caused problems for him; Guy Nassiff's essay in which he tries to work up the courage to write to a father whom he has never met; the airline flight attendants who explain in their flight logs the difficulties they encounter in their jobs.

    Other chapters contain similar evidence: Mel Lazarus remembering how his father refused to use physical punishment, although the other boys' fathers did ("Angry Fathers," Chapter 2); James McBride remembering how his mother struggled to provide for her 12 children (excerpt from *The Color of Water*, Chapter 3); Dan Holt realizing that one of his students came from a home where there was no heat ("Intrusion," Chapter 4); Rosemary Bray remembering the shame she felt when she discovered, through a visit to the home of a rich friend, that her family was poor (excerpt from *Unafraid of the Dark*, Chapter 5); Leah Hager Cohen uncovering the truth about her grandfather's death (excerpt from *Train Go Sorry*, Chapter 6); Caffilene Allen realizing that her teachers taught her much of value, but they also taught her to be ashamed of her mother ("First They Changed My Name," Chapter 7); Claudia Shear explaining the difficult temporary and hourly jobs at which she has worked ("Who Am I Today?", Chapter 8); Daniel Stolar trying to come to terms with James's death and trying to better understand his relationship with Lillie ("City Maps," Chapter 9).

    In your essay, refer to these or other readings, and be certain to include quotations from them to offer your reader proof of your statements and observations.

2. Of course it would be very difficult for you to find the time to write the story of your life as Jessie Brown did; after all, she took almost 20 years to complete her first memoir. Instead, return to the free write you completed before you read "Past Imperfect," and choose one chapter that interests you and about which you have a lot to say. Then write just one chapter of your life story. Do not worry about giving background information that would have been in earlier chapters; as you write, you can assume your reader knows that this is a chapter from a longer work.

Additional Writing Topics about Growing Older and Wiser

1. Think about the older people in your life: parents, grandparents, other relatives, neighbors, friends—and choose the one you admire the most. Then write a poem in which you praise the courage and hard work the person has exhibited over the course of his or her life. Remember to include specific examples and details (think of the details Jo Carson used in her poem, "I Am Asking You to Come Back Home"). To simply write a poem saying that a person is hardworking or courageous or loving is not convincing; it sounds too much like a greeting card slogan. In a poem, as in an essay, you must help your reader understand your meaning by providing details and evidence.
2. Return to the free write you completed before you began to read the selections in this chapter, and choose one of the older persons about whom you wrote who has had an interesting life and/or career. Interview this person (or use the information you already have about him or her), and write an essay explaining the differences between the circumstances, conditions, and opportunities that existed for the person when he or she was about your age, and the circumstances, conditions, and opportunities that exist for you today.